Christian Monastic Series

I0123856

A Monk's Topical Bible

Book 2

Volume 4

Revelation Insight Publishing Co.

2012'

Dear Reader

1 Corinthians 2: 7-15. We speak the hidden mystical wisdom of God, which God ordained before the world unto our Glory, Which none of the princes of this world knew, for had they known it, they would not have crucified the Lord of Glory. But, as it is written, eye has not seen, nor ear heard, neither has it entered into the Heart of man to conceive the things, which God has prepared for them that Love him. However, God has revealed them unto us by His Spirit, for the Spirit searches all things, yes, and the deep things of God. For what man knows the things of a man, save the spirit of a man, which is in him? Even so, the thing of God knows no man, but the Spirit of God. Now we have received, not the Spirit of this world, but the Spirit, which is of God; that we might know the things that are freely given us of God. Which things also we speak, not in your words which man's wisdom teaches, but which the, Holy Spirit teaches, comparing spiritual things with Spiritual. However, the natural man receives not the things of the Spirit of God, for they are foolishness unto him, neither can he know them, because they are spiritually discerned. Nevertheless, he that is spiritual judges or discerns all things.

A Monk's Topical Bible

Christian Monastic Series

Vol. 4

Behold I stand at the door and knock, if anyone hears my voice and opens the door; I will come in and dine with him, and he with Me. He who overcomes, I will grant to sit down with Me on My throne, as I also overcame and with My Father on His throne. " Rev. 3: 20 21

All rights reserved. No part of this book may be reproduced or transmitted in any form or means, electronic or mechanical including photocopying, or by any information storage and retrieval system without permission in writing from Revelation Insight.

ISBN # 978-1-936392-14-8

Library of Congress Cataloging in Publication Data.

#2010907136

BAISAC # REL- 006670

Printed and bound in the USA

Revelation – Insight © 2012

E Mail: Ripublishing@Mail.com

Christian Monastic Series

This series is designed and presented to accent a fine library of the essentials required for further in-depth investigation of this genre.

The focus of this series is to provide today's reader with the essentials of background writings on the monastic community that are a part of our Christian heritage. The selected written works are a culmination of screening the best of this genre from the numerous documents, which are available. We selected these works based on a number of factors. The greatest impact upon the body of Christ, their insight of the genre, their related impact on other writers, and the feasibility of this text to be used as a guide, or in a standalone application. They are the primary indicators used, coupled with other factors in making our selection.

Each text in this series is a premier stand-alone text in this genre. The intended corpus of works pooled together make for a reference library rivaling that of some great monastery or university library on this subject. These are re-edited for today's reader. These writings are not abridged, they are the complete text, completely redone in grammar, and syntax, verbiage and other literary components to ensure the spirit of these works are not lost in these important changes.

For many of these texts, this is the first time they are available in this format and to these standards. These are not a scholarly reference work editions. For that purpose, there are other publications available. This series is intended for those who have a fundamental familiarity with the subject, and some of the writers. The intent is to address the needs of the readers who are journeying forward on their quest in union with God.

There are other selections to be added as certain texts are processed. Please look forward to these great works in print, audio and E-book formats at your local bookstore, though us directly.

Staff at Revelation –Insight

Table of Contents

- Exhortations

- Exile

- Exorcism

- Faint heartedness

- Faith

- Fall

- False accusation

- Fantasy

- Fasting

- Fear

- Fear of god

- Flattery

- Flesh

- Food

- Forgetfulness

- Forgiveness

- Forgiving others

- Fornication

- Free will

- Freedom from anger

- Friendship

- Gelasius

- Generosity

- Giving advice

- Glossolia

- Gluttony

- God

- Good

- Gossip

- Grace

- Gratitude

- Great lent

- Great passion of Jesus Christ

- Greed

- Grief

- Grumbling

- Guardian Angel

- Guile

- Guilt

- Habits

- Happiness
- Hate
- Heart
- Heedfulness
- Hell
- Heresy
- Heresy Arianism
- Heterodoxy
- Holiness
- Holy Communion
- Holy Friday
- Holy Monday
- Holy spirit
- Holy tradition
- Holy trinity
- Holy Wednesday
- Holy week
- Honesty
- Hope
- Hospitality

- How to live

- Human nature

- Humiliation

- Humility

- Hypocrisy

- Icons

- Idle talk

- Idolatry

- Ignorance

- Illness

- Images

- Imagination

- Incarnation

- Incensive power

- Ingratitude

- Injustice

- Insensibility

- Instructions

- Insults

- Intellect

- Intelligence

- Intemperance

- Intention

- Jesus Christ

- Jesus Prayer

- Job

- Joy

- Joyful sorrow

- Judas

- Judging others

- Judgment

- Keeping a journal

- Kingdom of God

- Kingdom of heaven

- Knowledge

- Knowledge

- Kontakia of Romanos

Eating

...when you eat or drink, reflect that it is God, Who gives all food a taste which pleases us. So, delighting in Him alone, say: 'Rejoice, Oh my soul, for, although you can find no satisfaction, delight or comfort in anything outside God, you can know Him and cleave to Him, and can find every delight in Him alone, as David invites, saying: "*Oh taste and see that the Lord is good.*" (Ps. 34:8)...'   Lorenzo Scupoli

---

According to Gregory the Sinaite there are three degrees in eating: temperance, sufficiency, and satiety. Temperance is when someone wants to eat some more food but abstains, rising from the table still somewhat hungry. Sufficiency is when someone eats what is needful and sufficient for normal nourishment. Satiety is when someone eats more than enough and is more than satisfied. Now if you cannot keep the first two degrees and you proceed to the third, then, at least do not become a glutton, remembering the words of the Lord: "Woe to you that are full now, for you shall hunger" (Lk. 6:25).

Nicodemos of the Holy Mountain

Partake of the dishes, which are offered in silence and with prayer, and do everything as written above. At the same time guard yourself carefully also in this: Satisfy your body with food in such a way that you do not feel full or heavy, but have still a little hunger and thirst. Nourish rather your soul with the God-inspired words and lives of the Holy Fathers, which are read during trapeza. . . .   Nazarius of Valaam

---

Concerning the measure of continence in food and drink the Fathers say that one should use both the one and the other a little less than necessary, that is, one should not fill the stomach completely. In addition, everyone should determine for himself his measure both of cooked food and of wine. During wintertime no one drinks much; however, even then one should drink a little less than necessary, and he should act likewise with regard to food. In addition, the measure of continence is not limited only to food and drink, but extends also to conversations, to seep, to clothing, and to all the feelings; in all of this there should be a measure of continence. "   Barsanuphius

Constantly reflecting thus and reproaching yourself, decide for yourself how much you should eat and drink every day to satisfy the needs of nature. Avoid as much as possible not merely overeating, but even eating just enough to be full. Keep in mind what was said above, that one should eat and drink only to the point where one is still a little hungry and thirsty.

                                        Nazarius of Valaam

During a time of disturbance and warfare of thoughts, one should lessen a little even the ordinary quantity of food and drink.   Ibid

Having guarded ourselves against distractions and worries, let us turn our attention to our body on which mental vigilance is completely dependent. Human bodies differ widely from one another in strength and health. Some by their strength are like copper and iron; others are frail like grass. For this reason everyone should rule his body with great prudence, after exploring his physical powers. For a strong and healthy body, special fasts and vigils are suitable; they make it lighter, and give the mind a special wakefulness. A weak body should be strengthened by food and sleep according to one's physical needs, but on no account to satiety. Satiety is extremely harmful even for a weak body; it weakens it, and makes it susceptible to disease. Wise temperance of the stomach is a door to all the virtues. Restrain the stomach, and you will enter Paradise. Not if you please and pamper your stomach, you will hurl yourself over the precipice of bodily impurity, into the fire of wrath and fury, you will coarsen and darken your mind, and in this way you will ruin your powers of attention and self-control, your sobriety and vigilance....   Ignaty Brianchaninov

---

Having reflected thus, at least say to yourself from your whole soul and with heartfelt sorrow. Eat, unworthy one, enough so that you will not die. Dry up your body; confine your insatiable desires; grieve and belittle yourself. Will not the most merciful Lord look down upon this grief and contrition of my heart, which are justly deserved? Even though my contrition itself is imperfect and insufficient, will not God Who is endless in mercy still have mercy on me and forgive the great evils that I have done?

Nazarius of Valaam

He Who had everything in common with us except sin, and Who shared all our sufferings, did not think hunger a sin. Therefore He did not refuse Himself to undergo this experience, but accepted the natural instinct to desire food. Having remained forty days without food, He afterwards was hungry; for when He desired it, He allowed His human nature to act in its normal way. However, when the father of temptations realized that He, too, was affected by hunger, he advised Him to meet the desire with stones. Now this means to pervert the desire for natural food into something that is outside nature. He says, 'Command that these stones be made bread.'
Gregory of Nyssa

I have need of one hundred grams of bread a day, and God blesses it. He blesses those hundred grams, but not one gram more. Therefore, if I take 110 grams, I have stolen 10 grams from the poor.   Cosmas Aitilos

I shall speak first about control of the stomach, the opposite to gluttony, and about how to fast and what and how much to eat. I shall say nothing on my own account, but only what I have received from the Holy Fathers. They have not given us only a single rule for fasting or a single standard and measure for eating, because not everyone has the same strength; age, illness or delicacy of body create differences. Nevertheless, they have given us all a single goal: to avoid over-eating and the filling of our bellies... A clear rule for self-control handed down by the Fathers is this: stop eating while still hungry and do not continue until you are satisfied.   John Cassian

Let us be satisfied simply with what sustains our present life, not with what pampers it. Let us pray to God for this, as we have been taught, so that we may keep our souls unenslaved and absolutely free from domination by any of the visible things loved for the sake of the body. Let us show that we eat for the sake of living, and not be guilty of living for the sake of eating. The first is a sign of intelligence, the second proof of its absence.

Maximos the Confessor

Sitting at meals, do not look and do not judge how much anyone eats, but be attentive to yourself, nourishing your soul with prayer.   Seraphim of Sarov

According to Gregory the Sinaite there are three degrees in eating: temperance, sufficiency, and satiety. Temperance is when someone wants to eat some more food but abstains, rising from the table still somewhat hungry. Sufficiency is when someone eats what is needed and sufficient for normal nourishment. Satiety is when someone eats more than enough and is more than satisfied.

Now if you cannot keep the first two degrees and you proceed to the third, then, at least, do not become a glutton, remembering the words of the Lord: "Woe to you that are full now, for you shall hunger" (Lk 6:25). Remember also that rich man who ate in this present life sumptuously every day, but who was deprived of the desired bosom of Abraham in the next life, simply because of this sumptuous eating. Remember how he longed to refresh his tongue with a drop of water.

Basil not only did not forgive the young people who ate to satiety but also those who ate until satisfied; he preferred that all eat temperately. He said, "Nothing subdues and controls the body as does the practice of temperance. It is this temperance that serves as a control to those youthful passions and desires.'"

Gregory the Theologian has also noted in his poetry: "No satiety has brought forth prudent behavior; for it is in the nature of fire to consume matter. A filled stomach expels refined thoughts; it is the tendency of opposites to oppose each other."

Job, too, assuming that one could fall into sin through eating, offered sacrifice to God for his sons who were feasting among themselves. "And when the days of the feast had run their course, Job would send and sanctify them, and he would rise early in the morning and offer burnt offerings according to the number of them all; for Job said: 'It may be that my sons have sinned, and cursed God in their hearts'" (Jb 1:5-8). In interpreting this passage Olympiodoros wrote: "We learn from this that we ought to avoid such feasts which can bring on sinfulness. We must also purify ourselves after they have been concluded, even if these are conducted for the sake of concord and brotherly love as in the case of the sons of Job."

Surely then, if the sons of Job were not at a feast but in prayer or some other spiritual activity, the devil would not have dared to destroy the house and them, as Origen interpreted the passage: "The devil was looking for an opportunity to destroy them. Had he found them reading, he would not have touched the house, having no reason to put them to death. Had he found them in prayer, he would not have had any power to do anything against them. However, when he found an opportune time, he was powerful. What was the opportune time? It was the time of feasting and drinking." Do you see then, dear reader, how many evils are brought forth by luxurious foods and feasting in general?

Nicodemos

The question of Abbot Dorotheus to the Great : I am being strongly attacked by sexual passion; I am afraid that I may fall into despondency, and that from the infirmity of my body I will not be able to restrain myself; pray for me, for the Lord's sake, and tell me, my Father, what I should do?

A: Brother! The devil, out of envy, has raised up warfare against you. Guard your eyes and do not eat until you are full. Take a little wine for the sake of the body's infirmity of which you speak. In addition, acquire humility, which rends all the nets of the enemy.

I, who am nothing, will do what I can, entreating God that He might deliver you from every temptation and preserve you from every evil. Do not yield to the enemy, Oh brother, and do not give yourself over to despondency, for this is a great joy to the enemy. Pray without ceasing, saying: "Lord Jesus Christ, deliver me from shameful passions", and God will have mercy on you, and you will receive strength by the prayers of the Saints. Amen.

Barsanuphius

To act "according to one's strength" means to use a little less than necessary both of food, and drink, and sleep . . . . As for food, restrain yourself when you wish to eat a little more, and in this way you will always make use of it moderately.   Ibid

cumenical Dialogue

3. Theological dialogue must not in any way be linked with prayer in common, or by joint participation in any liturgical or worship services whatsoever; or in other activities which might create the impression that our Orthodox Church accepts, on the one hand, Roman Catholics as part of the fullness of the Church, or, on the other hand, the Pope as the canonical bishop of Rome. Activities such as these mislead both the fullness of the

Orthodox people and the Roman Catholics themselves, fostering among them a mistaken notion as to what Orthodoxy thinks of their teaching.

E cumenism

The life of Maximus is also instructive for us. Maximus, though only a simple monk, resisted and cut off communion with every patriarch, metropolitan, archbishop and bishop in the East because of their having been infected with the heresy of Monothelitism. During the first imprisonment of the , the messengers from the Ecumenical Patriarch asked him:"To which church do you belong? To that of Byzantium, of Rome, Antioch, Alexandria, or Jerusalem? For all these churches, together with the provinces in subjection to them, are in unity. Therefore, if you also belong to the Catholic Church, enter into communion with us at once, lest fashioning for yourself some new and strange pathway, you fall into that which you do not even expect!"

To this the righteous man wisely replied, "Christ the Lord called that Church the Catholic Church which maintains the true and saving confession of the Faith. It was for this confession that He called Peter blessed, and He declared that He would found His Church upon this confession. However, I wish to know the contents of your confession, on the basis of which all churches, as you say, have entered into communion. If it is not opposed to the truth, then neither will I be separated from it." The confession which they were proposing to the was not Orthodox, of course, and so he refused to comply with their coercions. Furthermore, they were lying about the See of Rome, which, in fact, had remained Orthodox. Some time later, at his last interrogation by the Byzantine authorities, the following dialogue took place:

The said, "They [the Patriarchs of Constantinople and Alexandria and all the other heretical bishops of the East] have been deposed and deprived of the priesthood at the local synod which took place recently in Rome. What Mysteries, then, can they perform? Or what spirit will descend upon those who are ordained by them?"

"Then you alone will be saved, and all others will perish?" they objected.

To this the   replied, "When all the people in Babylon were worshipping the golden idol, the Three Holy Children did not condemn anyone to perdition. They did not concern themselves with the doings of others, but took care only for themselves, lest they should fall away from true piety. In precisely the same way, when Daniel was cast into the lion's den, he did not condemn any of those who, fulfilling the law of Darius, did not wish to pray to God, but he kept in mind his own duty, and desired rather to die than to sin against his conscience by transgressing the Law of God. God forbid that I should condemn anyone or say that I alone am being saved! However, I shall sooner agree to die than to apostatize in any way from the true Faith and thereby suffer torments of conscience."

"But what will you do", inquired the envoys, "when the Romans are united to the Byzantines? Yesterday, indeed, two delegates arrived from Rome and tomorrow, the Lord's day, they will communicate the Holy Mysteries with the Patriarch. "

The   replied, "Even if the whole universe holds communion with the Patriarch, I will not communicate with him. For I know from the writings of the holy Apostle Paul: the Holy Spirit declares that even the angels would be anathema if they should begin to preach another Gospel, introducing some new teaching."

As history has demonstrated,   Maximus—who was only a simple monk and not even ordained—and his two disciples were the ones who were Orthodox, and all those illustrious, famous and influential Patriarchs and Metropolitans whom the   had written against were the ones who were in heresy. When the Sixth Ecumenical Synod was finally convened, among those condemned for heresy were four Patriarchs of Constantinople, one Pope of Rome, one Patriarch of Alexandria, two Patriarchs of Antioch and a multitude of other Metropolitans, Archbishops and Bishops. During all those years, that one simple monk was right, and all those notable bishops were wrong.

Maximus the Confessor

...But as for those who...severe themselves from communion with their president, that is, because he publicly preaches heresy and with bared head teaches it in the Church, such persons are not only not subject to canonical penalty..., but are worthy of due honor among the Orthodox. For not bishops, but false bishops and false teachers have they condemned, and they have not fragmented the Church's unity with schism, but from schisms and divisions have they earnestly sought to deliver the Church.

Canon 15 of the First-Second Council of Constantinople

Even more should this be happening now, when there is a discernible and lively interest on the part of the heterodox, particularly those of the West, in the Orthodox Church. But this gracious love which characterizes good zeal according to knowledge never forgets or overlooks the falsehood of heresy or who the heretics are, or, in this case, who the Pope of Rome is.

Nectarios of Aegina

All the teachers of the Church, and all the Councils, and all the Divine Scriptures advise us to flee from the heterodox and separate from their communion.   Mark of Ephesus

---

Among us, neither Patriarchs nor Councils were ever able to introduce innovations, because the defender of Religion is the very Body of the Church---that is, the people themselves --- which desire to have their Religion eternally unchanged and identical to that of their Fathers.

Reply of the Orthodox Patriarchs of the East to Pius IX, issued in 1848

The Lord said to Joshua, Rise up: why have you fallen upon your face? The people has sinned, and transgressed the covenant which I made with them; they have stolen from the accursed things (Greek: anathema), and put it into their store. In addition, the children of Israel will not be able to stand before their enemies, for they have become an accursed thing (anathema); I will no longer be with you, unless you remove the accursed thing (anathema) from yourselves.   Joshua 7.10-11

Any servant who kept his peace and did nothing in order to prevent thieves from breaking into his master house, would be condemned by his master as being treacherous thief like them even if he had not done nothing to assist them.   Symeon the New Theologian

---

Anyone who is able to speak the truth and does not do so will be condemned by God.   Justin the Philosopher

---

As we walk the unerring and life-bringing path, let us pluck out the eye that scandalizes us-not the physical eye, but the noetic one. For example, if a bishop or presbyter-who are the eyes of the Church-conduct themselves in an evil manner and scandalize the people, they must be plucked out. For it is more profitable to gather without them in a house of prayer, than to be cast together with them into the gehenna of fire together with Annas and Caiaphas .   Athanasius the Great

---

Be not unequally yoked together with unbelievers. For what partnership have righteousness and iniquity? Or what fellowship has light with darkness? What accord has Christ with Belial? What agreement has the temple of God with idols? For we are the temple of the living God.   2 Corinthians 6.14-16

Better is a praiseworthy war than a peace that separates us from God.

Gregory the Theologian

Although we, or an angel from Heaven, preach any other gospel unto you than that which we have preached unto you, let him be anathema. As we said before, so say I now again, If any man preach any other gospel unto you than that which you have received, let him be anathema' [Galatians 1:8-9]. I shall judge the bishop and the layperson. The sheep are rational and not irrational, so that no layman may ever say that, 'I am a sheep, and not a shepherd, and I give no account of myself, but the shepherd shall see to it, and he alone shall pay the penalty for me.' For even as the sheep that follows not the good shepherd shall fall to the wolves unto its own destruction, so too it is evident that the sheep that follows the evil shepherd shall acquire death; for he shall utterly devour it. Therefore, it is required that we flee from destructive shepherds. <u>Apostolic Constitutions, 10:19, PG 1:633</u>

Chrysostomos loudly declares not only heretics, but also those who have communion with them, to be enemies of God.

<u>Theodore the Studite, Epistle of Abbot Theophilus</u>

Come out of her, My people, lest you take part in her sins, lest you share in her plagues. <u>Revelation 18.4</u>

Concerning the Faith, the heretics were totally shipwrecked; but as for the others, even if in their thinking they did not founder, nonetheless, because of their communion with heresy, they too were destroyed with the others.

<u>Theodore the Studite</u>

Concerning the necessity of not permitting heretics to come into the house of God, so long as they persist in their heresy.

Canon 6 of the Council of Laodicea

Consider how contrary to the mind of God are the heterodox in regard to the grace of God which has come to us ... They abstain from the Eucharist and from prayer, because they do not admit that the Eucharist is the flesh of our Savior Jesus Christ, the flesh which suffered for our sins and which the Father, in His graciousness, raised from the dead."

Ignatius of Antioch 80-110 A.D.

Contentions," he means, with heretics, in which he would not have us labor to no purpose, where nothing is to be gained, for they end in nothing. For when a man is perverted and predetermined not to change his mind, whatever may happen, why should you labor in vain, sowing upon a rock, when you should spend your honorable toil upon your own people, in discoursing with them upon almsgiving and every other virtue?

How then does he elsewhere say, "If God peradventure will give them repentance" (2 Tim. ii.25); but here, "A man that is an heretic after the first and second admonition reject, knowing that he that is such is subverted and sins, being condemned of himself"? In the former passage he speaks of the correction of those of whom he had hope, and who had simply made opposition. However, when he is known and manifest to all, why do you contend in vain? why do you beat the air? What means, "being condemned of himself"? Because he cannot say that no one has told him, no one admonished him; since therefore after admonition he continues the same, he is self-condemned.   John Chrysostom

Do not err, my brethren: if anyone follows a schismatic, he will not inherit the Kingdom of God. If any man walks about with strange doctrine, he cannot lie down with the passion. Take care, then, to use one Eucharist, so that whatever you do, you do according to God: for there is one Flesh of our Lord Jesus Christ, and one cup in the union of His Blood; one altar, as there is one bishop with the presbytery and my fellow servants, the deacons."

Ignatius of Antioch

Even if one should give away all his possessions in the world, and yet be in communion with heresy, he cannot be a friend of God, but is rather an enemy

Theodore the Studite

Even if the whole universe holds communion with the [heretical] patriarch, I will not communicate with him. For I know from the writings of the holy Apostle Paul: the Holy Spirit declares that even the angels would be anathema if they should begin to preach another Gospel, introducing some new teaching. Maximus the Confessor

For when the [unbelievers and heretics], though established in a lie, use every means to conceal the shamefulness of their opinions, while we, the servants of the truth, cannot even open our mouths, how can they help condemning the great weakness of our doctrine? How can they help suspecting our religion to be fraud and folly? How shall they not blaspheme Christ as a deceiver, and a cheat . . . ? Moreover, we are to blame for this blasphemy, because we do not desire to be wakeful in arguments for piety, but deem these things superfluous, and care only for the things of earth

John Chrysostom

Grace and truth came by Jesus. They have forsaken the truth, in which the author of Proverbs boasts, saying, 'My throat shall meditate truth'; having embraced falsehood to themselves, it is clear that they have fallen away from grace   Acts of the Seventh Ecumenical Council

Guard yourselves from soul-destroying heresy, communion with which is alienation from Christ.   Theodore the Studite

Guard yourselves from soul-destroying heresy, communion with which is alienation from Christ.   Theodore the Studite

He that does not say 'Anathema' to those in heresy, let him be anathema.

Seventh Ecumenical Council

How then does Paul say, 'Obey them that have the rule over you, and submit yourselves' [Heb. 13:17]? After having said before, 'Whose faith follow, considering the end of their life [Heb. 13:7],' he then said, 'Obey them that have the rule over you, and submit yourselves.' What then (you say), when he is wicked, should we obey? Wicked? In what sense? If indeed in regard to matters of the Faith, flee and avoid him; not only if he be a man, but even if he be an angel come down from Heaven; but if in regard to his life, be not overly-curious   John Chrysostom

I adjure all the people in Cyprus who are true children of the Catholic Church to flee as fast as their feet can carry them from those priests who have fallen and submitted to the Latins; neither assemble in church with them, nor receive any blessing from their hands. For it is better for you to pray to God in your homes alone than to gather together in churches with the Latin-minded.   Germanos II, Patriarch of Constantinople

I am convinced that the further I depart from him [the Patriarch] and from those like him [the Latin-minded], the closer do I draw near God and all the faithful and the holy Fathers; and the more I am separated from them, by so much more am I united to the truth and the holy Fathers.

Mark of Ephesus

Is the shepherd a heretic? Then he is a wolf! You must flee from him; do not be deceived to approach him even if he appears gentle and tame. Flee from communion and conversation with him even as you would flee from a poisonous snake.   Photius the Great

It is a commandment of the Lord that we should not be silent when the Faith is in peril. So, when it is a matter of the Faith, one cannot say, 'What am I? A priest, a ruler, a soldier, a farmer, a poor man? I have no say or concern in this matter.' Alas! the stones shall cry out, and you remain silent and unconcerned?   Theodore the Studite

Just as the fishermen hide the hook with bait and covertly hook the fish, similarly, the crafty allies of the heresies cover their evil teachings and corrupt understanding with pietism and hook the more simple, bringing them to spiritual death.   Isidore of Pelusium

---

Let any Bishop, or Presbyter, or Deacon that merely joins in prayer with heretics be suspended, but if he has permitted them to perform any service as clergymen, let him be deposed.   Apostolic Canon 45

Let any clergyman or layman who enters a synagogue of Jews, or of heretics, to pray be both deposed and excommunicated.   Apostolic Canon 65

Let no one communicate who is not of the disciples. Let no Judas receive, lest he suffer the fate of Judas. I would give up my life rather than impart of the Lord's Blood to the unworthy; and I will shed my own blood rather than give such awful Blood contrary to what is right.   John Chrysostom

---

Let no one communicate who is not of the disciples. Let no Judas receive, lest he suffer the fate of Judas. I would give up my life rather than impart of the Lord's Blood to the unworthy; and I will shed my own blood rather than give such awful Blood contrary to what is right.   John Chrysostom

---

Let this, our decision, be plain: that if you do not preach the same doctrine concerning Christ our God as that embraced by the Church of the Romans, and of the Alexandrians, and of all the Catholic Church, which also the great Church of the Constantinopolitans so excellently embraced until you, and if within ten days---counting from the day of this notice---you do not openly and by a written confession reject this infidel innovation, which seeks to separate that which the Holy Scripture has united, you shall be cast out from the entire Catholic Church Pope Celestine I of Rome, Letter to the heretical Patriarch Nestorius of Constantinople, written in the name of the Local Council of Rome, which condemned Nestorius before the convocation of the Third Ecumenical Council.

Motivated by that which is right, the mind finds the truth; but motivated by some passion, it will reject it   Thalassius of Africa

---

Neither the Papist nor the Protestant church can be considered as the True church of Christ. The first was altered by a number of innovations and the accursed despotism (Primacy) due to which resulted the schism from the Orthodox. The same goes for the Protestants whose innumerable innovations lead to total anarchy and chaos. Only the Orthodox church maintained the teachings of Christ flawlessly without a single innovation. Only in the Orthodox church does unity exist. The unity which the Savior was petitioning from the Father saying, "Holy Father keep them in your Name those that you gave me so they can be one just like we were one." (John 17:11...)   Nektarios of Aegina

---

Not only if one posses rank or knowledge is one obliged to strive to speak and teach the doctrines of the orthodoxy ,but even if one were a disciple in rank ,one is obliged to speak truth boldly and openly.   Theodore the Studite

---

Not only if one possesses rank or knowledge is one obliged to strive to speak and to teach the doctrines of Orthodoxy, but even if one be a disciple in rank, one is obliged to speak the truth boldly and openly Letter Two (Book 2) to Monastics   Theodore the Studite

Now we command you, brethren, in the name of our Lord Jesus Christ, that you withdraw yourselves from every brother that walks disorderly, and not according to the tradition which he received from us.   2 Thessalonians 3:6

Put away from among yourselves that wicked person.   I Corinthians 5:13

Some have suffered final shipwreck with regard to the faith. Others, though they have not drowned in their thoughts, are nevertheless perishing through communion with heresy.   Theodore the Studite

Apraphat of Syria writes that the one house in which the Passover is to be eaten is the Church of Christ, and that just as the slave could not eat the Passover unless he was circumcised, so the sinner comes to Baptism, the true Circumcision, and is joined to the People of God, and communicates in the Body and Blood of Christ.   Demonstrations

John of Damascus writes: With all our strength let us beware lest we receive Communion from or give it to heretics. 'Give not what is holy to the dogs,' says the Lord. 'Neither cast you your pearls before swine', lest we become partakers in their dishonor and condemnation.

Exposition of the Orthodox Faith, 4, 13

John the Almsgiver said: We shall not escape sharing in that punishment which, in the world to come, awaits heretics, if we defile Orthodoxy and the holy Faith by adulterous communion with heretics.   John the Almsgiver

---

Maximus the Confessor said: "Even if the whole universe holds communion with the [heretical] patriarch, I will not communicate with him. For I know from the writings of the holy Apostle Paul: the Holy Spirit declares that even the angels would be anathema if they should begin to preach another Gospel, introducing some new teaching."   Maximus the Confessor

---

Do not submit yourselves to monk, nor to presbyters, who teach lawless things and evilly propound them. In addition, why do I say only monastics or presbyters? Follow not even after bishops who guilefully exhort you to do, say, and believe things that are not profitable. What pious man will keep silence, or who will remain altogether at peace? For silence means consent. Oftentimes war is known to be praiseworthy, and a battle proves to be better than a peace that harms the soul. For it is better to separate ourselves from them who do not believe aright than to follow them in evil concord, and by our union with them separate ourselves from God.   Meletius the Confessor

---

That one must not accept the blessings of heretics, which are rather misfortunes than blessings.   Canon 32 of the Council of Laodicea

---

That one must not join in prayer with heretics or schismatics.   Ibid

---

The divine and sacred canons say: 'He who has communion with an excommunicate, let him be excommunicated, as overthrowing the rule of the Church.' Again: 'He who receives a heretic is subject to the same indictment' The great apostle and evangelist John says: 'If anyone comes to you and does not bring this teaching with him, do not greet him and do not receive him into your house; for he who greets him communicates with his evil deeds' (2 John 10-11). If we are forbidden merely to greet him on the way, and if inviting him into our house is prohibited, how can it be otherwise not in a house, but in the temple of God, in the sanctuary at the mystical and terrible Supper of the Son of God Whoever belches out the commemoration of him who has been worthily cut off by the Holy Spirit for his arrogance towards God and the Divine things, becomes for that reason an enemy of God and the Divine things. an Epistle of the Martyred Fathers of the Holy Mountain to Emperor Michael Palaeologus against the heretical Patriarch.

<u>John Beccus of Constantinople</u>

The divine and sacred canons say: 'He who has communion with an excommunicate, let him be excommunicated, as overthrowing the rule of the Church.' And again: 'He who receives a heretic is subject to the same indictments' The great apostle and evangelist John says: 'If anyone comes to you and does not bring this teaching with him, do not greet him and do not receive him into your house; for he who greets him communicates with his evil deeds' (2 John 10-11). If we are forbidden merely to greet him on the way, and if inviting him into our house is prohibited, how can it be otherwise not in a house, but in the temple of God, in the sanctuary at the mystical and terrible Supper of the Son of God. Whoever belches out the commemoration of him who has been worthily cut off by the Holy Spirit for his arrogance towards God and the Divine things, becomes for that reason an enemy of God and the Divine things. an Epistle of the Martyred Fathers of the Holy Mountain to Emperor Michael Palaeologus against the heretical. <u>Ibid</u>

The fact that we do not become indignant over small matters is the cause of all our calamities; and because slight errors escape fitting correction, greater ones creep in. As in a body, a neglect of wounds generates fever, infection and death; so in the soul, slight evils overlooked open the door to graver ones . . . But if a proper rebuke had at first been given to those who attempted to depart from the divine sayings and change some small matter, such a pestilence would not have been generated, nor such a storm have seized upon the Church; for he that overturns even that which is minor in the sound Faith, will cause ruin in all. John Chrysostom

---

Do not think that I am come to send peace on earth; I came not to send peace, but a sword. For I am come to set a man at variance against his father, and the daughter against her mother, and the daughter in law against her mother in law. A man's foes shall be they of his own household. Matthew 10:34-36

This good zeal has always inspired our Most Holy Church to offer up liturgical petitions such as: "gather the dispersed; bring back those who have gone astray, and unite them to Your Holy, Catholic, and Apostolic Church." This good zeal expands the hearts of Orthodox Christians to pray unceasingly for the repentance and the return of those who belong to other denominations and other religions, and of the whole world , to the light of our Holy Faith.

Nectarios of Aegina

This is indeed peace, when that which is ailing is cut away, when that which is seditious is separated. John Chrysostom

---

Those that are not reborn by the divine grace in the only one, Holy, Catholic and Apostolic Church, they do not consist of (comprise) any church, neither visible nor invisible." Nektarios of Aegina

---

We exhort all pious and Orthodox Christians: remain in those things, which you learned and in which you were born and bred, and when the times and circumstances call for it, shed your very blood in order both to keep the Faith given us by our Fathers and to keep your confession.

The Bishops of the Synod who were present (Constantinople, 1583)

We forbid all the clergy who adhere to the Orthodox and Ecumenical Council in any way to submit to the bishops who have already apostatized or shall hereafter apostatize. Third Canon of the Third Ecumenical Council Ever rekindle this faith within yourselves and keep yourselves unblemished and undefiled, by neither having communion with the aforementioned [Nestorius], nor attending to him as though he were a teacher, so long as he remains a wolf and not a shepherd . . . We are in communion with those clergymen or laypeople that have separated themselves from him or who have been deposed by him on account of the right Faith, because we do not endorse his unjust sentence; rather, we praise those who have suffered, and we say to them, 'Blessed are you if you are reviled for the Lord's sake; for the Spirit and the might of God rest upon you'   Cyril of Alexandria

We make our protest to you in this third letter, and counsel you to refrain from such wicked and perverse doctrines, which you believe and teach, and that you choose the right Faith . . . Other-wise, unless Your Reverence does so by the time set in the letters sent to you by our concelebrant, the most righteous and God-fearing bishop of Rome, Celestine, know that you will have no portion with us, nor place or speech among the priests and bishops of God   Ibid

We have excised and cut them [the Papists] off from the common body of the Church, we have, therefore, rejected them as heretics, and for this reason we are separated from them"; they are, therefore, heretics, and we have cut them off as heretics.   Mark of Ephesus

We shall not escape sharing in that punishment which, in the world to come, awaits heretics, if we defile Orthodoxy and the holy Faith by adulterous communion with heretics.   John the Almsgiver

When Hypatius understood what opinions Nestorius held, immediately, in the Church of the Apostles, he erased his name from the diptychs, so that it should no longer be pronounced at the Oblation. [This was before Nestorius' condemnation by the Third Ecumenical Council.] When the most pious Bishop Eulalius learned of this, he was anxious about the outcome of the affair. In addition, seeing that it had been noised abroad, Nestorius also ordered him to reprimand Hypatius. For Nestorius was still powerful in the city. Bishop Eulalius spoke thus to Hypatius: 'Why have you erased his name without understanding what the consequences would be?' Hypatius replied: 'From the time that I learned that he said unrighteous things about the Lord, I have no longer been in communion with him and I do not commemorate his name; for he is not a bishop.' Then the bishop, in anger, said: 'Be off with you! Make amends for what you have done, for I shall take measures against you.' Hypatius replied: 'Do as you wish. As for me, I have decided to suffer anything, and it is with this in mind that I have done this'   Hypatius

With all our strength let us beware lest we receive Communion from or give it to heretics. 'Give not what is holy to the dogs,' says the Lord. 'Neither cast you your pearls before swine', lest we become partakers in their dishonor and condemnation.   Exposition of the Orthodox Faith, IV, 13

You told me that you feared to tell your presbyter not to commemorate the heresiarch; . . . I will not presume to say anything about this to you for the present, except that the communion is defiled simply by commemorating him, even if he who is commemorating is Orthodox.

Theodore the Studite

'The sixteenth century gave birth to four great beasts: the heresy of Luther, the heresy of Calvin, the heresy of the Jesuits, and the heresy of the new calendar. The heresies of Luther and Calvin were refuted by [such and such] . . . As for the heresy of the new calendar, this was condemned by a decision of the great Ecumenical Council that met in Constantinople in 1593'.

Dositheus, Patriarch of Jerusalem

The life of Maximus is also instructive for us. Maximus, though only a simple monk, resisted and cut off communion with every patriarch, metropolitan, archbishop and bishop in the East because of their having been infected with the heresy of Monothelitism. During the first imprisonment of the , the messengers from the Ecumenical Patriarch asked him, "To which church do you belong? To that of Byzantium, of Rome, Antioch, Alexandria, or Jerusalem? For all these churches, together with the provinces in subjection to them, are in unity. Therefore, if you also belong to the Catholic Church, enter into communion with us at once, lest fashioning for yourself some new and strange pathway, you fall into that which you do not even expect!"

To this the righteous man wisely replied, "Christ the Lord called that Church the Catholic Church which maintains the true and saving confession of the Faith. It was for this confession that He called Peter blessed, and He declared that He would found His Church upon this confession. However, I wish to know the contents of your confession, on the basis of which all churches, as you say, have entered into communion. If it is not opposed to the truth, then neither will I be separated from it." The confession which they were proposing to the was not Orthodox, of course, and so he refused to comply with their coercions. Furthermore, they were lying about the See of Rome, which, in fact, had remained Orthodox. Some time later, at his last interrogation by the Byzantine authorities, the following dialogue took place:

The   said, "They [the Patriarchs of Constantinople and Alexandria and all the other heretical bishops of the East] have been deposed and deprived of the priesthood at the local synod which took place recently in Rome. What Mysteries, then, can they perform? Or what spirit will descend upon those who are ordained by them?"

"Then you alone will be saved, and all others will perish?" they objected.

To this the   replied, "When all the people in Babylon were worshipping the golden idol, the Three Holy Children did not condemn anyone to perdition. They did not concern themselves with the doings of others, but took care only for themselves, lest they should fall away from true piety. In precisely the same way, when Daniel was cast into the lion's den, he did not condemn any of those who, fulfilling the law of Darius, did not wish to pray to God, but he kept in mind his own duty, and desired rather to die than to sin against his conscience by transgressing the Law of God. God forbid that I should condemn anyone or say that I alone am being saved! However, I shall sooner agree to die than to apostatize in any way from the true Faith and thereby suffer torments of conscience."

"But what will you do", inquired the envoys, "when the Romans are united to the Byzantines? Yesterday, indeed, two delegates arrived from Rome and tomorrow, the Lord's day, they will communicate the Holy Mysteries with the Patriarch. "

The   replied, "Even if the whole universe holds communion with the Patriarch, I will not communicate with him. For I know from the writings of the holy Apostle Paul: the Holy Spirit declares that even the angels would be anathema if they should begin to preach another Gospel, introducing some new teaching."

As history has demonstrated, Maximus—who was only a simple monk and not even ordained—and his two disciples were the ones who were Orthodox, and all those illustrious, famous and influential Patriarchs and Metropolitans whom the had written against were the ones who were in heresy. When the Sixth Ecumenical Synod was finally convened, among those condemned for heresy were four Patriarchs of Constantinople, one Pope of Rome, one Patriarch of Alexandria, two Patriarchs of Antioch and a multitude of other Metropolitans, Archbishops and Bishops. During all those years, that one

simple monk was right, and all those notable bishops were wrong.
Maximus   the   Confessor

Concerning the Patriarch I shall say this, lest it should perhaps occur to him to show me a certain respect at the burial of this my humble body, or to send to my grave any of his hierarchs or clergy or in general any of those in communion with him in order to take part in prayer or to join the priests invited to it from amongst us, thinking that at some time, or perhaps secretly, I had allowed communion with him. And lest my silence give occasion to those who do not know my views well and fully to suspect some kind of conciliation, I hereby state and testify before the many worthy men here present that I do not desire, in any manner and absolutely, and do not accept communion with him or with those who are with him, not in this life nor after my death, just as (I accept) neither the Union nor Latin dogmas, which he and his adherents have accepted, and for the enforcement of which he has occupied this presiding place, with the aim of overturning the true dogmas of the Church. I am absolutely convinced that the farther I stand from him and those like him, the nearer I am to God and all the saints, and to the degree that I separate myself from them am in union with the Truth and with the Holy Fathers, the Theologians of the Church; and I am likewise convinced that those who count themselves with them stand far away from the Truth and from the blessed Teachers of the Church. Thus, for this reason I say: just as in the course of my whole life I was separated from them, so at the time of my departure, yea and after my death, I turn away from intercourse and communion with them and vow and command that none (of them) shall approach either my burial or my grave, and likewise anyone else from our side, with the aim of attempting to join and concelebrate in our Divine services; for this would be to mix what cannot be mixed. However, it befits them to be absolutely separated from us until such time as God shall grant correction and peace to His Church.   Mark of Ephesus

E lijah

This man of God sought nothing for himself, but all for God. God was everything to him: all glory, all strength, and all good. Therefore God crowned him with deathless glory, fearsome might and good things that do not decay and that moth does not corrupt (cf.. Mt. 6:20). This is why God did not allow Elijah to die, but caught him up into heaven like Enoch. Holy Elijah had a soul as pure as morning dew, a body as chaste as a child's and a heart and mind as stainless as that of an angel of God, and therefore he was and remains a vessel of God's power. Therefore he wrought marvels then and works them now.   Nikolai Velimirovich

---

Elisha

Naaman, the commander of the Syrian army, came to Elisha with many gifts. Moreover, what did the prophet do? Did he go out to meet him? Did he run towards him? No, he sent a lad to find out why Naaman had come, and did not even admit him to his presence. This was to prevent anyone thinking that he had cured Naaman in return for the gifts that he brought (cf. 2King 5:8-16). This story, without teaching us to be arrogant, shows us that we should not flatter, because of our needs, those who value highly the very things it is our vocation to despise.   Neilos the Ascetic

---

Empathy

When can someone understand human suffering? When he also suffers. When he goes through the same, he learns and understands the other person's suffering. Otherwise, he is callous and is not grieved, unless he happens to have a good nature. However, all natural attributes merit neither honor nor dishonor; achievements and falls depend on our own free will

Joseph the Hesychast

End Times

The more calamities afflict them, the more evil will they become, instead of repenting ,they will be angered at God. The evil deeds of people will surpass those of people of the time of flood. All will speak only of evil, plan only evil, consent to evil, and meet other only for evil.   Nilus the Myrrh

---

ndurance

Have courage, faith, hope and love in God patience unto the end, to gain your immortal soul, which the whole world is not equal to.   Joseph the Hesychast

---

...the chief thing that every man needs is endurance, just as the earth needs water. On this earth he should lay the foundation of faith (cf. 2 Pet. 1:5). Then discrimination, like an experienced builder, can set about slowly building the house of the soul with clay taken from the earth of humility, successively binding one stone to another - that is, one virtue to another - until the roof, which is perfect love, is put in place. Then, when it has posted good doorkeepers, always bearing arms - that is to say, luminous thoughts and godlike actions capable of protecting the king from being disturbed - the master of the house comes and takes up residence in it.

Peter of Damaskos

Because we do not believe, endurance is far from us.   Ephrem the Syrian

---

No matter what misfortune might befall you, no matter what unpleasantness might occur, say "I will endure this for Jesus Christ's sake!" Just say that, and you will feel better, for the Name of Jesus Christ is powerful. Before It, all difficulties abate, and demons disappear. Your annoyance and faintness of heart will abate when you repeat His most sweet Name. Lord, grant unto me to see my transgressions. Lord, grant unto me patience, magnanimity, and meekness.   Antony of Optina

...God has shown how close He is to those who are willing to endure trials for His sake, and who will not abandon virtue out of cowardice because of the suffering involved, but cleave to the law of God by patiently enduring what befalls them, rejoicing in the hope of salvation.   Peter of Damaskos

Endurance is like an unshakable rock in the winds and waves of life. However the tempest batters him, the patient man remains steadfast and does not turn back; and when he finds relief and joy, he is not carried away by self-glory: he is always the same, whether things are hard or easy, and for this reason, he is proof against the snares of the enemy.   Ibid

It is always possible to make a new start by means of repentance. 'For a righteous man may fall seven times And rise again' (Prov. 24:16). In addition, if you fall again, then rise again, without despairing at all of your salvation, no matter what happens. So long as you do not surrender yourself willingly to the enemy, your patient endurance, combined with self-reproach, will suffice for your salvation. 'For we ourselves were also once foolish, disobedient,' says Paul, '...not by works of righteousness which we have done, but according to His mercy He saved us' (Tit. 3:3,5).   Ibid

Patient endurance kills the despair that kills the soul; it teaches the soul to take comfort and not to grow listless in the face of its many battles and afflictions.   Ibid

The patient endurance of the saints exhausts the evil power that attacks them, since it makes them glory in sufferings undergone for the sake of truth.   Ibid

ntertainment

Most men not only bear Satan's burden willingly in their hearts, but they become so accustomed to it that they often do not feel it, and even imperceptibly increase it. Sometimes, however, the evil enemy increases his burden tenfold, and then they become terribly despondent and fainthearted, they murmur and blaspheme God's name. The usual means that men...take to drive away their anguish are...entertainments...But such means afterwards increase still more the anguish and weariness of their hearts. If, happily, they turn to God, then the burden is removed from their heart, and they clearly see that previously the heaviest burden was lying on their heart, though frequently they did not feel it.   John of Kronstadt

ntrance of the Theotokos

As the Virgin's parents led her to the doors of the Temple, she was surrounded by angels, and all the heavenly hosts rejoiced. Although the angels knew nothing of the power of this mystery, as the Lord's servants they obeyed His command to serve at her entry. They marveled when they saw that the most pure vessel of the virtues bore the tokens of everlasting purity and were amazed that while she was clothed in flesh, no stain of sin could ever dray near her; then they preceded to do the will of the Lord and to perform what they had been instructed to do.   George of Nicomedia

Envy

As for your own envy, you will be able to check it if you rejoice with the man whom you envy whenever he rejoices, and grieve whenever he grieves.

Maximos the Confessor

Envy has alienated wives from their husbands, and changed that saying of our father Adam, "This is now bone of my bones, and flesh of my flesh." Envy and strife have overthrown great cities and rooted up mighty nations.

Epistle of Clement To The Corinthians

My children, desire to purify your hearts from envy and from anger with each other, lest death should overcome you, and you will be counted among the murderers. For whosoever hates his brother, kills a soul.

Abbot Anthony the Great

What separates us from the love of friends is envying or being envied, causing or receiving harm, insulting or being insulted, and suspicious thoughts. Would that you had never done or experienced anything of this sort and in this way separated yourself from the love of a friend.

Maximos the Confessor

---

ternal life

We were created for eternal life by our Creator, we are called to it by the word of God, and we are renewed by holy Baptism. Moreover, Christ the Son of God came into the world for this that He should call us and take us there, and He is the one thing needful. For this reason your very first endeavor and care should be to receive it. Without it everything is as nothing, though you have the whole world under you.   Abbot Epiphanios

---

ternal Security

Christ will not die again on behalf of those who now commit sin because death shall no more have dominion over Him.... Therefore we should not be puffed up.... However, we should beware lest somehow, after [we have come to] the knowledge of Christ, if we do things displeasing to God, we obtain no further forgiveness of sins but rather be shut out from His kingdom (Heb. 6:4-6).   Irenaeus, pupil of Polycarp

---

It is written, 'He who endures to the end, the same shall be saved' [Matt. 10:22]. Therefore, whatever precedes the end is only a step by which we ascend to the summit of salvation. It is not the final point wherein we have already gained the full result of the ascent.   Cyprian (200-258 AD)

Some people act as though God were under an obligation to bestow even on the unworthy His intended gift. They turn His liberality into slavery.... For do not many afterwards fall out of grace? Is not this gift taken away from many?

Tertullian

For Christians above all men are forbidden to correct the stumblings of sinners by force ... It is necessary to make a man better not by force but by persuasion. We neither have authority granted us by law to restrain sinners, nor, if it were, should we know how to use it, since God gives the crown to those who are kept from evil, not by force, but by choice.   John Chrysostom

Let us also imitate Him, and despair of no one. For the fishermen, too, when they have cast many times have not succeeded; but afterwards having cast again, have gained all. Therefore, we also expect that you will all at one show to us ripe fruit. For the husbandman, too, after he has sown, waits one day or two days, and is a long while in expectation; and all at once he sees the fruits springing up on every side.   Ibid

When the zeal of the religious emperor (Constantine I) had brought together priests of God from all over the earth (to the council of Nicaea in 325), rumor of the event gathered as well philosophers and dialecticians of great renown and fame.

One of them who was celebrated for his ability in dialectic used to hold ardent debates each day with our bishops, men likewise by no means unskilled in the are of disputation, and there resulted a magnificent display for the learned and educated men who gathered to listen. Nor could the philosopher be cornered or trapped in any way by anyone, for he met the questions proposed with such rhetorical skill that whenever he seemed most firmly trapped, he escaped like a slippery snake.

However, that God might show that the kingdom of God is based upon power rather than speech, one of the confessors (who had suffered tortures during the persecutions), a man of simplest character who knew only Christ Jesus and him crucified, was present with the other bishops in attendance.

When he saw the philosopher insulting our people and proudly displaying his skills in dialectic, he asked everyone for a chance to exchange a few words with the philosopher. Nevertheless, our people, who knew only the man's simplicity and lack of skill in speech, feared that they might be put to shame in case his holy simplicity became a source of laughter to the clever.

However, the elder insisted, and he began his discourse in this way: "In the name of Jesus Christ, Oh philosopher," he said, "listen to the truth! There is one God who made heaven and earth, who gave breath to man whom he had formed from the mud of the earth, and who created everything, what is seen and what is not seen, with the power of his word and established it with the sanctification of his Spirit. The word and wisdom, whom we call "Son", took pity on the errors of humankind, was born of a Virgin, by suffering death freed us from everlasting death, and by his resurrection conferred on us eternal life. Him we await as the judge to come of all that we do. Do you believe this is so, Oh philosopher?"

The philosopher, as though he had nothing whatever that he could say in opposition to this, so astonished was he at the power of what had been said, could only reply that he thought that it was so, and that what had been said was the only truth. Then the elder said, "If you believe that this is so, arise, follow me to the church, and receive the seal of this faith."

The philosopher, turning to his disciples and to those who had gathered to listen, said, "Listen, Oh learned men: so long as it was words with which I had to deal, I set words against words and what was said I refuted with my rhetoric. However, when power rather than words came out of the mouth of the speaker, words could not withstand power, nor could man oppose God. And therefore, if any one of you was able to feel in what was said what I feel, let him believe Christ and follow this old man in whom God has spoken." Thus the philosopher became a Christian and rejoiced at last to have been vanquished.   Rufinus

You were not worthy of having what you possess and what you keep through the grace of the giver. Do not hesitate, then, to distribute To those who ask, just as the woman of Samaria once shared. For having drawn from the well by herself, she shared with others what she received. No one asked her, and yet she gave to all ungrudgingly of her free gift. She thirsts, yet gives lavishly, not drinking, she gives to drink. When she has not yet tasted, still as one who is drunk, she cries out to those of her race: "Come, I have found a spring; is not this the One who furnishes Exceeding great joy and redemption?   Romanos the Melodist

---

vening

The farmer's wealth is gathered on the threshing floor and in the winepress, but the wealth and knowledge of monks is gathered during the evenings and the night hours while standing at prayer and engaged in spiritual activity.

John Climacus

---

vening Prayer

Do not neglect evening prayer. Pray with eagerness like those who are going to a feast. They are awake and feel joy alone. Thus, since you are going to speak with your Bridegroom, do not listen when the Tempter tells you various things in order to hinder you, because you know there is someone who cares for you.   Amphilochios Makris

---

vil

Evil is not an actual substance, but absence of good; just as darkness is nothing but absence of light.   Evagrius

---

Evil is not to be imputed to the essence of created beings, but to their erroneous and mindless motivation.   Maximos the Confessor

Inside us evil is at work suggesting unworthy inclinations. However, it is not in us in the same way as, to take as an example, water mixes with wine. Evil is in us without being mixed with good. We are a field in which wheat and weeds are growing separately. We are a house in which there is a thief, but also the owner. We are a spring, which rises from the middle of the mud, but pours out pure water. All the same, it is enough to stir up the mud and the spring is fouled. It is the same with the soul. If the evil is spread, it forms a unity with the soul and makes it dirty. With our consent, evil is united with the soul; they become accomplices. Yet there comes a moment when the soul can free itself and remain separate again: in repentance, contrition, prayer, recourse to God. The soul could not benefit from these habits if it were always sunk in evil. It is like a marriage. A woman is united with a man and they become one flesh. However, when one of them dies, the other is left alone. Nevertheless, union with the Holy Spirit is complete. So, let us become a single spirit with Him. Let us be wholly absorbed by grace. Macarius the Great

The beginning of evil is heedlessness. Abbot Poemen

You know that evil entered into us through the transgression of the commandments. Hence it is obvious that by keeping them, evil departs from us. However, without the doing of the commandments we should not even aspire or hope for purity of soul, because at the very outset we do not walk on the path that leads us to purity of soul. Do not say that God can give us the grace of purity of soul even without our keeping the commandments.

Isaac the Syrian

Evil Thoughts

A PRAYER AGAINST EVIL THOUGHTS

"Oh Master, Lord my God, in Whose hands are my lots, help me according to Your mercy and do not allow me to be destroyed with mine iniquities, nor permit me by my will to follow the desires of my flesh against my spirit. I was fashioned by You; do not forsake the works of Your hands.

Turn not Your face, have pity, do not despise me, neither forsake me, Oh Lord, for I am weak; and it is to You, my protecting God, that I have come for refuge. Heal my soul, for I have sinned against You. Save me for the sake of Your mercy, for upon You have I cast myself from my very youth.

May those who war against me be put to shame, and may those who seek to separate me from You through immodest acts, unseemly thoughts, and unprofitable reflections be turned back.

Chase far from me every filthiness, which is superabundance of evil.

For You alone are holy; You alone are mighty; You alone are immortal, having unfathomable power against all things; and it is through You that every power is given against the Devil and his forces.

Unto You is due all glory, honor and worship, to the Father, and to the Son, and to the Holy Spirit, now and ever, and unto the ages of ages. Amen."

The Trebnic

When evil thoughts become active within us, we should blame ourselves and not ancestral sin.   Kosmas Aitolos

---

The roots of evil thoughts are the obvious vices, which we keep trying to justify in our words and actions.   Ibid

---

If you do not want evil thoughts to be active within you, accept humiliation of soul and affliction of the flesh; and this not just on particular occasions, but always, everywhere and in all things.   Ibid

xhortations

Do not be despondent when fighting against the incorporeal enemy, but even in the midst of your afflictions and oppression praise the Lord, Who has found you worthy to suffer for Him, by struggling against the subtlety of the serpent, and to be wounded for Him at every hour; for had you not lived piously, and endeavored to become united to God, the enemy would not have attacked and tormented you.   John of Kronstadt

If you are a Christian, no earthly city is yours; while our City 'the Builder and Maker is God.' Though we may gain possession of the whole world, we are withal but strangers and sojourners in it all! We are enrolled in Heaven: our citizenship is there! Let us not, after the manner of little children, despise things that are great, and admire those which are little.   John Chrysostom.

"Let the eye look on no evil thing, and it has become a sacrifice; let your tongue speak nothing filthy, and it has become an offering; let your hand do no lawless deed, and it has become a whole burnt offering … Let us then from our hands and feet and mouth and all other members, yield a first-fruit to God."   Ibid

In all your works, either at home or at the place of your service, do not forget that all your strength, your light and your success are in Christ and His Cross; therefore, do not fail to call upon the Lord before beginning any work, saying: Jesus, help me! Jesus, enlighten me! Thus your heart will be supported and warmed by lively faith and hope in Christ, for His is the power and glory unto ages of ages.   John of Kronstadt

Your Lord is Love: love Him and in Him all men, as His children in Christ. Your Lord is a fire: do not let your heart be cold, but burn with faith and love. Your Lord is light: do not walk in darkness of mind, without reasoning or understanding, or without faith. Your Lord is a God of mercy and bountifulness: be a source of mercy and bountifulness to your neighbors. If you will be such, you will find salvation yourself with everlasting glory.

Ibid

Knowing, therefore, that "as we brought nothing into the world, so we can carry nothing out", let us arm ourselves with the armor of righteousness; and let us teach, first of all, ourselves to walk in the commandments of the Lord. Next, [teach] your wives [to walk] in the faith given to them, and in love and purity tenderly loving their own husbands in all truth, and loving all [others] equally in all chastity; and to train up their children in the knowledge and fear of God. Teach the widows to be discreet as respects the faith of the Lord, praying continually for all, being far from all slandering, evil-speaking, false-witnessing, love of money, and every kind of evil; knowing that they are the altar s of God, that He clearly perceives all things, and that nothing is hid from Him, neither reasonings, nor reflections, nor any one of the secret things of the heart.   The Epistle of Polycarp to the Philippians

Let the young men also be blameless in all things, being especially careful to preserve purity, and keeping themselves in, as with a bridle, from every kind of evil. For it is well that they should be cut off from the lusts that are in the world, since "every lust wars against the spirit"; and "neither fornicators, nor effeminate, nor abusers of themselves with mankind, shall inherit the kingdom of God," nor those who do things inconsistent and unbecoming.

Ibid

Your Lord is Love: love Him and in Him all men, as His children in Christ. Your Lord is a fire: do not let your heart be cold, but burn with faith and love. Your Lord is light: do not walk in darkness of mind, without reasoning or understanding, or without faith. Your Lord is a God of mercy and bountifulness: be a source of mercy and bountifulness to your neighbors. If you will be such, you will find salvation yourself with everlasting glory. Ibid

---

Thirst for Jesus, so that he may fill you to overflowing with His love. Blind your eyes to all that is held in honor in the world, so that you may be held worthy to have the peace, which comes from God reign in your heart. Fast from the attractions that make the eyes glitter, in order that you may become worthy of spiritual joy. If your way of life is unworthy of God, then do not ask Him for glorious things, otherwise, you will appear as someone who tempts God. Prayer conforms strictly with behavior.   Isaac of Nineveh

---

 **xile**

Exile means that we leave forever everything in our own country that prevents us from reaching the goal of piety. Exile means modest manners, wisdom which remains unknown, prudence not recognized as such by most, a hidden life, an invisible intention, unseen meditation, desire for humiliation, longing for hardship, constant determination to love God, abundance of love, renunciation of vainglory, depth of silence.

John Climacus

Run from places of sin as from the plague. For when fruit is not present, we have no frequent desire to eat it. Ibid

There is such a thing as exile, an irrevocable renunciation of everything in one's familiar surroundings that hinders one from attaining the ideal of holiness. Exile is a disciplined heart, unheralded wisdom, an unpublicized understanding, a hidden life, masked ideals. It is unseen meditation, the striving to be humble, a wish for poverty, the longing for what is divine. It is an outpouring of love, a denial of vainglory, a depth of silence. Ibid

Those who have come to love the Lord are at first unceasingly and greatly disturbed by this thought, as if burning with divine fire. I speak of separation from their own, undertaken by the lovers of perfection so that they may live a life of hardship and simplicity. Yet great and praiseworthy as this is, yet it requires great discretion; for not every kind of exile, carried to extremes, is good. Ibid

Exorcism

One day a man possessed with a devil came to Scetis, and they prayed over him, but the devil did not leave him, for it was obstinate. The priests said, "What can we do against this devil? No one can drive him away, except Abbot Bessarion, but if we call him, he will not come, even to the church. Therefore let us do this: since he comes to church early, before anyone else, let us make the possessed sleep here, and when he comes, let us keep to our prayer, and say to him, 'Abbot, awaken the brother.'" This is what they did. When the old man came early, they kept to their prayer and said to him, "Awaken the brother." The old man said to him, "Arise and go." Immediately the devil departed from him and from that hour he was healed.

Bessarion of Egypt

Some visitors came to the Thebaid one day to visit an old man, bringing one possessed with a devil that he might heal him. When they persistently asked him, the old man said to the devil, "Come out of God's creature." In addition, the devil said to the old man, "I am going to come out, but I am going to ask you a question. Tell me, who are the goats and who are the sheep?" The old man said, "I am one of the goats, but as for the sheep, God alone knows who they are." When he heard this, the devil began to cry out with a loud voice, "Because of your humility, I am driven away!" and he departed at the same hour.   The Desert Fathers

Faint-Heartedness

Amma Theodora said, "It is good to live in peace, for the wise man practices perpetual prayer. It is truly a great thing for a virgin or a monk to live in peace, especially for the younger ones. However, you should realize that as soon as you intend to live in peace, at once evil comes and weighs down your soul through accidie, faintheartedness, and evil thoughts. It also attacks your body through sickness, debility, weakening of the knees, and all the members. It dissipates the strength of soul and body, so that one believes one is ill and no longer able to pray. Nevertheless, if we are vigilant, all these temptations fall away. There was, in fact a monk who was seized by cold and fever every time he began to pray, and he suffered from headaches, too. In this condition, he said to himself, 'I am ill, and near to death; so now I will get up before I die and pray.' By reasoning in this way, he did violence to himself and prayed, When he had finished, the fever abated also. So, by reasoning in this way, the brother resisted, and prayed and was able to conquer his thoughts."   Ibid

To the Monk Andrew, when he became faint from the temptations that had come upon him:

"Andrew! My brother one in soul (with me), do not grow faint. God has not abandoned you and will not abandon you. However, know that the sentence pronounced by the Master to our common father Adam: "In the sweat of your brow you shall earn your bread" (Genesis 3:19) is immutable. Moreover, just as this commandment is given to the outward man, so to the inward man it is commanded to aid the prayers of the Saints by means of one's own ascetic labors; and these prayers greatly help a man so that he will not remain fruitless. For just as gold which is heated in a furnace, held with pincers and beaten with a hammer, becomes pure and fit for a royal crown, so also a man being supported by the mighty and much-performing prayer of the Saints is heated by sorrows, receives the blows of temptations and, if he endures everything with gratitude, becomes a son of the Kingdom.

Therefore, everything that might happen to you occurs for your benefit, so that you also might receive boldness before God, both through the intercession of the Saints and through your own labors. And do not be ashamed to offer now to God the beginning of these labors, lest in place of spiritual joy, sorrow should overtake you; and believe that He who has given the promises will fulfill them (Hebrews 10:23). Prosper in the Lord, my beloved.   Barsanuphius and John

---

Faith

"When Scripture says, 'He will reward every man according to his works' (Matt. 16:27), do not imagine that works in themselves merit either hell or the Kingdom. On the contrary, Christ rewards each man according to whether his works are done with faith or without faith in Himself; and He is not a dealer bound by contract, but God our Creator and Redeemer.

Mark the Ascetic

...a man has no right to be called faithful, if his faith is a bare word and if he has not in him a faith made active by love or the Spirit. Thus faith must be made evident by progress in works, or it must act in the light and shine in works, as the divine Apostle says: Show me your faith without your works, and I will show you my faith by my works' (James 2:18), thus showing that the faith of grace is made evident by works performed in accordance with the commandments, just as the commandments are fulfilled in deed and are made bright through the faith which is in grace.   Gregory of Sinai

---

...all things that are accomplished in the world, even by those who are aliens from the Church, are accomplished by faith.   Cyril of Jerusalem

---

...faith is that which completes our argument.   Gregory Nazianzen

---

...there is one kind of faith, the dogmatic, involving an assent of the soul on some particular point...But there is a second kind of faith, which is bestowed by Christ as a gift of grace...The faith then which is given of grace from the Spirit is not merely doctrinal, but also works things above man's power.

Cyril of Jerusalem

...there is, first, the ordinary faith of all Orthodox Christians, that is to say, correct doctrinal belief concerning God and His creation, both visible and invisible, as the Holy Catholic Church, by God's grace, has received it; and there is, second, the faith of contemplation or spiritual knowledge, which is not in any way opposed to the first kind of faith; on the contrary, the first gives birth to the second, while the second strengthens the first.

Peter of Damaskos

...though remission of sins is given equally to all, the communion of the Holy

Spirit is bestowed in proportion to each man's faith. If you have labored little, you receive little; but if you have wrought much, the reward is great. You are running for yourself, see to your own interest.   Cyril of Jerusalem

---

...while the Lord's victory is certainly an accomplished fact, my personal participation in that victory is as yet far from complete...My trust is, therefore in Christ, not in myself, and I am confident that Christ is faithful and stands firm.   Kallistos Ware

---

For the method of godliness consists of these two things, pious doctrines, and virtuous practice: and neither are the doctrines acceptable to God apart from good works, nor does God accept the works, which are not perfected with pious doctrines.   Cyril of Jerusalem

---

A brother questioned Abbot Poemen saying, "Give me a word." In addition, he said to him, "The fathers put compunction as the beginning of every action." The brother said again, "Give me another word." The old man replied, "As far as you can, do some manual work so as to be able to give alms, for it is written that alms and faith purify from sin." The brother said, "What is faith?" The old man said, "Faith is to live humbly and to give alms."
                                                                        The Desert Fathers

---

A fiery dart of desire of base indulgence is often cast forth from the devil: but faith, suggesting a picture of the judgment, cools down the mind, and quenches the dart.   Cyril of Jerusalem

---

A man advises his neighbor in accordance with what his neighbor knows. Correspondingly, God acts on one who hears Him according to the degree of his faith.   Abbot Mark the Evergetinos

---

An old man and a brother led their life together. Now the old man was charitable. It happened that there was a famine and the people came to his door seeking alms, and in charity the old man gave to all who came. Seeing what was happening, the brother said to the old man, "Give me my share of the loaves, and do what you like with yours." The old man divided the loaves and gave alms from his share.

Now many people hastened to the old man, learning that he supplied everyone, and God -- seeing that he supplied everyone -- blessed these loaves. Yet when the brother had consumed his own food he said to the old man, "Since I have only a little food left, Abbot, take me back into the common life again." The old man said, "I will do as you wish." Therefore, they began to again to live in common.

When scarcity came again, the needy came back seeking alms. Now one day the brother came in and saw they were short of loaves. A poor man came, and the old man told the brother to give him alms. He said, "It is no longer possible, father." The old man said to him, "Go in and look." The brother went inside and found the bin full of loaves. When he saw that, he was filled with fear, and taking some he gave to the poor. In this way he learned the faith and virtue of the old man, and he gave glory to God. The Desert Fathers

---

Just as tools without the workmen and the workmen without tools are unable to do anything, just so neither is faith without the fulfillment of the commandments, nor the fulfillment of the commandments without faith able to renew and re-create us, nor make us new men from the old. Yet, whenever we do possess both within a heart free of doubt, then we shall become the Master's vessels, be made fit for the reception of the spiritual myrrh. Then, too, will He Who makes darkness His hiding-place renew us by the gift of the Holy Spirit and raise us up new instead of old, and part the veil of His darkness and carry our mind away and allow it to peek as through some narrow opening, and grant it to see Him, still somehow dimly, and one might look on the disk of the sun or moon. It is then that the mind is taught -- or, put better -- knows and is initiated, and is assumed that that truly in no other way does one arrive at even partial participation in the ineffable good things of God except by way of the heart's humility, unwavering faith, and the resolve of the whole soul to renounce all the world and everything in it, together with one's own will, in order to keep all of God's commandments.

Symeon the New Theologian

As the memory of fire does not warm the body, so faith without love does not bring about the illumination of knowledge in the soul.

Maximus Confessor

Before anything else one must believe in God, "that He is, and that He is a rewarder of them that diligently seek Him" (Hebrews 11:6).

Seraphim of Sarov

Belief is a matter of dying for Christ and His commandments. It is believing that such a death is life giving. It is to count poverty as riches, and to consider the lowest humiliation as true honor and nobility. Faith is believing that when one has nothing, one has everything. More than this, it is to possess the incomprehensible riches of the knowledge of Christ and to look upon all visible things as but clay and smoke.

Symeon the New Theologian

God said, I require mercy, and not sacrifice; and the acknowledgement of God, and not whole burnt offerings" Hosea 6:6. What is meant by mercy? What by sacrifice? By mercy then is signified Justification and grace in Christ; even that which is by faith. For we have been justified, not by the works of the law that we have done, but by His great mercy. Sacrifice means the law of Moses.   Cyril of Alexandria

Citizens fear enemy invasions so long as they have no help from the king. When the news comes that a military commander has entered their town, they cease to worry in the knowledge that the authorities will take care of them. Even if they hear that the enemy approaches, they are not afraid since they have a protector. In the same way, if we believe in God, we do not fear the demons, for God sends us His help.   Barsanuphius and John

Complete salvation depends not on the faith of the heart alone, but also upon confessing it, for the Lord said, `Whosoever shall deny Me before men, him will I also deny before my Father which is in Heaven' (Mt. 10:33). Also, the divine Apostle teaches: `For with the heart man believeth unto righteousness; and with the mouth confession is made unto salvation' (Rom. 10:10). If, then, God and the divine Prophets and Apostles command that the mystery of faith be confessed in words and with the tongue, and this mystery of faith brings salvation to the whole world, then people must not be forced to keep silence with regard to confession, lest the salvation of people be hindered.

Maximus the Confessor

Faith and love, which are gifts of the Holy Spirit, are such great and powerful means that a person who has them can easily, and with joy and consolation, go the way Jesus Christ went. Besides this, the Holy Spirit gives man the power to resist the delusions of the world so that although he makes use of earthly good, yet he uses them as a temporary visitor, without attaching his heart to them. Now a man who does not have the Holy Spirit, despite all his learning and prudence, is always more or less a slave and worshipper of the world. <u>Innocent of Irkutsk</u>

Faith consists not only of being baptized in Christ, but also in fulfilling His commandments. Holy Baptism is perfect and gives us perfection, but does not make perfect those who do not follow the commandments.

<u>Mark the Ascetic</u>

Faith gives wings to prayer, and without it we cannot fly up to Heaven.

<u>John Climacus</u>

Faith is a comprehensive knowledge of the essentials, and knowledge is the strong and sure demonstration of what is received by faith, built upon faith by the Lord's teaching, conveying the soul on to infallibility, science, and comprehension. In my view, the first saving change is that from heathenism to faith, and the second, that from faith to knowledge. Also, the latter terminating in love, thereafter gives the loving to the loved, that which knows to that which is known. <u>Clement of Alexandria</u>

Faith is the beginning of love; the end of love is knowledge of God.

<u>Evagrius</u>

Faith, according to the teaching of Antioch, is the beginning of our union with God. One who truly believes is a stone in the temple of God; he is prepared for the edifice of God the Father, raised to the heights by the power of Jesus Christ, that is, of the Cross, with the aid of ropes, that is, the grace of the Holy Spirit.   Seraphim of Sarov

Faith, like active prayer, is a grace. For prayer, when activated by love through the power of the Spirit, renders true faith manifest - the faith that reveals the life of Jesus. If, then, you are aware that such faith is not at work within you, that means your faith is dead and lifeless. In fact you should not even speak of yourself as one of the 'faithful' if your faith is merely theoretical and not actualized by the practice of the commandments or by the Spirit. Thus, faith must be evidenced by progress in keeping the commandments, or it must be actualized and translucent in what we do. This is confirmed by James when he says, 'Show me your faith through your works and I will show you the works that I do through my faith" (cf. Jas. 2:18.)   Gregory of Sinai

For the man who believes, all things are possible because: 'Faith is counted as righteousness,' and `Christ is the end of the Law.' Belief in Him justifies and perfects the believer, for belief in Christ is considered to correspond to the works of the law. It is confirmed and witnessed by the evangelic precepts and so earns for the faithful a participation in eternal life, in Christ Himself.

                                                        Symeon the New Theologian

God the blessed Creator and Source of saintly men does not choose only the foolish and feeble elements of the decaying world to destroy the lofty. As He Himself said, He now draws all things upward, and claims the lofty things of the world also. For He made both the weak and the strongest, and unites them both in grace. Those whom the Creator fashioned by the one act He renews by the one gift. A general lack of belief circumscribed all men so that faith could heal all, so that the whole world might become subject to God, and every tongue, every power should proclaim that Jesus alone rules above every name in the glory of the Father. <u>Paulinus of Nola</u>

He that does not believe in the God Who saves us in difficult circumstances, but is faint-hearted; he that does not wish to render glory to God, that represents Him as not vigilant, but sleeping, not all-powerful and not merciful, thinks falsely of the God of truth, and thus sins grievously. Especially inexcusable are faint-heartedness and unbelief in the man who has already been deemed worthy of often receiving marvelous help God the Savior. Oh, how great a sinner I am!" <u>John of Kronstadt</u>

Hold faith and humility fast within you; for through them you will find mercy, help, and words spoken by God in the heart, along with a protector who stands beside you both secretly and manifestly. Do you wish to obtain these things, which are a fountain of life? From the very onset take hold of simplicity. Walk before God in simplicity and not with knowledge. Simplicity is attended by faith; but subtle and intricate deliberations, by conceit; and conceit is attended by separation from God. <u>Isaac the Syrian</u>

If any here is a slave of sin, let him promptly prepare himself through faith for the new birth into freedom and adoption; and having put off the miserable bondage of his sins, and taken on him the most blessed bondage of the Lord, so may he be counted worthy to inherit the kingdom of heaven.

<u>Cyril of Jerusalem</u>

If we desire to acquire faith the foundation of all blessings, the door to God's mysteries, unflagging defeat of our enemies, the most necessary of all the virtues, the wings of prayer and the dwelling of God within the soul--we must endure every trial imposed by our enemies and by our many and various thoughts....if we forcibly triumph over the trials and temptations that befall us, it will not be we who are victorious, but Christ, Who is present in us through faith.   Peter of Damaskos

If you have faith in the Lord you will fear punishment, and this fear will lead you to control the passions. Once you control the passions you will accept affliction patiently, and through such acceptance you will acquire hope in God. Hope in God separates the intellect from every worldly attachment, and when the intellect is detached in this way it will acquire love for God.

Maximos the Confessor

It is by faith that all things, both human and spiritual are sustained. For without faith neither does the farmer cut his furrow, nor does the merchant commit his life to the raging waves of the sea on a small piece of wood, nor are marriages contracted, nor any other step in life taken.

John Damascene

Let us contemplate with faith the mystery of the divine incarnation and in all simplicity let us simply praise Him who in His great generosity became man for us. For who, relying on the power of rational demonstration, can explain how the conception of the divine Logos took place? How was flesh generated without seed? How was there an engendering without loss of maidenhood? How did a mother after giving birth remain a virgin? How did He who was supremely perfect develop as He grew up (cf. Luke 2:52)? How was He who was pure baptized? How did He who was hungry give sustenance (cf. Matt. 4:2; 14:14-21)? How did He who was weary impart strength (cf. John 4:6)?

How did He who suffered dispense healing? How did He who was dying bestow life? In addition, to put the most important last, how did God become man?...Faith alone can embrace these mysteries, for it is faith that makes real for us things beyond intellect and reason (cf. Heb. 11:1).

Maximos the Confessor

Let us, then, cling to His blessing, and study the ways and means of securing this blessing. Let us unroll the records of antiquity. For what reason was our father Abraham blessed? Was it not that he did what was right and lived up to the truth, enabled by faith? With confidence because he knew the future, Isaac cheerfully let himself be led to the altar. Jacob was humble enough to leave his country because of his brother, and went to Laban and lived in servitude, and the twelve tribes were given to him. Whoever considers these details without bias will appreciate the splendor of the gifts conferred by Him. Clement of Rome

---

Listen to a parable against base thoughts. The grape, when it is cut from the vine and cast into the press and trampled down and yields its wine, to begin with the wine bubbles up so much as though it were being boiled by a ferocious heat; so that open vats, unable to bear the violence, break under the strain; so it is with human thoughts, whenever they pass over from this vain world and its care to things of heaven.

For the demons, unable to bear the zeal, trouble the human mind in varied ways, as they wish to engineer for it a turbid overthrow; so that they find a ready vessel, that is an unfaithful and doubting soul, they will rend it. For the demons are ravening wolves, who go round the cells of the monks looking for an open door for them, so that when they have got inside they may destroy a soul which obeys them. Now if they find the door shut in their faces, they go away extremely disappointed; I am speaking of a soul which is firmly founded on faith. Ephrem the Syrian

---

My soul measured the mighty workings of God, wrought on the scale of His eternal omnipotence, not by its own powers of perception but by a boundless faith; and therefore refused to disbelieve, because it could not understand, that God was in the beginning with God, and that the Word became flesh and dwelt among us, but bore in mind the truth that with the will to believe would come the power to understand.   Hilary of Poitiers

Remember that while you pray, God expects from you a positive answer to His question: "Do you believe that I can fulfill your prayer?" You must be able to answer from the bottom of your heart: "Yes, I believe, Oh God," and then you will be answered according to your faith.   John of Kronstadt

Stand therefore firm in your hearts, that no one overthrow you that no one is able to make you fall. The Apostle has taught us what it is "to stand," that is what was said to Moses: "The place whereon you stand is holy ground;" for no one stands unless he stand by faith, unless he stands fixed in the determination of his own heart.   Ambrose of Milan

The eternal dogmatic truths, the divine dogmas, are the subject of the faith, and the faith is an exercise of man, and therefore, the human mind. All of the evangelical virtues of the exercise and of the grace, with faith first, are the heavenly bread of the eternal life, with which man nourishes, makes worthy, sanctifies, perfects himself, and is restored in his God-likeness. Life within the Church, through grace, inevitably becomes the source of knowledge, through grace, of the eternal dogmatic truths. Living them as the content of his life, man comes nearer to the authority, the Truth, and the saving power. Just as the Lord has said: "If any man will do his will", (namely, of God the Father, "he shall know the doctrine", for the dogmas, if they are derived "from God." (John 7:17) .   Justin Popovich

The first and unique effect of the divine gift of genuine spiritual knowledge is to produce within us by faith the resurrection of God. Faith needs to be accompanied by the right ordering of our will and purpose - that is to say, by discrimination - which makes it possible for us bravely to withstand the spate of trials and temptations, sought or unsought. Thus faith, rightfully expressing itself through the fulfillment of the commandments, is the first resurrection within us of the God whom we have slain through our ignorance.

Maximos the Confessor

There is a knowledge that precedes faith, and there is a knowledge born of faith. Knowledge that precedes faith is natural knowledge; and that which is born of faith is spiritual knowledge. What is natural knowledge? Knowledge is natural that discerns good from evil, and this is also called natural discernment, by which we know to discern good from evil naturally, without being taught. God has implanted this in rational nature, and with teaching it receives growth and assistance; there is no one who does not have it.

Isaac the Syrian

There is nothing impossible unto those who believe; lively and unshaken faith can accomplish great miracles in the twinkling of an eye. Besides, even without our sincere and firm faith, miracles are accomplished, such as the miracles of the sacraments; for God's Mystery is always accomplished, even though we were incredulous or unbelieving at the time of this celebration.

John of Kronstadt

Through faith man apprehends all that is invisible and apprehensible by the mind. Faith is a free conviction of the soul as to the truth of what is proclaimed from God.   Antony the Great

To have faith in Christ means more than simply despising the delights of this life. It means we should bear all our daily trials that may bring us sorrow, distress, or unhappiness, and bear them patiently for as long as God wishes and until He comes to visit us. For it is said: `I waited on the Lord and He came to me.'   Symeon the New Theologian

Your past and present torments and sufferings are poured down upon you to test your faith and 'steel' it; they also work to curb your lusts and passions. Humble yourself. God gives help to the humble. Judgment of others, insistence on their shortcomings, can only increase the bitterness of your sorrow. Choose the better part.   Macarius of Optina

Faith is the door to mysteries. What the bodily eyes are to sensory objects, the same is faith to the eyes of the intellect that gaze at hidden treasures.

Isaac the Syrian

"For behold, all our lofty doctrines, how destitute they are of reasonings, and dependent on faith alone. God is not anywhere, and is everywhere. What has less reason than this (What idea makes less logical sense)? He was not made, He did not make Himself, and He never began to be. What reasoning will receive this if there is no faith?"   John the Chrysostom

"If only with firm resolve we begin to live according to God's Law, we do not need to fear any sort of attack from those who do not understand. For to him who has truly begun to live according to God's Law, all that happens to him at the hand of men, happens for his profit and to the glory of God."

One commandment is higher than another; consequently one level of faith is more firmly founded than another. There is faith 'that comes by hearing' (Rm 10:17) and there is faith that 'is the substance of things hoped for' (Hb 11:1).

Kosmas Aitolos

By contrast, if faith is lacking in those who bring forward the sick, then it will not be permitted, even to those with the gift of healing , to work a cure. The evangelist Mark had this to say: 'And Jesus could not work miracles among them because of their unbelief'. It was at this time that the Lord said: 'There were many lepers in Israel in the days of Elisseus the prophet and no one of them was cured except Neman the Syrian' (Luke 4:27).

John Cassian

Correct faith does not benefit in anything, when life is corrupted.

John Chrysostom

If we desire to acquire faith -- the foundation of all blessings, the door to God's mysteries, unflagging defeat of our enemies, the most necessary of all the virtues, the wings of prayer and the dwelling of God within our soul -- we must endure every trial imposed by our enemies and by our many and various thoughts.

Only the inventor of evil, the devil, can perceive these thoughts or uncover and describe them. But we should take courage; because if we forcibly triumph over the trials and temptations that befall us, and keep control over our intellect so that it does not give in to the thoughts that spring up in our heart, we will once and for all overcome all the passions; for it will not be we who are victorious, but Christ, who is present in us through faith.

Peter of Damaskos

The man of faith acts, not as one endowed with free will, but as a beast that is led by the will of God. He says to God: "I became as a beast before You; yet I am continually with You" (Psalms 73:22 - 23).

If Your desire is that I should be at rest in Your knowledge, I shall not refuse. If it is that I should experience temptation so as to learn humility, again I am with You. Of myself, there is absolutely nothing I can do. For without You I would not have come into existence from non- existence; without You I cannot live or be saved. Do what You wilt to Your creature; for I believe that, being good, You bestow blessings on me, even if I do not recognize that they are for my benefit. Nor am I worthy to know, nor do I claim to understand, so as to be at rest: this might not be to my profit.   Ibid

---

Just as certain readings and certain words, tears and prayers are appropriate for one engaged in ascetic practice, so his is a different kind of faith from that superior faith which gives birth to stillness.

The former is the faith of hearsay, the latter is the faith of contemplation, as Isaac says. Contemplation is more sure than hearsay.

For the ordinary initial faith of the Orthodox is born of natural knowledge, and from this faith are born devotion to God, fasting and vigil, reading and psalmody, prayer and the questioning of those with experience. It is such practices that give birth to the soul's virtues, that is, to the constant observance of the commandments and of moral conduct. Through this observance come great faith, hope, and the perfect love that ravishes the intellect to God in prayer, when one is united with God spiritually, as Neilos puts it.   Ibid

Fall

The gates of Paradise were opened for Adam, but it was fitting that they be closed when he fell from the state in which he ought to have remained. These gates Christ Himself opened, "Who committed no sin" (1Pet. 2:22) and cannot sin, for as it says, "His righteousness remained for ever" (Ps. 111:3). Wherefore they must of necessity remain open and lead to life, but without providing a way out of life, for "I came," says the Savior, "that they might have life" (Jn. 10:10). This is the life, which the Lord came to bring, that those who come through these Mysteries should be partakers of His death and share in His passion. Apart from this it is impossible to escape death. It is not possible for him who has not been "baptized in water and the Spirit" (Jn. 3:5) to enter into life, nor can those who have not eaten the Flesh of the Son of man and drunk His Blood have life in themselves. (Jn. 6:24)

Nicholas Cabasilas

False Accusation

Another day, Theodore (of Tabennesi) went off to a monastery to visit the brothers, and straightway they brought him a brother they accused of having stolen something, that he should expel him from among the brothers for this reason. The culprit, however, was not this brother, but another who passed for a faithful man among all the brothers. They were accusing the former because he was somewhat negligent in their view.

When the thief realized that he had not only committed the first fault but that, moreover, because of him they were going to drive the other brother away from the monastery, he went to see Theodore privately and said to him, "Forgive me, my father; I am the one who committed the theft." Theodore said to him, "The Lord has forgiven you the fault you have committed, for clearing the innocent in our presence." Then he called the one who had been falsely accused and said to him, "I know that you are not the perpetrator of this fault. But even if the brothers afflicted you a little for the fault you have not committed, nevertheless do not be proud of your innocence in this case.

For you are doubtless indebted to the Lord for other faults you have committed.

Therefore, give Him thanks and be in fear of Him all you life long." Then he said to the brothers about this matter, "Have you not entrusted me with judgment so that I might pass sentence? Well, it is God's will that he should be absolved. Indeed, we are all in need of God's mercy." Life of Pachomius

---

Another day, Theodore (of Tabennesi) went off to a monastery to visit the brothers, and straightway they brought him a brother they accused of having stolen something, that he should expel him from among the brothers for this reason. The culprit, however, was not this brother, but another who passed for a faithful man among all the brothers. However, they were accusing the former because he was somewhat negligent in their view.

When the thief realized that he had not only committed the first fault but that, moreover, because of him they were going to drive the other brother away from the monastery, he went to see Theodore privately and said to him, "Forgive me, my father; I am the one who committed the theft." Theodore said to him, "The Lord has forgiven you the fault you have committed, for clearing the innocent in our presence."

Then he called the one who had been falsely accused and said to him, "I know that you are not the perpetrator of this fault. Now even if the brothers afflicted you a little for the fault you have not committed, nevertheless do not be proud of your innocence in this case. For you are doubtless indebted to the Lord for other faults you have committed. Therefore, give Him thanks and be in fear of Him all you life long." Then he said to the brothers about this matter, "Have you not entrusted me with judgment so that I might pass sentence? Well, it is God's will that he should be absolved. Indeed, we are all in need of God's mercy." Ibid

---

Fantasy

God reveals Himself to the humble, who live in accordance with virtue. Those who take up the wings of the imagination attempt the flight of Ikaros and have same end. Those who harbor fantasies do not pray; for he that prays lifts his mind and heart towards God, whereas he that turns to fantasies diverts himself. Those who are addicted to the imagination have withdrawn from God's grace and from the realm of Divine revelation. They have abandoned the heart in which grace is revealed and have surrendered themselves to the imagination, which is devoid of all grace. It is only the heart that receives knowledge about things that are not apprehended by the senses, because God, Who dwells and moves within it, speaks within it and reveals to it the substance of things hoped for.   Nectarios of Aegina

---

Fasting

People have to answer greatly for not keeping the rules of the Church with respect to the fasts. People justify themselves by saying that they never considered it a sin to eat dairy products during the fasts. They repent and consider themselves sinners in every other respect, but they do not think to repent about not keeping the fasts. Meanwhile, they are transgressing the commandment of our holy Mother, the Church, and according to the teaching of the Apostle Paul, they are as the heathen and publicans because of their disobedience.   Ambrose of Optina

---

Fasting is an exceptional virtue; it represses bodily impulses and gives strength to the soul to fight against the poisoning of the heart through the senses, and provides it with a remedy against any past poisoning. Fasting causes the mind to be cleansed constantly. It withers up every evil thought and brings healthy, godly thoughts -- -holy thoughts that enlighten the mind and kindle it with more zeal and spiritual fervor.   Ephraim of Philotheou

---

'This fasting,' he says, 'if the commandments of the Lord are kept, is very good. This, then, is the way that you shall keep the fast. First of all, keep yourself from every evil word and every evil device, and purify your heart from all the vanities of this world. If you keep these things, your fast shall be perfect for you. And thus shall you do. Having fulfilled what is written, on that day on which you fastest, you shall taste nothing but bread and water; and from my meals which you would have eaten, you shall reckon up the amount of that day's expenditure, which you would have incurred, and shall give it to a widow, or an orphan, or to one in want, and so shall you humble your soul, that he that received from your humiliation may satisfy his own soul, and may pray for you to the Lord. If then you shall so accomplish this fast, as I have commanded you, your sacrifice shall be acceptable in the sight of God, and this fasting shall be recorded; and the service, so performed is beautiful and joyous, and acceptable to the Lord.'   The Shepherd of Hermas

A Constitution Concerning the Great Passover Week

Do you therefore fast on the days of the Passover, beginning from the second day of the week until the preparation, and the Sabbath, six days, making use of only bread, and salt, and herbs, and water for your drink. But do you abstain on these days from wine and flesh, for they are days of lamentation and not of feasting. Do you who are able fast the day of the preparation and the Sabbath day entirely, tasting nothing till the cock-crowing of the night. But if any one is not able to join them both together, at least let him observe the Sabbath day. For the Lord says somewhere, speaking of Himself: "When the bridegroom shall be taken away from them, in those days shall they fast." In these days, therefore, He was taken from us by the Jews, falsely so named, and fastened to the cross, and "was numbered among the transgressors."

Constitutions of the Holy Apostles

A worker takes the trouble to get hold of the instruments that he requires. He does so not simply to have them and not use them. Nor is there any profit for him in merely possessing the instruments. What he wants is, with their help, to produce the crafted objective for which these are the efficient means.

In the same way, fasting, vigils, scriptural meditation, nakedness and total deprivation do not constitute perfection but are the means to perfection. They are not in themselves the end point of a discipline, but an end is attained to through them.   John Cassian

Abbot Isidore said, "If you fast regularly, do not be inflated with pride; if you think highly of yourself because of it, then you had better eat meat. It is better for a man to eat meat than to be inflated with pride and glorify himself."   The Desert Fathers

Abbot John the Dwarf said, "If a king wanted to take possession of his enemy's city, he would begin by cutting off the water and the food and so his enemies, dying of hunger, would submit to him. It is the same with the passions of the flesh; if a man goes about fasting and hungry the enemies of his soul grow weak.   Ibid

An old man was asked, 'How can I find God?' He said, 'In fasting, in watching, in labors, in devotion, and, above all, in discernment. I tell you, many have injured their bodies without discernment and have gone away from us having achieved nothing. Our mouths smell bad through fasting, we know the Scriptures by heart, we recite all the Psalms of David, but we have not that which God seeks: charity and humility.'   Ibid

According to Gregory the Sinaite there are three degrees in eating: ;temperance, sufficiency, and satiety. Temperance is when someone wants to eat some more food but abstains, rising from the table still somewhat hungry. Sufficiency is when someone eats what is needed and sufficient for normal nourishment. Satiety is when someone eats more than enough and is more than satisfied. Now if you cannot keep the first two degrees and you proceed to the third, then, at least, do not become a glutton, remembering the words of the lord: "Woe unto you that are full now, for you shall hunger" (Lk. 6:25). Remember also that rich man who ate in this present life sumptuously every day, but who was deprived of the desired bosom of Abraham in the next life, simply because of this sumptuous eating.

Nicodemos of the Holy Mountain

According to Gregory the Sinaite there are three degrees in eating: temperance, sufficiency, and satiety. Temperance is when someone wants to eat some more food but abstains, rising from the table still somewhat hungry. Sufficiency is when someone eats what is needful and sufficient for normal nourishment., Satiety is when someone eats more than enough and is more than satisfied. Now if you cannot keep the first two degrees and you proceed to the third, then, at least do not become a glutton, remembering the words of the Lord: "Woe to you that are full now, for you shall hunger" (Lk. 6:25).

Ibid

Almsgiving heals the soul's incensive power; fasting withers sensual desire; prayer purifies the intellect and prepares it for contemplation of created beings. For the Lord has given us commandments which correspond to the powers of the soul.   Maximos the Confessor

And just as a ship, after having run through innumerable surges, and having escaped many storms, then in the very mouth of the harbor having been dashed against some rock, loses the whole treasure which is stowed away in her — so truly did this Pharisee, after having undergone the labors of the fasting, and of all the rest of his virtue, since he did not master his tongue, in the very harbor underwent shipwreck of his cargo. For the going home from prayer, from which he should have derived gain, having rather been so greatly damaged, is nothing else than undergoing shipwreck in harbor.

BROTHER: Is there any man who fasts that shall not be redeemed?

OLD MAN: There is one kind of fasting which is from habit, and another from desire, and another from compulsion, and another from sight, and another from the love of vainglory, and another from affliction, and another from repentance, and another from spiritual affection; for although each of these seems to be the same as the other in the mind externally, yet in the word of knowledge they are distinct. Now the way in which each is performed by the body is the same, and the way in which each is to be undertaken is wholly the same by him who travels straightly on the path of love, and who bears his burden with patient endurance spiritually, and who doth not rejoice in his honor. The Holy Fathers

BROTHER: What are fasting and prayer?

OLD MAN: Fasting is the subjugation of the body, prayer is converse with God, vigil is a war against Satan, abstinence is being weaned from meats, humility is the state of the first man, kneeling is the inclining of the body before the Judge, tears are the remembrance of sins, nakedness is our captivity which is caused by the transgression of the command, and service is constant supplication to and praise of God.

BROTHER: Are these able to redeem the soul?

OLD MAN: When internal things agree with external, and manifest humility appears in the hidden works, which are from within, verily, a man shall be redeemed from the weight of the body. Ibid

Beware of limiting the good of fasting to mere abstinence from meats. Real fasting is alienation from evil. 'Loose the bands of wickedness.' For give your neighbor the mischief he has done you. Forgive him his trespasses against you. Do not 'fast for strife and debate.' You do not devour flesh, but you devour your brother. You abstain from wine, but you indulge in outrages. You wait for evening before you take food, but you spend the day in the law courts. Woe to those who are 'drunken, but not with wine.' Anger is the intoxication of the soul, and makes it out of its wits like wine.   Basil

Bodily purity is primarily attained through fasting, and through bodily purity comes spiritual purity. Abstinence from food, according to the words of that son of grace, Ephraim the Syrian, means: 'Not to desire or demand much food, either sweet or costly; to eat nothing outside the stated times; not to give oneself over to gratification of the appetite; not to stir up hunger in oneself by looking at good food; and not to desire one or another sort of food.   Nikolai Velimirovich

But let not your fasts be with the hypocrites; for they fast on the second and fifth day of the week (meaning Monday and Thursday); but do you fast on the fourth day and the day of Preparation (meaning Wednesday and Friday). Neither pray as the hypocrites; but as the Lord commanded in His Gospel, thus pray: Our Father who are in heaven, hallowed be Your name. Your kingdom come. Your will be done, as in heaven, so on earth. Give us today our daily (needful) bread, and forgive us our debt as we also forgive our debtors. And bring us not into temptation, but deliver us from the evil one (or evil); for Yours is the power and the glory for ever. Three times in the day thus pray.   Didache

Concerning the watching all the night of the Great Sabbath, and Concerning the Day of the Resurrection:

This is why we exhort you to fast on those days, as we also fasted till the evening, when He was taken away from us; but on the rest of the days, before the day of the preparation, let every one eat at the ninth hour (3 PM) or the evening, or as every one is able. But from the evening of the fifth day till cock-crowing break your fast when it is daybreak of the first day of the week, which is the Lord's day (Sunday). From the evening till cock-crowing keep awake, and assemble together in the church. Watch and pray, and entreat God; reading, when you sit up all night, the Law, the Prophets, and the Psalms, until cock-crowing, and baptizing your catechumens, and reading the Gospel with fear and trembling, and speaking to the people such things as tend to their salvation. Put an end to your sorrow, and beseech God that Israel may be converted, and that He will allow them place of repentance, and the remission of their impiety... For this reason do you also, now the Lord is risen, offer your sacrifice, concerning which He made a constitution by us, saying, "Do this for a remembrance of me;" and henceforth leave off your fasting, and rejoice, and keep a festival, because Jesus Christ, the pledge of our resurrection, is risen from the dead.

And let this be an everlasting ordinance till the consummation of the world, until the Lord come. For to Jews the Lord is still dead, but to Christians He is risen: to the former, by their unbelief; to the latter, by their full assurance of faith. For the hope in Him is immortal and eternal life.

After eight days let there be another feast observed with honor, the eighth day itself, on which He gave me Thomas, who was hard of belief, full assurance, by showing me the print of the nails, and the wound made in His side by the spear.

And again, from the first Lord's day count forty days, from the Lord's day till the fifth day of the week, and celebrate the feast of the ascension of the Lord, whereon He finished all His dispensation and constitution, and returned to that God and Father that sent Him, and sat down at the right hand of power, and remains there until His enemies are put under His feet; who also will come at the consummation of the world with power and great glory, to judge the quick and the dead, and to recompense to every one according to his works. And then shall they see the beloved Son of God whom they pierced; and when they know Him, they shall mourn for themselves, tribe by tribe, and their wives apart.   Constitutions of the Holy Apostles

---

Consider well my soul: Do you fast? Then despise not your neighbor. Do you abstain from food? Condemn not your brother.   The Lenten Triodion

Considering all these things then, and counting the recompense, which is given in this case, and remembering that to wipe away sins does not entail much labor and zeal, let us pardon those who have wronged us. For that which others scarcely accomplish, I mean the blotting out of their own sins by means of fasting and lamentations, and prayers, and sackcloth, and ashes, this it is possible for us easily to effect without sackcloth and ashes and fasting if only we blot out anger from our heart, and with sincerity forgive those who have wronged us.   John Chrysostom

Eat simply, and stop before satiety. What do I mean by this? First eating simply means that one's food preparation should not be of the normal, non-fasting type: sumptuous, fattened, and designed to entice the palate. This only reinforces one's love for food. This does not mean that one's preparation should result in food that is repugnant. Rather it means that it should not inflame one's desire for more, nor incite one (e.g. overly spicy or rich tasting recipes). It should be such that it is simple, meager, and life-sustaining. It is still permissible for the food to be interesting and pleasant to eat (after all it is not a sin to enjoy food in moderation)."   Anonymous

Fasting appears gloomy until one steps into its arena. But begin and you will see what light it brings after darkness, what freedom from bonds, what release after a burdensome life.   Theophan the Recluse

Fasting is absolutely indispensable for man. From the external aspect, it is a struggle of filial obedience to God, Who has given us the rules of fasting through His Holy Spirit. From the inner aspect, fasting is a struggle of restraint and self-limitation. In this lies the great value and sense of fasting, since a strict observance of fasts tempers one's will and perfects the character of one who is firm in his religious convictions and actions. Let us not forget that Christ Himself fasted, and foretold that His apostles would also fast.

Metropolitan Philaret

Fasting is acceptable to God when abstention from food is accompanied by refraining from sins, from envy, from hatred, from calumny, from vainglory, from wordiness, from other evils. He who is fasting the true fast 'that is agreeable' to God ought to shun all these things with all his strength and zeal, and remain impregnable and unshakeable against all the attacks of the Evil one that are planned from that quarter. On the other hand, he who practices abstention from food, but does not keep self-control in the face of the aforesaid passions, is like unto one who lays down splendid foundations for a house, yet takes serpents and scorpions and vipers as fellow-dwellers therein.

Photios the Great

Fasting is the champion of every virtue, the beginning of the struggle, the crown of the abstinent, the beauty of virginity and sanctity, the resplendence of chastity, the commencement of the path of Christianity, the mother of prayer, the well-spring of sobriety and prudence, the teacher of stillness, and the precursor of all good works. Just as the enjoyment of light is coupled with healthy eyes, so desire for prayer accompanies fasting that is practiced with discernment.   Isaac the Syrian

---

Fasting is wonderful, because it tramples our sins like a dirty weed, while it cultivates and raises truth like a flower.   John Chrysostom

---

Fasting was ordained in Paradise. The first injunction was delivered to Adam, 'Of the tree of the knowledge of good and evil you shall not eat.'

'You shall not eat' is a law of fasting and abstinence." The general argument is rather against excess than in support of ceremonial abstinence. In Paradise there was no wine, no butchery of beasts, no eating of flesh. Wine came in after the flood. Noah became drunk because wine was new to him. So fasting is older than drunkenness. Esau was defiled, and made his brother's slave, for the sake of a single meal. It was fasting and prayer that gave Samuel to Hannah. Fasting brought forth Samson. Fasting begets prophets, strengthens strong men. Fasting makes lawgivers wise, is the soul's safeguard, the body's trusty comrade, the armor of the champion, the training of the athlete.   Basil

Fasts and vigils, the study of Scripture, renouncing possessions and everything worldly are not in themselves perfection, as we have said; they are its tools. For perfection is not to be found in them; it is acquired through them. It is useless, therefore, to boast of our fasting, vigils, poverty, and reading of Scripture when we have not achieved the love of God and our fellow men. Whoever has achieved love has God within himself and his intellect is always with God.   John Cassian

Great infirmity constrains us, dearest brother, from which if we were free, we should seem justly blamable. But since, while we are in this fragile body, we cannot subsist but by subservience to its weaknesses, we ought not to blush for what necessity imposes on us. And so, since physicians all say that to those who suffer from eruption of blood fasts are injurious, we exhort your Fraternity by this present address that, recalling to mind what you have been accustomed to endure from sickness, you by no means impose on yourself the labor of fasting. If, however, by the mercy of God, you know yourself to be so far improved in health as to have sufficient strength, we permit you to fast once or twice in the week. But of this it befits you before all things to take care, that you in no wise subject yourself to any feeling of irritation, so that the sickness, which is believed to be now lighter and as it were suspended, should be experienced afterwards more heavily through exasperation.   Gregory the Great

I know a man who kept no long strict fasts, no vigils, did not sleep on bare earth, imposed on himself no other specially arduous tasks; but, recollecting in memory his sins, understood his worthlessness and, having judged himself, became humble - and for this alone the most compassionate Lord saved him; as the divine David says: 'The Lord is near to them that are of a broken heart; and saves such as be of a contrite spirit' (Ps. 34:18). In short, he trusted the words of the Lord and for his faith the Lord received him."

Simeon the New Theologian

I shall speak first about control of the stomach, the opposite to gluttony, and about how to fast and what and how much to eat. I shall say nothing on my own account, but only what I have received from the Holy Fathers. They have not given us only a single rule for fasting or a single standard and measure for eating, because not everyone has the same strength; age, illness or delicacy of body create differences. But they have given us all a single goal: to avoid over-eating and the filling of our bellies... A clear rule for self-control handed down by the Fathers is this: stop eating while still hungry and do not continue until you are satisfied.   John Cassian

---

I shall speak first about control of the stomach, the opposite to gluttony, and about how to fast and what and how much to eat. I shall say nothing on my own account, but only what I have received from the Holy Fathers. They have not given us only a single rule for fasting or a single standard and measure for eating, because not everyone has the same strength; age, illness or delicacy of body create differences. But they have given us all a single goal: to avoid over-eating and the filling of our bellies... A clear rule for self-control handed down by the Fathers is this: stop eating while still hungry and do not continue until you are satisfied.   John Cassian

---

If you can begrudge the stomach, your mouth will stay closed, because the tongue flourishes where food is abundant.　　　　　　　　　John Climacus

---

Inasmuch then as our Master knew that if He carved out only one road for us, many must shrink from it, He carved out diverse roads. You can not enter the kingdom it may be by the way of virginity. Enter it then by the way of single marriage. Can you not enter it by one marriage? By chance you may by means of a second marriage. You can not enter by the way of continence: enter then by the way of almsgiving: or you can not enter by the way of almsgiving? Then try the way of fasting. If you can not use this way, take that — or if not that, then take this.　　　　　　　　　Ibid

---

Keep the body properly slim so that you reduce the burden of the heart's warfare, with full benefit to yourself.　　　　　　Ieronymos of Aegina

---

Let those of us who have wisely finished the course of fasting And who celebrate with love the beginning of the suffering of the Passion of the Lord, Let us all, my brothers, zealously imitate the purity of self-controlled Joseph; Let us fear the sterility of the fig tree; Let us dry up through almsgiving the sweetness of passion. In order that we may joyously anticipate the Resurrection, Let us procure like myrrh pardon from on high Because the eye that never sleeps observes all things.　　　　Romanos the Melodist

---

Let us love that fasting of the soul, which, by the cooperation of the Spirit, doth wither the grievous passions and doth strengthen us to do godly deeds, and doth uplift our mind towards Heaven, and doth obtain our sins' forgiveness, grant unto us by the compassionate God.　　　　Triodion

Many abstain from meat, milk and other food which God has not forbidden and which was even given as a blessing of people who have learned the truth and know how to partake of these things with thanksgiving (1 Tim. 4:34). However, the same abstemious, devout-living people, give scandal by their action, and spread scandal with their tongue like an incendiary fire.

Tikhon of Zadonsk

He therefore charged us Himself to fast these six days on account of the impiety and transgression of the Jews, commanding us to bewail over them, and lament for their perdition. For even He Himself "wept over them, because they knew not the time of their visitation." Nevertheless, He commanded us to fast on the fourth and sixth days of the week (Wednesday and Friday); the former on account of His being betrayed, and the latter on account of His passion. However, He appointed us to break our fast on the seventh day at the cock crowing, but to fast on the Sabbath day. Not that the Sabbath day is a day of fasting, being the rest from the creation, but because we ought to fast on this one Sabbath only (Holy Saturday), while on this day the Creator was under the earth. For on their very feast-day (Jewish Passover) they apprehended the Lord, that that oracle might be fulfilled, which says: "They placed their signs in the middle of their feast, and knew them not." You ought therefore to bewail over them, because when the Lord came they did not believe on Him, but rejected His doctrine, judging themselves unworthy of salvation.   Constitutions of the Holy Apostles

On Feast Days and Fast Days a Catalogue of the Feasts of the Lord which are to be kept, and when each of them ought to be observed

Brethren, observe the festival days. First of all the birthday (of our Lord) which you are to celebrate on the twenty-fifth of the ninth month (December); after which let the Epiphany be to you the most honored, in which the Lord made to you a display of His own Godhead, and let it take place on the sixth of the tenth month (January); after which the fast of Lent is to be observed by you as containing a memorial of our Lord's mode of life and legislation. (As we learned last weekend, at first Great Lent was in emulation of our Lord's fast of 40 days after His baptism, and took place directly after Epiphany, rather than just before Pascha & Holy Week.) However, let this solemnity be observed before the fast of the Passover, beginning from the second day of the week (Monday), and ending at the day of the preparation (Friday). After which solemnities, breaking off your fast, begin the holy week of the Passover, fasting in the same all of you with fear and trembling, praying in them for those that are about to perish. (Passover here is the Greek word Pascha, and refers to the resurrection and not the Jewish Passover.)   Constitutions of the Holy Apostles

Our virtue, therefore, must not be contaminated with fault, but must be single minded and blameless, and free from all that can bring reproach. For what profit is there in fasting twice in the week, if your so doing serve only as a pretext for ignorance and vanity, and make you supercilious and haughty, and selfish?   Cyril of Alexandria

Sear your loins by abstaining from food, and prove your heart by controlling your speech, and you will succeed in bringing the desiring and incensive powers of your soul into the service of what is noble and good.

Ilias the Presbyter

Sleep is a particular state of nature, an image of death, inactivity of the senses. Sleep is one, but, like desire, its sources and occasions are many; that is to say, it comes from nature, from food, from demons, or perhaps, sometimes, from extreme and prolonged fasting, through which the flesh is weakened and at last longs for the consolation of sleep.   John Climacus

Some are convinced that we should eat all foods, at all times, without discretion. They say that we should cast off all the restrictions of the fast and make wide the road to the belly. However, we have a teaching from the Savior Christ that the demons are not cast out except by prayer and fasting. His holy disciples and Apostles ministered to the Lord with fasting, as it is written: 'As they ministered to the Lord and fasted ...' (Acts 13:1).

Cleopa of Romania

Suppose you have ordered yourself not to eat fish; you will find that the enemy continually makes you long to eat it. You are filled with an uncontrollable desire for the thing that is forbidden. In this way you can see how Adam's fall typifies what happens to all of us. Because he was told not to eat from a particular tree, he felt irresistibly attracted to the one thing that was forbidden him.

John of Karpathos

A question of no small importance arose at that time. For the parishes of all Asia, as from an older tradition, held that the fourteenth day of the moon, on which day the Jews were commanded to sacrifice the lamb, should be observed as the feast of the Savior's Passover. It was therefore necessary to end their fast on that day, whatever day of the week it should happen to be. However, it was not the custom of the churches in the rest of the world to end it at this time, as they observed the practice, which, from apostolic tradition, has prevailed to the present time, of terminating the fast on no other day than on that of the resurrection of our Savior. Synods and assemblies of bishops were held on this account, and all, with one consent, through mutual correspondence drew up an ecclesiastical decree, that the mystery of the resurrection of the Lord should be celebrated on no other but the Lord's day, and that we should observe the close of the paschal fast on this day only.

The Church History of Eusebius

According to Gregory the Sinaite there are three degrees in eating: temperance, sufficiency, and satiety. Temperance is when someone wants to eat some more food but abstains, rising from the table still somewhat hungry. Sufficiency is when someone eats what is needed and sufficient for normal nourishment. Satiety is when someone eats more than enough and is more than satisfied.

Now if you cannot keep the first two degrees and you proceed to the third, then, at least, do not become a glutton, remembering the words of the Lord: "Woe to you that are full now, for you shall hunger" (Lk 6:25). Remember also that rich man who ate in this present life sumptuously every day, but who was deprived of the desired bosom of Abraham in the next life, simply because of this sumptuous eating. Remember how he longed to refresh his tongue with a drop of water.

Basil not only did not forgive the young people who ate to satiety but also those who ate until satisfied; he preferred that all eat temperately. He said, "Nothing subdues and controls the body as does the practice of temperance. It is this temperance that serves as a control to those youthful passions and desires.'"

Gregory the Theologian has also noted in his poetry: "No satiety has brought forth prudent behavior; for it is in the nature of fire to consume matter. And a filled stomach expels refined thoughts; it is the tendency of opposites to oppose each other."

Job, too, assuming that one could fall into sin through eating, offered sacrifice to God for his sons who were feasting among themselves. "And when the days of the feast had run their course, Job would send and sanctify them, and he would rise early in the morning and offer burnt offerings according to the number of them all; for Job said: 'It may be that my sons have sinned, and cursed God in their hearts'" (Jb 1:5-8). In interpreting this passage Olympiodoros wrote: "We learn from this that we ought to avoid such feasts which can bring on sinfulness. We must also purify ourselves after they have been concluded, even if these are conducted for the sake of concord and brotherly love as in the case of the sons of Job."

Surely then, if the sons of Job were not at a feast but in prayer or some other spiritual activity, the devil would not have dared to destroy the house and them, as Origen interpreted the passage: "The devil was looking for an opportunity to destroy them. Had he found them reading, he would not have touched the house, having no reason to put them to death. Had he found them in prayer, he would not have had any power to do anything against them. Nevertheless, when he found an opportune time, he was powerful. What was the opportune time? It was the time of feasting and drinking." Do you see then, dear reader, how many evils are brought forth by luxurious foods and feasting in general?   Nicodemos

---

The old man (Abbot Moses) was asked, "What is the good of the fasts and watchings which a man imposes on himself?" and he replied, "They make the soul humble. For it is written, "Consider my affliction and my trouble, and forgive all my sins" (Psalm 25:18). So if the soul gives itself all this hardship, God will have mercy on it."   Desert Fathers

---

The partaking of food has three degrees: abstinence, adequacy and satiety. To abstain, means to remain a little hungry after eating; to eat adequately, means neither to be hungry, nor weighed down. However, eating beyond satiety is the door to belly-madness, through which lust comes in. Nevertheless, you, firm in knowledge, choose what is best for you, according to your powers, without overstepping the limits.   Gregory of Sinai

---

The reason that fasting has an effect on the spirits of evil rests in its powerful effect on our own spirit. A body subdued by fasting brings the human spirit freedom, strength, sobriety, purity, and keen discernment.   Ignaty

---

The right practice of abstinence is needful not only to the mortification of the flesh but also to the purification of the mind. For the mind then only keeps holy and spiritual fast when it rejects the food of error and the poison of falsehood.   Leo the Great

The undefiled beauty of fasting is the pure mother of character. It causes philosophy to gush forth, and offers a crown. It negotiates Paradise for us And grants a paternal family for those who fast. Of this Adam was deprived, and he attracted death When he dishonored the worth of feasting. For at the time when it was treated scornfully, The God of all, the Creator and the Master was at once displeased. To those who honor it He grants eternal life.

Kontakia of Romanos

There was a certain old man who lived a life of such strict self-denial that he never drank wine. In addition, when I arrived at his cell we sat down to eat. Dates were brought and he ate, and he took water and drank. In addition, I said unto him laughingly, "So you are angry with absinthe, Father? Since you have eaten dates and have drank water, why do you not drink wine?"

Moreover, he answered and said unto me, "If you take a handful of dust and throw it on a man, will it hurt him?" In addition, I said unto him, "No." In addition, he said unto me, "If you take a handful of water and throw it over a man, will he feel pain?" Moreover, I said unto him, "No." In addition, he said unto me, "And again, if you take a handful of chopped straw and throw it over a man, will it cause him pain?" In addition, I said unto him, "No."

Then he said unto me, "But if you bring them all together and mix them, and knead them well, and dry them, you may throw the mass on the skull of a man and you will not break it." In addition, I said unto him, "Yes, father, that is true." And he said unto me, "The monks do not abstain from certain things without good reason, and you must not listen to the men who are in the world who say, 'Why do they not eat this and why do they not drink that?' Is there not sin in them? Such people do not know. Now we abstain from certain things not because the things themselves are bad, but because the passions are mighty, and when they have waxed strong they kill us."

The Desert Fathers

There was a man who at a lot and was still hungry, and another who ate little and was satisfied. The one who ate a lot and was still hungry received a greater reward than he who ate little and was satisfied.   John of Kronstadt

Those pursuing the spiritual way should train themselves to hate all uncontrolled desires until this hatred becomes habitual. With regard to self-control in eating, we must never feel loathing for any kind of food, for to do so is abominable and utterly demonic. It is emphatically not because any kind of food is bad in itself that we refrain from it. Now by not eating too much or too richly we can to some extent keep in check the excitable parts of our body. In addition we can give to the poor what remains over, for this is the mark of sincere love.   Diadochos of Photiki

Those who struggle, regain their original state by keeping two commandments - obedience and fasting; for all evil entered into the generation of mortals through practices opposed to them. Moreover, those who keep the commandments through obedience ascend to God more quickly, and those who keep them through fasting - more slowly. Besides, obedience is more suitable for beginners, and fasting for those on the way, who possess courage and vision of mind. But in fulfilling the commandments it is given to very few always to obey God undeceived, and even for the most valiant this achievement is very difficult.   Gregory of Sinai

True fasting lies is rejecting evil, holding one's tongue, suppressing one's hatred, and banishing one's lust, evil words, lying, and betrayal of vows.

Basil the Great

We are told: It is no big deal to eat non-Lenten food during Lent. It is no big deal if you wear expensive beautiful outfits, go to the theater, to parties, to masquerade balls, use beautiful expensive china, furniture, expensive carriages and dashing steeds, amass and hoard things, etc. Yet what is it that turns our heart away from God, away from the Fountain of Life? Because of what do we lose eternal life? Is it not because of gluttony, of expensive clothing like that of the rich man of the Gospel story, is it not because of theaters and masquerades? What turns us hard-hearted toward the poor and even toward our relatives? Is it not our passion for sweets, for satisfying the belly in general, for clothing, for expensive dishes, furniture, carriages, for money and other things? Is it possible to serve God and mammon, to be a friend to the world and a friend to God, to serve Christ and Belial? That is impossible. Why did Adam and Eve lose paradise, why did they fall into sin and death? Was it not because of one evil? Let us attentively consider why we do not care about the salvation of our soul, which cost the Son of God so dearly. Why do we compound sin upon sin, fall endlessly into opposing to God, into a life of vanity? Is it not because of a passion for earthly things and especially for earthly pleasures? What makes our hearts become crude? Why do we become flesh and not spirit, perverting our moral nature? Is it not because of a passion for food, drink, and other earthly comforts? How after this can one say that it does not matter whether you eat non-Lenten food during Lent? The fact that we talk this way is in fact pride, idle thought, disobedience, refusal to submit to God, and separation from Him. Holy Righteous   John of Kronstadt

---

What does spoil repentance is being again entangled in the same evils. "For there is one" we read, "who builds, and one who pulls down, what have they gained more than toil? He who is dipped in water because of contact with a dead body, and then touches it again, what has he gained by his washing?" Even so if a man fasts because of his sins, and goes his way again, and does the same things, who will hear his prayer? And again we read "if a man goes back from righteousness to sin the Lord will prepare him for the sword," and, "as a dog when he has returned to his vomit, and become odious, so is a fool who by his wickedness has returned to his sin."   John Chrysostom

---

When you fast and are nourished with abstinence, do not store the leftovers for tomorrow, but, as the Lord became poor and enriched us, feed someone who does not want to be hungry, you who hungers willingly. Then your fast will be like the dove who brings and joyfully proclaims salvation to your soul from the flood.   Gregory Palamas

---

Which days of the week we are to fast, and which not, and for what reasons. But let not your fasts be with the hypocrites; for they fast on the second and fifth days of the week. But do you either fast the entire five days, or on the fourth day of the week (Wednesday), and on the day of the Preparation (Friday), because on the fourth day the condemnation went out against the Lord, Judas then promising to betray Him for money; and you must fast on the day of the Preparation, because on that day the Lord suffered the death of the cross under Pontius Pilate. But keep the Sabbath, and the Lord's day festival (non-fasting, that is feasting); because the former is the memorial of the creation, and the latter of the resurrection. But there is one only Sabbath to be observed by you in the whole year, which is that of our Lord's burial, on which men ought to keep a fast, but not a festival. For inasmuch as the Creator was then under the earth, the sorrow for Him is more forcible than the joy for the creation; for the Creator is honorable by nature and dignity than His own creatures.   Constitutions of the Holy Apostles

---

While fasting and sitting on a certain mountain, and giving thanks to the Lord for all His dealings with me, I see the Shepherd sitting down beside me, and saying, "Why have you come hither [so] early in the morning?" "Because, sir," I answered, "I have a station." "What is a station?" he asked. "I am fasting, sir," I replied. "What is this fasting," he continued, "which you are observing?" "As I have been accustomed, sir," I reply, "so I fast." "You do not know," he says, "how to fast unto the Lord: this useless fasting which you observe to Him is of no value." "Why, sir," I answered, "do you say this?" "I say to you," he continued, "that the fasting which you think you observe is not a fasting. But I will teach you what is a full and acceptable fasting to the Lord. Listen," he continued: "God does not desire such an empty fasting. For fasting to God in this way you will do nothing for a righteous life; but offer to God a fasting of the following kind: Do no evil in your life, and serve the Lord with a pure heart: keep His commandments, walking in His precepts, and let no evil desire arise in your heart; and believe in God. If you do these things, fear Him, and abstain from every evil thing, you will live unto God; and if you do these things, you will keep a great fast, and one acceptable before God.   Shepherd of Hermas

[To a sick monk] Concerning fasting, do not grieve, as I have said to you before: God does not demand of anyone labors beyond his strength. And indeed, what is fasting if not a punishment of the body in order to humble a healthy body and make it infirm for passions, according to the word of the Apostle: "When I am weak, then am I strong" (2 Corinthians 12:10)

Barsanuphius and John

It is necessary most of all for one who is fasting to curb anger, to accustom himself to meekness and condescension, to have a contrite heart, to repulse impure thoughts and desires, to examine his conscience, to put his mind to the test and to verify what good has been done by us in this or any other week, and which deficiency we have corrected in ourselves in the present week. This is true fasting.   John Chrysostom

"And finally, did not the Lord Jesus Himself begin His divine ministry of the salvation of mankind with a long, forty day fast? And did not He, in this way, clearly show that we must make a serious beginning to our life as Christians with fasting? First, the fast, and then all the rest comes together with, and through, the fast.

By His own example, the Lord showed us how great a weapon fasting is. With this weapon, He vanquished Satan in the wilderness, and with it was victorious over the three chief satanic passions with which Satan tempted Him: love of ease love of praise and love of money. These are three destructive greeds, the three greatest traps into which the evil enemy of the human race lures Christ's soldiers." <u>Nikolai Velimirovic</u>

Fear

...fear is of two kinds: the first is introductory, while the second, which grows out of the first is perfect.

He who is afraid of God's punishment has a slave-like fear of God, and it is this that makes him refrain from evil: 'Out of fear of the Lord men shun evil' (Prov. 16:6. LXX)... through fear of what threatens us we sinners may be led to repent and may seek deliverance from our sins...

The more a man struggles to do good, the more fear grows in him, until it shows him his slightest faults, those which he thought of as nothing while he was still in the darkness of ignorance.

When fear in this way has become perfect, he himself becomes perfect through inward grief: he no longer desires to sin but, fearing the return of the passions, he remains in this pure fear invulnerable. As the psalm puts it, 'The fear of the Lord is pure, and endures for ever' (Ps. 19:9. LXX). The first kind of fear is not pure, for it arises in us because of our sins. But, independent of sin, the person who has been purified continues to feel fear, not because he sins, but because, being human, he is changeable and prone to evil.

In his humility, the further he advances through the acquisition of the virtues, the more he fears. This is natural; for everyone who possesses wealth greatly fears loss, punishment, dishonor, and the consequent fall from his high estate...The sign of the first kind of fear is hatred of sin and anger towards it, like someone wounded by a wild beast. The sign of perfect fear is the love of virtue and the fear of relapsing, since no one is unalterable.

<u>Peter of Damaskos</u>

As it is not possible to cross over the great ocean without a ship, so no one can attain to love without fear. The fetid sea, which lies between us and the noetic paradise, we may cross by the boat of repentance, whose oarsmen are those of fear. But if fear's oarsmen do not pilot the barque of repentance whereby we cross over the sea of this world to God, we shall be drowned in the fetid abyss. Repentance is the ship and fear is the pilot; love is the divine haven.   Isaac the Syrian

---

As it is not possible to cross over the great ocean without a ship, so no one can attain to love without fear. The foetid sea, which lies between us and the noetic paradise, we may cross by the boat of repentance, whose oarsmen are those of fear. But if fear's oarsmen do not pilot the barque of repentance whereby we cross over the sea of this world to God, we shall be drowned in the foetid abyss. Repentance is the ship and fear is the pilot; love is the divine haven.   Isaac the Syrian

---

Do not hesitate to go late at night to those places where you usually feel afraid. But if you yield only a little to such weakness, then this childish and ridiculous infirmity will grow old with you. As you go on your way, arm yourself with prayer. When you reach the place, stretch out your hands. Flog your enemies with the name of Jesus, for there is no stronger weapon in heaven or earth. When you get rid of the disease of fear, praise Him who has delivered you. If you continue to be thankful, He will protect you forever.

John Climacus

Fear is a rehearsing of danger beforehand; or again, fear is a trembling sensation of the heart, alarmed and troubled by unknown misfortunes. Fear is a loss of assurance.   John Climacus

He who has acquired purity of heart has conquered fear. But a man who is still in process of purification, at times is conquered by fear, and at times conquers it. A man, however, who does not strive at all after purity, is either for ever sunk into a state of insensibility and, being a friend of passions and demons and filled with vanity and conceit, 'think(s) himself to be something, when he is not' (Gal. 6:3); or he is a slave, delivered into the hands of fear and, being of a childish mind, trembles and is afraid, where for those who fear God there is no fear or trembling.   Simeon the New Theologian

He who has become the servant of the Lord will fear his Master alone, but he who does not yet fear Him is often afraid of his own shadow. John Climacus

Q: Pray for me, my Father, I am very much disturbed by thoughts of sexual sin, despondency, and fear; and a thought says to me that I should converse with a brother to whom I feel attracted when I see him, lest by my silence I give him occasion for suspicion. I feel likewise that the demons are somehow pressing me, and I fall into fear.

A: Brother! You are not yet instructed in warfare with the enemy, which is why there come to you thoughts of fear, despondency, and sexual sin. Stand against them with a firm heart, for combatants, unless they labor, are not crowned, and warriors, unless they show the King their skill in battles, do not become worthy of honors. Remember what David was like. Do you not also sing: "Test me, Oh Lord, and try me, kindle my inwards parts and my heart" (Psalms 25:2). And again: "If a regiment arm itself against me, I will hope in Him" (Psalms 26:3). Likewise, concerning fear: "For if I should go in the midst of the shadow of death, I will fear no evil, for You are with me" (Psalms 22:4). And concerning despondency: "If the spirit of the powerful one should come upon you, do not leave your place" (Ecclesiastes 10:4).

Do you not wish to be skilled? But a man who is not tested by temptations is not skilled. It is battles that make a man skilled. The work of a monk consists of enduring battles and opposing them with manfulness of heart. But since you do not know the cunning traps of the enemy, he brings thoughts of fear and weakens your heart. You must know that God will not allow against you battles and temptations above your strength; the Apostle also teaches this, saying: "Faithful is the Lord, Who will not leave you to be tempted more than you can bear" (1 Corinthians 10:13).

Brother! I also in my youth was many times and powerfully tempted by the demon of sexual sin, and I labored against such thoughts, contradicting them and not agreeing with them, but presenting before my own eyes eternal tortures. For five years I acted thus every day, and God relieved me of these thoughts. This warfare is abolished by unceasing prayer with weeping.

And the fact that the demons are pressing you proceeds from their envy; if they could, they would chase you out of your cell also; but God does not allow them to take possession of you, for they do not have authority for this. God could swiftly relive you, but then you would not begin to oppose another passion (when it comes). May the demons not weaken you so as to turn your attention to a brother (to whom you are attracted), or to converse with him; but If you should happen unexpectedly to come together with him, against your desire, restrain your glance with fear and decency and do not listen attentively to his voice. And if this brother, out of ignorance, should himself begin to speak with you or sit next to you, then skillfully avoid him, but not suddenly, rather with decorum. Say to your thought: "Remember the terrible Judgment of God and the shame which will then overtake those who are attracted by these shameful passions." Compel your thought, and you will receive help, by the prayers of the Saints, and God will have mercy on you. Do not be a child in mind, "but a child in malice" (1 Corinthians 14:20); in mind, Oh brother, be perfect. Pay heed to yourself, as to how you will meet God. Amen. "   Barsanuphius

The fact that repentance furnishes hope should not be taken by us as a means to rob ourselves of the feeling of fear, so that one might more freely and fearlessly commit sin. For behold how God in every wise preached fear in all the Scriptures and showed Himself to be a hater of sin.   Isaac the Syrian

The first good which actively affects us, namely fear, is reckoned by Scripture as the most remote from God, for it is called 'the beginning of wisdom' (Ps. 111:10, Prov. 1:7; 9:10). Setting out from this towards our ultimate goal, wisdom, we come to understanding, and this enables us to draw close to God Himself, for we have only wisdom lying between us and our union with Him. Yet it is impossible for a man to attain wisdom unless first, through fear and through the remaining intermediary gifts, he frees himself completely from the mist of ignorance and the dust of sin. That is why, in the order established by Scripture, wisdom is placed close to God and fear close to us. In this way we can learn the rule and law of good order.

Maximos the Confessor

The origin and consummation of every man's salvation is wisdom, which initially produces fear but when perfected gives rise to loving desire. Or, rather, initially and providentially wisdom manifests itself for our sakes as fear, so as to make us who aspire to wisdom desist from evil; but ultimately it exists in its natural state for its own sake as loving desire, so as to fill with spiritual mirth those who have abandoned all existing things in order to dwell with it.   Maximos the Confessor

The soul that is given over to the will of God fears nothing: neither thunder nor thieves nor any such thing. Whatever may come, 'Such is God's pleasure,' she says. If she falls sick she thinks, 'This means that I need sickness, or God would not have sent it.'   Staretz Silouan

Those who mourn and those who are insensitive are not subject to fear, but the cowardly often have become deranged. And this is natural. For the Lord rightly forsakes the proud that the rest of us may learn not to be puffed up.

John Climacus

To those who do not long for it, wisdom is fear, because of the loss, which they suffer through their flight from it; but in those who cleave to it, wisdom is loving desire, promoting an inner state of joyous activity. For wisdom creates fear, delivering a person from the passions by making him apprehensive of punishment; and it also produces loving desire, accustoming the intellect through the acquisition of the virtues to behold the blessings held in store for us.   Maximos the Confessor

Fear of God

A man who has taken upon himself to travel the path of internal mindfulness must have above all the fear of God, which is the beginning of wisdom.

Seraphim of Sarov

Abbot John, the Dwarf, said, "Humility and the fear of God are above all virtues."   Desert Fathers

---

Abbot Poemen said, "As the breath which comes out of his nostrils, so does a man need humility and the fear of God.   Desert Fathers

---

Die daily, that you might live eternally, for one who fears God will live forever.   Anthony the Great

---

Dispassion engenders love, hope in God engenders dispassion, and patience and forbearance engender hope in God; these in turn are the product of complete self-control, which itself springs from fear of God. Fear of God is the result of faith in God.   Maximos the Confessor

Fear of God is of two kinds. The first is generated in us by the threat of punishment. It is through such fear that we develop in due order self-control, patience, hope in God and dispassion; and it is from dispassion that love comes. The second kind of fear is linked with love and constantly produces reverence in the soul, so that it does not grow indifferent to God because of the intimate communion of its love. "The first kind of fear is expelled by perfect love when the soul has acquired this and is no longer afraid of punishment (cf. I John 4:18). The second kind, as we have already said, is always found united with perfect love. The first kind of fear is referred to in the following two verse: 'Out of fear of the Lord men shun evil' (Prov. 16:6), and 'Fear of the Lord is the beginning of wisdom' (Ps. 111:10). The second kind is mentioned in the following verses: 'Fear of the Lord is pure, and endures forever' (Ps. 19:9. LXX), and 'Those who fear the Lord will not want for anything' (Ps. 34:10. LXX).   Maximos the Confessor

He who has obtained the fear of the Lord has forsaken lying, having within himself an incorruptible judge – his own conscience.   John Climacus

Holy Scripture says of the midwives who kept alive the Israelites' male children, that through the God-fearing midwives they made themselves houses. Does it mean they made visible houses? How can they say they acquired houses through the fear of God when we do the opposite, and learn in time, through fear of God to give up the houses we have? Evidently this does not refer to visible houses but to the houses of the soul which each one builds by for himself by keeping God's commandments. Through this Holy Scripture teaches us that the fear of God prepares the soul to keep the commandments, and through the commandments the house of the soul is built up. Let us take hold of them, brothers, and let us fear God, and we shall build houses for ourselves where we shall find shelter in winter weather, in the season of storm-cloud, lightning, and rain; for not to have a home in winter-time is a great hardship.   Dorotheos of Gaza

---

If a man wishes to attain to love of God, he must have fear of God. Fear gives birth to mourning, and mourning to courage. When all this has ripened in the soul, it begins to bear fruit in all things. And, seeing these beautiful fruits in the soul, God draws it to Himself, like choice incense, takes joy in it with His Angels for all time, fills it with rejoicing, and protects it in all its ways, to let it reach its place of rest without harm. Then, seeing the Most High Guardian encompassing it, the devil no longer attacks it; indeed he fears to come near it owing to this great power. Obtain this power that the demons may fear you, your labors be light and Divine things a sweet joy. This sweetness of Divine love is far sweeter than honey. Many monks and virgins, living in communities, having had no taste of this Divine sweetness nor received Divine power, have thought that they had it already. But, since they had made no effort to gain it, God did not give it to them. He who strives to obtain it will surely gain it through God's mercy; for God is no respecter of persons. When a man wishes to have in himself the light of God and His power, and so disregards both the abuse and the honors of this world, hates all things of the world and ease of the body, and purifies his heart of all bad thoughts, when he unceasingly brings to God fasting and tears day and night, as well as pure prayers, then God enriches him with that power. Strive to obtain this power - and you will do all your works with calm and ease, will receive a great daring towards God and He will grant all that you ask.

Anthony the Great

Like the sun's rays passing through a crack and lighting up the house, show up even the finest dust, the fear of the Lord on entering the heart of a man show up all his sins. .   John Climacus

---

No one can love God consciously in his heart unless he has first feared Him with all his heart. Through the action of fear the soul is purified and, as it were, made malleable and so it becomes awakened to the action of love.

Diadochos of Photiki

Only those who fear the Lord and keep His commandments have life with God. But as to those who do not keep His commandments, there is no life in them.... All, therefore, who despise Him and do not follow His commands deliver themselves to death, and each will be guilty of his own blood. But I implore you to obey His commands, and you will have a cure for your former sins. "

Hermas Shepherd

The Fathers tell us that a man gains possession of the fear of God by keeping the thought of death before his mind and remembering eternal punishment, by examining himself each evening about how he has passed the day and each morning about how he has passed the night; by never giving rein to his tongue and by keeping in close and continual touch with a man possessed of the fear of God, as his spiritual director.

Dorotheos of Gaza

The beginning of repentance proceeds from fear of God and heedfulness, as the holy martyr Boniface says (Lives of Saints, Dec. 19): The fear of God is the father of heedfulness, and heedfulness is the mother of inner peace, and the latter gives birth to conscience, which causes the soul to behold its own ugliness as in a certain pure and undisturbed water; and thus are both the beginnings and roots of repentance.

Seraphim of Sarov

The fear of the Lord is twofold. The first type is produced in us from threats of punishment, and from it arises in proper order self-control, patience, hope in God, and detachment, from which comes love. The second is coupled with love itself and constantly produces reverence in the soul, lest through the familiarity of love it becomes presumptuous of God. <u>Maximus the Confessor</u>

The growth of fear is the beginning of love, but a complete state of purity is the foundation of theology.   <u>John Climacus</u>

The prophet Jeremiah, speaking in the place of God, tells us that from above there comes the very fear of God by which we may cling to Him. `I shall give them one heart and one-way so that they may fear me during all their days, so that all will be well for them and for their sons after them. And I will make an everlasting covenant with them and I shall not cease to do good things for them and, as a gift, I shall put fear of Me in their hearts so that they may never go away from Me' (Jer. 32:39-40). Ezekiel speaks in similar terms: `And I shall give them a single heart and I will put a new spirit in them and I will remove the strong heart from their bodies and I will give them a heart of flesh instead. And I shall do this so that they may walk as I command and respect my decisions and carry them out. Then they shall be my people and I shall be their God' (Ez. 11:19-20). <u>John Cassian</u>

The prophet Jeremiah, speaking in the place of God, tells us that from above there comes the very fear of God by which we may cling to Him. `I shall give them one heart and one-way so that they may fear me during all their days, so that all will be well for them and for their sons after them. And I will make an everlasting covenant with them and I shall not cease to do good things for them and, as a gift, I shall put fear of Me in their hearts so that they may never go away from Me' (Jer. 32:39-40). , I will put a new spirit in them, I will remove the strong heart from their bodies, and I will give them a heart of flesh instead. And I shall do this so that they may walk as I command and respect my decisions and carry them out. Then they shall be my people and I shall be their God' (Ez. 11:19-20). <u>John Cassian</u>

The spirit of the fear of God is abstention from evil deeds.

Maximos the Confessor

There is a humility that comes from the fear of God, and there is a humility that comes from the fervent love of God. One man is humbled because of his fear of God, another is humbled because of his joy. The man humbled from fear of God is possessed of modesty in his members, a right ordering of his senses, and a heart contrite at all times. But the man humbled because of joy is possessed of great exuberance and an open and insuppressible heart.

Isaac of Syria

When a man walks in the fear of God he knows no fear, even if he were to be surrounded by wicked men. He has the fear of God within him and wears the invincible armor of faith. This makes him strong and able to take on anything, even things which seem difficult or impossible to most people. Such a man is like a giant surrounded by monkeys, or a roaring lion among dogs and foxes. He goes forward trusting in the Lord and the constancy of his will to strike and paralyze his foes. He wields the blazing club of the Word in wisdom.   Symeon the New Theologian

---

"Beholding the undreamed-of richness of God's gifts, an obedient man is filled with fear and amazement both at God's almightiness and his own sin. He would then want to hide from God, that God should depart from him and he himself return to his old spirit and his old life. But as soon as God's splendor and His mercy are revealed to a man, his own sinfulness, unworthiness and long estrangement from God are instantly revealed to him."   Nikolai Velimirovich

138. Acts of kindness and generosity are spoilt by self-esteem, meanness and pleasure, unless these have first been destroyed by fear of God.

Kosmas Aitolos

205. The fear of God compels us to fight against evil; and when we fight against evil, the grace of God destroys it.   Ibid

219. Fear of God and reproof induce remorse; hardship and vigils make us intimate with suffering.   Ibid

Flattery

Naaman, the commander of the Syrian army, came to Elisha with many gifts. And what did the prophet do? Did he go out to meet him? Did he run towards him? No, he sent a lad to find out why Naaman had come, and did not even admit him to his presence. This was to prevent anyone thinking that he had cured Naaman in return for the gifts that he brought (cf. 2King 5:8-16). This story, without teaching us to be arrogant, shows us that we should not flatter, because of our needs, those who value highly the very things it is our vocation to despise.   Neilos the Ascetic

The flatterer is a servant of devils, a guide to pride, a destroyer of contrition, a ruiner of virtues, a misleader. Those who pronounce you blessed, lead you astray, says the prophet. (Isaiah 3:12)   John Climacus

Flesh

He who keeps his flesh in strict subjection will reach passionlessness. He who feeds it will suffer from it.   Evagrius

Food

According to Gregory the Sinaite there are three degrees in eating: ;temperance, sufficiency, and satiety. Temperance is when someone wants to eat some more food but abstains, rising from the table still somewhat hungry. Sufficiency is when someone eats what is needed and sufficient for normal nourishment. Satiety is when someone eats more than enough and is more than satisfied. Now if you cannot keep the first two degrees and you proceed to the third, then, at least, do not become a glutton, remembering the words of the lord: "Woe unto you that are full now, for you shall hunger" (Lk. 6:25). Remember also that rich man who ate in this present life sumptuously every day, but who was deprived of the desired bosom of Abraham in the next life, simply because of this sumptuous eating.

Nicodemos of the Holy Mountain

Sleep is a particular state of nature, an image of death, inactivity of the senses. Sleep is one, but, like desire, its sources and occasions are many; that is to say, it comes from nature, from food, from demons, or perhaps, sometimes, from extreme and prolonged fasting, through which the flesh is weakened and at last longs for the consolation of sleep.   John Climacus

---

The partaking of food has three degrees: abstinence, adequacy and satiety. To abstain, means to remain a little hungry after eating; to eat adequately, means neither to be hungry, nor weighed down. But eating beyond satiety is the door to belly-madness, through which lust comes in. But you, firm in knowledge, choose what is best for you, according to your powers, without overstepping the limits.   Gregory of Sinai

---

Forgetfulness

...often a thought has occurred to me, and it was by writing it down that I committed it to memory. Thus in time of spiritual struggle I had it as a source of aid or relief or gratitude, supported as it was by the testimony of divine Scripture. Had I been negligent about writing it down, I would not have found it when I had need of it, and I would have been deprived of its help by that greatest of evils, forgetfulness."   Peter of Damaskos

---

When the mind forgets the purpose of piety, then visible works of virtue become useless.   Mark the Ascetic

---

Forgiveness

Even if all spiritual fathers, patriarchs, hierarchs, and all the people forgive you, you are unforgiven if you do not repent in action.   Kosmas Aitolos

---

'And forgive us our debts as we also forgive our debtors.' For we have many sins. For we offend both in word and in thought, and very many things we do worthy of condemnation; and 'if we say that we have no sin' (1 Jn. 1:8), we lie, as John says...The offenses committed against us are slight and trivial, and easily settled; but those which we have committed against God are great, and need such mercy as His only is. Take heed, therefore, lest for the slight and trivial sins against you, you shut out for yourself forgiveness from God for your very grievous sins.   Cyril of Jerusalem

Although remission of sins is given equally to all, the communion of the Holy Spirit is bestowed in proportion to each man's faith. If you have labored little, you receive little; but if you have wrought much, the reward is great. You are running for yourself, see to your own interest.   Cyril of Jerusalem

Abbot Poemen also said this about Abbot Isidore that whenever he addressed the brothers in church he said only one thing, "Forgive your brother, so that you also may be forgiven."   Desert Fathers

Do we forgive our neighbors their trespasses? God also forgives us in His mercy. Do we refuse to forgive? God, too, will refuse to forgive us. As we treat our neighbors, so also does God treat us. The forgiveness, then, of your sins or unforgiveness, and hence also your salvation or destruction, depend on you yourself, man. For without forgiveness of sins there is no salvation. You can see for yourself how terrible it is.   Philotheos of Sinai

Do we forgive our neighbors their trespasses? God also forgives us in His mercy. Do we refuse to forgive? God, too, will refuse to forgive us. As we treat our neighbors, so also does God treat us. The forgiveness, then, of your sins or unforgiveness, and hence also your salvation or destruction, depend on you yourself, man. For without forgiveness of sins there is no salvation. You can see for yourself how terrible it is.   Tikhon of Zadonsk

For God seeks nothing else from us, save a good purpose. Say not, How are my sins blotted out? I tell you, By willing, by believing. What can be shorter than this? But if, while your lips declare you willing, your heart be silent, He knows the heart, who judges you. Cease from this day from every evil deed. Let not your tongue speak unseemly words, let your eye abstain from sin, and from roving after things unprofitable.   Cyril of Jerusalem

---

Hence, in whatever state a person is, he sometimes finds himself making pure and intense prayers. For even from that first and lowest sort, which has to do with recalling the future judgment, the one who is still subject to the punishment of terror and the fear of judgment is occasionally so struck with compunction that he is filled with no less joy of spirit from the richness of his supplication than the one who, examining the kindnesses of God and going over them in the purity of his heart, dissolves into unspeakable gladness and delight. For, according to the words of the Lord, the one who realizes that more has been forgiven him begins to love more.   John Cassian

---

If we remember that thief who, for a single confession, was taken into Paradise, we shall realize that it was not for the merit of the life he lived that he obtained so great blessedness, but that it was his by the gift of God, Who had mercy on him. Or let us think of David, the king, whose two such grievous and awful crimes were wiped away by one word of penitence. Neither here do we see that the merit of what he did was equal to obtaining pardon for such great offense, but the grace of God did the more abound when on the occasion of true penitence He did away with all that weight of sin for one single word of genuine confession. Again, when we consider the beginnings of man's calling and salvation, which, as the Apostle tells us, is not of ourselves or of our words, but we are saved by the gift and grace of God, we shall be able clearly to perceive how the end of perfection is not "of him that wills, nor of him that runs, but of God Who shows mercy," Who makes us victors over our vices, although we have no merit at all of life or labors to weigh against them, nor does the effort of our will avail for us to reach the steep summit of righteousness, or to subdue the flesh which we are bound to use... For the outcome of all good flows from His grace, Who has bestowed so great an eternity of bliss and such immeasurable glory , with manifold generosity, upon the weak will and the short life-work of man.

John Cassian

If your heart has been softened either by repentance before God or by learning the boundless love of God towards you, do not be proud with those whose hearts are still hard. Remember how long your heart was hard and incorrigible.

Seven brothers were ill in one hospital. One recovered from his illness, got up, and rushed to serve his other brothers with brotherly love, to speed their recovery. Be like this brother. Consider all men to be your brothers, and sick brothers at that. And if you come to feel that God has given you better health than others, know that it is given through mercy, so in health you may serve your frailer brothers.   Nikolai Velimirovic

Let no man deceive himself, let none be misled. Only the Lord can grant mercy. Sins committed again Him can be cancelled by Him alone Who bore our sins and suffered for us, by Him whom God delivered up for our sins. Man cannot be above God, nor can the servant by any indulgence of his own remit or condone the graver sort of crime committed against his Lord, for that would make the lapsed liable to this further charge, that he knows not the words of the prophet: "Cursed be the man that puts his hope in man." It is Our Lord we must pray to, it is Our Lord we must win over by our satisfaction; for He has said He will deny the man that denies Him, and He alone has received all power of judgment from His Father.   Cyprian

No one is as good and kind as the Lord is; but He does not forgive one who does not repent.   Mark the Ascetic

Not only is it wonderful that He forgives us our sins, but also that He neither uncovers them nor does He make them stand forth clearly revealed. Nor does He force us to come forward and publicly proclaim our misdeeds, but He bids us to make our defense to Him alone and to confess our shins to Him. And yet, if any judge of a worldly tribunal were to tell some captured highwayman or grave robber to confess his crime and be excused from paying the penalty, this prisoner would with all alacrity admit the truth and scorn the disgrace in his desire to go free. But this is not the case in baptism. God forgives our sins and does not force us to make a parade of them in the presence of others. He seeks one thing only: that he who benefits by the forgiveness make learn the greatness of the gift.   John Chrysostom

Often during the day I have been a great sinner, and at night, after prayer, I have gone to rest, justified and whiter than snow by the grace of the Holy Ghost, with the deepest peace and joy in my heart! How easy it will be for the Lord to save us too in the evening of our life, at the decline of our days! Oh! save, save, save me, most gracious Lord; receive me in Your heavenly Kingdom! Everything is possible to You.   John of Kronstadt

Sometimes we do not see any outlet, any escape from our sins, and they torment us: on account of them, the heart is oppressed with sorrow and weary. But Jesus looks upon us, and streams of tears flow from our eyes, and with the tears all the tissue of evil in our soul vanishes. We weep with joy that such mercy has suddenly and unexpectedly been sent to us.

John of Kronstadt

The deeper the contrition, the better. Now however deep the contrition, never admit a shadow of doubt about forgiveness. Forgiveness is already fully prepared and the record of all sins has been torn up on the Cross. Repentance and contrition alone are expected of every man, before he too can participate in the power of the redemption of the sins of the world through the Crucifixion.   Lorenzo Scupoli

The drunkard, the fornicator, the proud - he will receive God's mercy. But he who does not want to forgive, to excuse, to justify consciously, intentionally... ...that person closes himself to eternal life before God, and even more so in the present life. He is turned away and not heard.

Sampson of Russia

You do not so much desire your sins to be forgiven, as He desires to forgive you your sins. In proof that you do not so desire it, consider that you have no mind either to practice vigils, or to give your money freely: but He, that He might forgive our sins, spared not His Only-Begotten and True Son, the partner of His throne   John Chrysostom

You do not so much desire your sins to be forgiven, as He desires to forgive you your sins. In proof, that you do not so desire it, consider that you have no mind either to practice vigils, or to give your money freely; but He, that He might forgive our sins, spared not His Only Begotten and True Son, the partner of His throne."   John Chrysostom

Thus should we weep for the forgiveness of our sins. The words of the bearer of the purple should convince us of this: 'Going they went and wept, casting their seed; but coming they shall come with joyfulness, carrying their sheaves (Ps. 125:6);' as well as the words of Isaac the Syrian: 'Moisten your cheeks with the tears of your eyes, that the Holy Spirit may abide in you, and cleanse the filth of your malice. Move your lord with your tears, that He may help you.'   Seraphim of Sarov

It is impossible for a man to be freed from the habit of sin before he hates it, just as it is impossible to receive forgiveness before confessing his trespasses.   <u>Monks Callistus and Ignatius</u>

'And forgive us our debts as we also forgive our debtors.' For we have many sins. For we offend both in word and in thought, and very many things we do worthy of condemnation; and 'if we say that we have no sin (1 John 1:8), we lie, as John says.... The offenses committed against us are slight and trivial, and easily settled; but those, which we have committed against God, are great, and need such mercy as His only is. Take heed, therefore, lest for the slight and trivial sins against you, you shut out for yourself forgiveness from God for your very grievous sins.   <u>Cyril of Jerusalem</u>

---

orgiving Others

He who would be reconciled to God and have peace with God must first be reconciled with his neighbor.   <u>Tikhon of Zadonsk</u>

...to forgive our enemies and to do good to them is true magnanimity - one of the greatest traits of likeness to God.   <u>Lorenzo Scupoli</u>

Abbot Poemen also said this about Abbot Isidore that whenever he addressed the brothers in church he said only one thing, "Forgive your brother, so that you also may be forgiven."   <u>Desert Fathers</u>

Abbot Zeno said, 'If a man wants God to hear his prayer quickly, then before he prays for anything else, even his own soul, when he stands and stretches out his hands towards God, he must pray with all his heart for his enemies. Through this action God will hear everything that he asks.'   Ibid

---

Considering all these things then, and counting the recompense, which is given in this case, and remembering that to wipe away sins does not entail much labor and zeal, let us pardon those who have wronged us. For that which others scarcely accomplish, I mean the blotting out of their own sins by means of fasting and lamentations, and prayers, and sackcloth, and ashes, this it is possible for us easily to effect without sackcloth and ashes and fasting if only we blot out anger from our heart, and with sincerity forgive those who have wronged us.   John Chrysostom

---

Do we forgive our neighbors their trespasses? God also forgives us in His mercy. Do we refuse to forgive? God, too, will refuse to forgive us. As we treat our neighbors, so also does God treat us. The forgiveness, then, of your sins or unforgiveness, and hence also your salvation or destruction, depend on you yourself, man. For without forgiveness of sins there is no salvation. You can see for yourself how terrible it is.   Philotheos of Sinai

---

Do we forgive our neighbors their trespasses? God also forgives us in His mercy. Do we refuse to forgive? God, too, will refuse to forgive us. As we treat our neighbors, so also does God treat us. The forgiveness, then, of your sins or unforgiveness, and hence also your salvation or destruction, depend on you yourself, man. For without forgiveness of sins there is no salvation. You can see for yourself how terrible it is.   Tikhon of Zadonsk

Do we forgive our neighbors their trespasses? God also forgives us in His mercy. Do we refuse to forgive? God, too, will refuse to forgive us. As we treat our neighbors, so also does God treat us. The forgiveness, then, of your sins or unforgiveness, and hence also your salvation or destruction, depends on you yourself, man. For without forgiveness of sins there is no salvation. You can see for yourself how terrible it is. <u>Philotheos of Sinai</u>

Do you not see, brethren that we toil for nothing when we pray, if we have enmity against someone? And again the Lord says, 'If you offer your gift at the altar, and there you remember that someone has something against you, leave your gift before the altar, and go first and be reconciled to your brother, and then come and offer your gift'. Therefore, it is clear that if you do not do this first, all that you offer will be unacceptable, but if you do the Master's bidding, then implore the Lord with boldness, saying, 'Forgive me my debts, Master, as I have forgiven my brother, so fulfilling your commandment. I, weak though I am, have forgiven'. For the Lover of mankind will answer, 'If you have forgiven, I too will forgive. If you have pardoned, I too will pardon your sins. For I have authority on earth to forgive sins. Forgive and you will be forgiven'. <u>Ephrem the Syrian</u>

For an offense, whatever kind may have been given, one must not only not avenge oneself, but on the contrary must all the more forgive from the heart, even though it may resist this, and must incline the heart by conviction of the word of God: "If you forgive not men their trespasses, neither will your Father forgive your trespasses" (Matt. 6:15). <u>Seraphim of Sarov</u>

God is long-suffering and merciful to you: this you experience many times every day. Be long-suffering and merciful to your brethren, also fulfilling the words of the Apostle, who thus speaks of love before everything: "Love suffers long, and is kind." You desire that the Lord should rejoice you by His love, rejoice on your part the hearts of others by your tender love and kindness. <u>John of Kronstadt</u>

If a man insults me, kills my father, my mother, my brother, and then gouges out my eye, as a Christian it is my duty to forgive him. We who are pious Christians ought to love our enemies and forgive them. We ought to offer them food and drink, and entreat God for their souls. And then we should say: "My God, I beseech You to forgive me, as I have forgiven my enemies. Teachings of   Kosmas Aitolos

If the Emperor had laid down a law that all those who were enemies should be reconciled to one another, or have their heads cut off, should we not every one make haste to a reconciliation with his neighbor? Yes, truly, I think so! What excuse then have we, in not ascribing the same honor to the Lord that we should do to those who are our fellow servants? For this reason we are commanded to say, "Forgive us our debts, as we forgive our debtors" (Matt. 6:12).

What can be more mild, what more merciful, than this precept! He has made you a judge of the pardon of your own offenses! If you forgive few things, He forgives you few! If you forgive many things, He forgives you many! If you pardon from the heart, and sincerely, God in like manner also pardons you.

Do not tell me, "I have besought him many times , I have entreated, I have supplicated, but I have not effected a reconciliation." Never desist till you have reconciled him. For He said not, "Leave your gift, and go your way". Although you may have made many entreaties, yet you must not desist until you have persuaded. God entreats us every day, and we do not hear; yet He does not cease entreating. And do not then disdain to entreat your fellow servant. How is it then possible for you ever to be saved? In proportion as the good work is accomplished with greater difficulty, and the reconciliation is one of much labor, so much the greater will be the judgment on him, and so much the brighter will be the crowns of victory for your forbearance.

John Chrysostom

If you want to cure your soul, you need four things. The first is to forgive your enemies. The second is to confess thoroughly. The third is to blame yourself. The fourth is to resolve to sin no more. If we wish to be saved, we must always blame ourselves and not attribute our wrong acts to others. For God, who is most compassionate, will forgive us.   Kosmas Aitolos

If, in the case of one human being who has done wrong to another, God in His grace has commanded that we should be forgiving to the offender seventy times seven, how much more will God forgive the person who offers up supplication for his sins?   John the Solitary

Imagine the vanity of thinking that your enemy can do you more damage than your enmity.   Augustine

It is characteristic of generous, valiant souls not to despair in the midst of perils; and it is the work of one who is grateful not only to give thanks to the Lord in good fortune, but to show the same thankfulness in misfortunes as well. Nothing can embitter the virtuous soul, but everything that he suffers he considers to be gain for himself. And what can be better than to bear one's lot generously and without complaint? There is nothing more generous than to forget the offenses made against one.   Abbot Nazarius

Let us love one another, and we shall be loved by God. Let us be long-suffering toward one another, and He will be longsuffering toward our sins. Let us not render evil for evil, and He will not render to us according to our sins. We shall find remission of our transgressions in forgiving our brethren; for God's mercy toward us is concealed in our mercifulness toward our neighbor. This is also why the Lord said: Forgive, and you shall be forgiven

(Luke 6:37). If you forgive men their trespasses, your heavenly Father will also forgive you (Matthew 6:14). After this, our salvation is already in our power.   Maximus the Confessor

---

Rightly did the Lord say, 'My burden is light'. For what sort of weight is it, what sort of toil is it to forgive one's brother his offences, which are light and of no importance, and to be pardoned for one's own, and immediately justified?

He did not say, 'Bring me money, or calves, or goats, or fasting, or vigils', so that you could say, 'I have none, I cannot', but he ordered you to bring what is light and easy and immediate, saying, 'Pardon your brother his offences, and I will pardon yours. You pardon small faults, a few halfpennies, or three pennies, while I give you the ten thousand talents. You only pardon without giving anything, I nevertheless both grant you pardon and give you healing and the Kingdom.

I accept your gift, when you are reconciled to the one who is your enemy, when you have enmity against no one, when the sun does not go down on your anger.

When you have peace and love for all, then your prayer is acceptable, and your offering well-pleasing, and your house blessed and you blessed. But if you are not reconciled with your brother, how can you seek pardon from me? You trample on my words, and do you demand pardon? I, your Master, demand, and you pay no attention, and do you, a slave, dare to offer me prayer, or sacrifice, or first fruits, while you have enmity against someone? Just as you turn your face from your brother, so I too turn my eyes from your gift and your prayer.'   Ephrem the Syrian

---

Some, for the sake of forgiveness, give themselves up to labor and struggles, but a man who is forgetful of wrongs excels them. If you forgive quickly, then you will be generously forgiven.   John Climacus

---

The brothers said, "What kind of prayer is that which is not acceptable before God?" The old man said, "The prayer for the destruction of enemies. When we ask that evil things may come upon those who do harm to us, and for bodily health, and abundance of possessions, and fertility in respect of children, these requests are not acceptable before God. If God bears with us, who are sinners and who offend Him, how much more is it right that we should bear each with the other? It is, then, not meet that we should ask for the things which concern the body, for the wisdom of God provides everything necessary."   Desert Fathers

There is no prayer so quickly heard as the prayer whereby a man asks to be reconciled with those who are wroth with him. For when he charges himself with the offence, this prayer is immediately answered.   Isaac the Syrian

This is the ladder by which Christians ascend toward perfection that is toward love of enemies. What, then, Christian? When you are commanded to love your enemies, and to do good to those that hate you - commanded by Him Who created you and redeemed the lost by His blood and death, and Who holds your death and life in His hand - will you consent and forgive him who offended you? If an earthly king had commanded you not only to forgive your neighbor his offense, but also to serve him, or else be put to death, which had you better choose? To die or to forgive and serve your neighbor? I hope that you would rather wish to forgive and serve your neighbor than to die.. The Heavenly King commands you not only to forgive him that offended you, but also to love your enemies, and to do good to those that hate you. Otherwise eternal death will follow those that do not hear the commandment of the Heavenly King, `Not every one that says unto Me, Lord, Lord, shall enter into the Kingdom of Heaven, but he that doeth the will of My Father which is in heave' (Mt. 7:21).   Tikhon of Zadonsk

What are you saying? "Shall I forgive him?" Christ is saying, "Yes!" This sacrifice was instituted for the sake of peace with your brother. Accordingly, if the sacrifice was instituted for the sake of peace with your brother, but you do not establish peace, you partake of the sacrifice in vain, the work has become of no profit to you. Do first, then, that for the sake of which the sacrifice is offered, and then you will properly enjoy its benefits. The Son of God came down for this purpose, to reconcile our human nature to the Lord. But He did not come down for that purpose alone, but also for the purpose of making us, if we do likewise, sharers of His title. For He says: "Blessed are the peacemakers, for they shall be called sons of God" (Mt. 5:9). You, according to human capacity, must do what the Only begotten Son of god has done, be an agent of peace, for yourself and for others. For this reason, at the very time of sacrifice He recalls to us no other commandment that that of reconciliation with one's brother, showing that it is the greatest of all.

John Chrysostom

Do we forgive our neighbors their trespasses? God also forgives us in His mercy. Do we refuse to forgive? God, too, will refuse to forgive us. As we treat our neighbors, so also does God treat us. The forgiveness, then, of your sins or unforgiveness, and hence also your salvation or destruction, depend on you yourself, man. For without forgiveness of sins there is no salvation. You can see for yourself how terrible it is.　　　　　Tikhon of Zadonsk

'And forgive us our debts as we also forgive our debtors.' For we have many sins. For we offend both in word and in thought, and very many things we do worthy of condemnation; and 'if we say that we have no sin (1 John 1:8), we lie, as John says.... The offenses committed against us are slight and trivial, and easily settled; but those, which we have committed against God, are great, and need such mercy as His only is. Take heed, therefore, lest for the slight and trivial sins against you, you shut out for yourself forgiveness from God for your very grievous sins.　　　　　Cyril of Jerusalem

Antioch had another Patriarch who was compassionate and merciful; his name was Alexander. One of his secretaries once stole some gold from him, fled in fear and came to the Thebaid in Egypt. He was found wandering around by the bloodthirsty barbarians of Egypt and of the Thebaid; they took him to the remotest corner of their land. When the godly Alexander heard about this, he ransomed him from captivity at the cost of eighty-five pieces of gold. When the captive returned, the bishop was so loving and gentle with him that one of the inhabitants of the city once said: 'There is nothing more profitable or advantageous for me than to sin against Alexander."

John Moscos

Fornication

A vigilant monk is a foe to fornication, but a sleepy one is its mate.

John Climacus

Even if you already appear to be with God, beware the demon of fornication; for it has great fascination and is full of cunning, constantly trying to overcome the transport of your sober mind and to draw it away from God, even when it stands before God with reverence and fear. "

Nilus of Mt Sinai

He who cherishes his stomach and hopes to overcome the spirit of fornication, is like one who tries to put out a fire with oil.   John Climacus

---

Satiety in food is the father of fornication; but affliction of the stomach is an agent of purity.   John Climacus

Freewill

God in His wisdom, power and compassion knows how to change for the better the lapses we suffer as a result of our freely willed perversion.

Gregory Palamas

...in spite of the fact that you are weak and faulty, you are accounted guilty for all the wrong things you do. For since you possess a will, all that comes forth from you is subject to it, and so everything good is counted in your favor and everything bad - to your detriment. Therefore, conscious of your general wickedness, admit yourself guilty also in the particular wickedness into which you have fallen at the present moment. Judge and condemn yourself, and only yourself; do not look around, seeking on whom you could put the blame. Neither the people around you nor the circumstances are guilty of your sin. Your bad will alone is to blame. So blame yourself.

Lorenzo Scupoli

Unless questioned by the brethren we should not say anything by way of giving help, so that any benefit is a consequence of their own free choice.

Peter of Damaskos

A man by himself working and toiling at freedom from sinful desires achieves nothing. But if he plainly shows himself to be very eager and earnest about this, he attains it by the addition of the power of God. God works together with willing souls. But if the person abandons his eagerness, the spirit from God is also restrained. To save the unwilling is the act of one using compulsion; but to save the willing, that of one showing grace.

Clement of Alexandria

All the creatures that God made, He made very good. And He gave to every individual the sense of free will, by which standard He also instituted the law of judgment.... And certainly whoever will, may keep the commandments. Whoever despises them and turns aside to what is contrary to them, shall yet without doubt have to face this law of judgment.... There can be no doubt that every individual, in using his own proper power of will, may shape his course in whatever direction he pleases."   Archelaus

Baptism does not take away our free will or freedom of choice, but gives us the freedom no longer to be tyrannized by the devil unless we choose to be. After baptism it is in our power either to persist willingly in the practice of the commandments of Christ, into Whom we were baptized, and to advance in the path of His ordinances, or to deviate from this straight way and to fall again into the hands of our enemy, the devil.   Symeon the New Theologian

For Christians above all men are forbidden to correct the stumblings of sinners by force ... It is necessary to make a man better not by force but by persuasion. We neither have authority granted us by law to restrain sinners, nor, if it were, should we know how to use it, since God gives the crown to those who are kept from evil, not by force, but by choice.   John Chrysostom

Good and evil deeds are the offspring of freedom. Where freedom is lacking, the doing of [good and evil] deeds is superfluous with respect to receiving a recompense. There is no recompense for what is natural. A reward is bestowed for a conflict, and one does not speak of a victory where there is no struggle. When opposition is taken away, freedom also vanishes with it. Henceforth nature has no more struggle.   Isaac the Syrian

---

Grace has been given mystically to those who have been baptized into Christ; and it becomes active within them to the extent that they actively observe the commandments. Grace never ceases to help us secretly; but to do good - as far as lies in our power - depends on us.   Mark the Ascetic

---

He makes Himself known to those who, after doing all that their powers will allow, confess that they need help from Him."   Origen

---

In making us in His image, after His likeness, God placed us before Him, not as an action of His, entirely subject to Him, but as fact even for Him - as free beings. And by virtue of this, relations between man and God are based on the principle of freedom. When we take advantage of this freedom and commit sin, we thrust God aside. This liberty to turn away from God is the negative, tragic aspect of free will, but it is a sine qua non if we are to take hold of the life which is truly divine, life which is not predetermined."

Archimandrite Sophrony

It is not God's foreknowledge of those who, by their free choice and zeal, will prevail, which is the cause of their victory, just as, again, it is not His knowing beforehand who will fall and be vanquished which is responsible for their defeat. Instead, it is the zeal, deliberate choice, and courage of each of us, which effects the victory. Our faithlessness and sloth, our irresolution and indolence, on the other hand, comprise our defeat and perdition. So, while reclining on our bed of worldly affection He predestined,' without perceiving just what it is we are saying. Yes, indeed, He truly knew you beforehand as inattentive and disobedient and lazy, but this is certainly not because He ordered or foreordained it that you should have no power to repent yourself nor, if you will it, to get up and obey.

Symeon the New Theologian

Man is made in the image of God, Who is humble but at the same time free. Therefore it is normal and natural that he should be after the likeness of his Creator - that he should recoil from exercising control over others while himself being free and independent by virtue of the presence of the Holy Spirit within him. Those who are possessed by the lust for power cloud the image of God in themselves.   Archimandrite Sophrony

Neither praise nor condemnation, neither rewards nor punishments, are right if the soul does not have the power of choice and avoidance, if evil is involuntary."   Clement of Alexandria

Therefore, since the time of this life is a time for repentance, the mere fact that a sinner who desires to return to God can still live, proves that one is accepted by Him. For here in this life is always present freedom of choice. Free will, then, is founded upon the possibility of the acceptance or repudiance of the above-mentioned way of life and death. A person possesses the ability to chose whenever one wishes.   Gregory Palamas

Those [pagans] who decide that man does not have free will, but say that he is governed by the unavoidable necessities of fate, are guilty of impiety toward God Himself, making Him out to be the cause and author of human evils. "   Methodius

To him who has been baptized into Christ grace has been mysteriously given already. But it acts in proportion to his fulfillment of commandments. Although this grace never ceases to help us in secret, it lies in our power to do or not to do good according to our own will.

In the first place, it fittingly arouses conscience, through which even evildoers have been accepted by God when they repented.

Again, it may be concealed in the advice of a brother. Sometimes it follows thought during reading and teaches its truth to the mind by means of a natural deduction (from that thought). Thus, if we do not bury this talent bestowed upon us on these and similar occasions, we shall in truth enter into the joy of the Lord.   Mark the Ascetic

We are each born into a world in which it is easy for us to do evil and hard for us to do good.   Kallistos Ware

We have learned from the prophets, and we hold it to be true, that punishments, chastisements, and rewards are rendered according to the merit of each man's actions. Otherwise, if all things happen by fate, then nothing is in our own power. For if it be predestined that one man be good and another man evil, then the first is not deserving of praise or the other to be blamed. Unless humans have the power of avoiding evil and choosing good by free choice, they are not accountable for their actions-whatever they may be.... For neither would a man be worthy of reward or praise if he did not of himself choose the good, but was merely created for that end. Likewise, if a man was evil, he would not deserve punishment, since he was not evil of himself, being unable to do anything else than what he was made for.
                                                          Justin Martyr

When we lay bare the hidden meaning of the history, scripture is seen to teach that the birth, which distresses the tyrant, is the beginning of the virtuous life. I am speaking of the kind of birth in which free will serves as the midwife, delivering the child amid great pain. For no one causes grief to his antagonist unless he exhibits in himself those marks, which give proof of his victory over the other.   Gregory of Nyssa

Now if anyone has drawn close to God, he has evidently approached Him by means of His energy. In what way? By natural participation in that energy? But this is common to all created things. It is not, therefore, by virtue of natural qualities, but by virtue of what one achieves through free choice that one is close to or distant from God.

But free choice pertains only to beings endowed with intelligence. So among all creatures only those endowed with intelligence can be far from or close to God, drawing close to Him through virtue or becoming distant through vice. Thus such beings alone are capable of wretchedness or blessedness. Let us strive to lay hold of blessedness.   Gregory Palamas

...we experience temptations even against our will; and we grieve over passions (when they arise), yet we love to prolong their impulses and their sweetness. Sins we do not desire; yet we accept with enjoyment the impulses, which lead us to them. So in practice the latter become for us the cause of the former. He who enjoys the sweetmeats of passions becomes involuntarily subjected to them and is a slave to his passions against his will.
                                     Callistus and Ignatius

(Then we say): "Your will be done on earth as it is in heaven." In this statement, brothers, our free will is expressed, and whatever harm the persuasion of the ancient serpent has done us is removed, if we so will, for the will of the Lord heals us.

As the apostle says: "You do not always carry out your good intentions." The spirit chooses to have the will of the Lord done in us, so that the soul no longer does what it had been persuaded to do by the concupiscence of corrupt flesh. We therefore pray that the will of the Lord will be done in us

If this His will is always done in us, on the day of judgment there will be no self-will to be condemned after being examined for faults. For the will of the Lord is holy. It knows how to remove fear of judgment. This His will promises that those in whom it is accomplished will judge even angels.

Benedict of Nursia

F reedom from anger

As the gradual pouring of water on a fire completely extinguishes the flame, so the tears of mourning are able to quench every flame of anger and irritability. Therefore, we place this next in order. (after mourning)

John Climacus

Freedom from anger is an insatiable appetite for dishonor, just as in the vainglorious there is no unbounded desire for praise. Freedom from anger is victory over nature and insensibility to insults, acquired by struggles and sweat.   Ibid

The beginning of freedom from anger is silence of the lips when the heart is agitated; the middle is silence of the thoughts when there is a mere disturbance of soul; and the end is an imperturbable calm under the breath of unclean winds.   Ibid

riendship

A true friend is one who in times of trial calmly and imperturbably suffers with his neighbor the ensuing afflictions, privations and disasters as if they were his own.   Maximos the Confessor

---

Never form a close friendship with someone who enjoys noisy and drunken feasts, or who likes telling dirty stories, even though he may have been a monk for many years. Do not let his filth defile you; do not fall under the influence of people who are unclean and uncircumcised in heart.

John of Karpathos

'A faithful friend is beyond price' (Eccles. 6:15), since he regards his friend's misfortunes as his own and suffers with him, sharing his trials until death.

Maximos the Confessor

---

elasius

It was said of Abbot Gelasius that he had a leather Bible worth eighteen pieces of silver. In fact it contained the whole of the Old and New Testaments. He had put it in the church so that any of the brethren who wished, could read it.

A strange brother came to see the old man and, seeing the Bible, wished to have it, and stole it as he was leaving. The old man did not run after him to take it from him, although he knew what he was doing. So the brother went to the city and tried to sell it, and finding a purchaser, he asked thirteen pieces of silver for it. The purchaser said to him, "Lend it to me, first, so that I may examine it, then I will give you a price." So he gave it to him.

Taking it, the purchaser brought it to Abbot Gelasius for him to examine it and told him the price, which the seller had set. The old man said to him, "Buy it, for it is beautiful and worth the price you tell me." This man, when he returned, said something quite different to the seller, and not what the old man had said to him. "I have shown it to Abbot Gelasius," he said, "and he replied that it was dear, and not worth the price you said."

Hearing this, he asked, "Didn't the old man say anything else?" "No," he replied. Then the seller said, "I do not want to sell it any more." Filled with compunction, he went to find the old man, to do penance and ask him to take his book back. but he did not wish to make good his loss.

So the brother said to him, "If you do not take it back, I shall have no peace." The old man answered, "If you won't have any peace, then I will take it back." So the brother stayed there until his death, edified by the old man's way of life. "   Desert Fathers

---

Generosity

Look at all the earth supplies in summer and in autumn! Every Christian, especially the priest, ought to imitate God's bountifulness. Let your table be open to everybody, like the table of the Lord. The avaricious is God's enemy.

John of Kronstadt

Acts of kindness and generosity are spoilt by self-esteem, meanness and pleasure, unless these have first been destroyed by fear of God.

Kosmas Aitolos

Giving Advice

...unless questioned by the brethren the fathers said nothing that might contribute to the soul's salvation; they regarded unsolicited advice as vain chatter. This is quite right; for it is because we think that we know more than others that we speak unbidden.   Peter of Damaskos

---

We you see a person who is spiritually tired do not burden him any further, because his knees will not be able to bear it.   Amphilochios Makris

---

Glossolia

The multitude of the hearers was confounded; - it was a second confusion in the room of that first evil one at Babylon. For in that confusion of tongues there was division of purpose, because their thought was at enmity with God; but here minds were restored and united, because the object of interest was godly.   Cyril of Jerusalem

---

Gluttony

According to Gregory the Sinaite there are three degrees in eating: ;temperance, sufficiency, and satiety. Temperance is when someone wants to eat some more food but abstains, rising from the table still somewhat hungry. Sufficiency is when someone eats what is needed and sufficient for normal nourishment. Satiety is when someone eats more than enough and is more than satisfied. Now if you cannot keep the first two degrees and you proceed to the third, then, at least, do not become a glutton, remembering the words of the lord: "Woe unto you that are full now, for you shall hunger" (Lk. 6:25). Remember also that rich man who ate in this present life sumptuously every day, but who was deprived of the desired bosom of Abraham in the next life, simply because of this sumptuous eating.

Nicodemos of the Holy Mountain

Constantly reflecting thus and reproaching yourself, decide for yourself how much you should eat and drink every day to satisfy the needs of nature. Avoid as much as possible not merely overeating, but even eating just enough to be full. Keep in mind what was said above, that one should eat and drink only to the point where one is still a little hungry and thirsty.

Nazarius of Valaam

Gluttony is hypocrisy of the stomach; for when it is glutted, it complains of scarcity; and when it is loaded and bursting, it cries out that it is hungry.

John Climacus

Having guarded ourselves against distractions and worries, let us turn our attention to our body on which mental vigilance is completely dependent. Human bodies differ widely from one another in strength and health. Some by their strength are like copper and iron; others are frail like grass. For this reason everyone should rule his body with great prudence, after exploring his physical powers. For a strong and healthy body, special fasts and vigils are suitable; they make it lighter, and give the mind a special wakefulness. A weak body should be strengthened by food and sleep according to one's physical needs, but on no account to satiety. Satiety is extremely harmful even for a weak body; it weakens it, and makes it susceptible to disease. Wise temperance of the stomach is a door to all the virtues. Restrain the stomach, and you will enter Paradise. But if you please and pamper your stomach, you will hurl yourself over the precipice of bodily impurity, into the fire of wrath and fury, you will coarsen and darken your mind, and in this way you will ruin your powers of attention and self-control, your sobriety and vigilance.   Ignaty Brianchaninov

---

He who cherishes his stomach and hopes to overcome the spirit of fornication, is like one who tries to put out a fire with oil.   John Climacus

---

I shall speak first about control of the stomach, the opposite to gluttony, and about how to fast and what and how much to eat. I shall say nothing on my own account, but only what I have received from the Holy Fathers. They have not given us only a single rule for fasting or a single standard and measure for eating, because not everyone has the same strength; age, illness or delicacy of body create differences. But they have given us all a single goal: to avoid over-eating and the filling of our bellies... A clear rule for self-control handed down by the Fathers is this: stop eating while still hungry and do not continue until you are satisfied.   John Cassian

---

If you can begrudge the stomach, your mouth will stay closed, because the tongue flourishes where food is abundant.   John Climacus

---

It is known that the body has three kinds of carnal movements.

The first is a natural movement, inherent in it, which does not produce anything (sinful, burdening the conscience) without the consent of the soul and merely lets it be known that it exists in the body.

The second kind of movement in the body is produced by too abundant food and drink, when the resulting heat in the blood stimulates the body to fight against the soul and urges it towards impure lusts. This is the reason the Apostle says: "be not drunk with wine, wherein is excess" (Ephesians 5:18).

In the same way the Lord commands His disciples in the Gospels: "take heed to yourselves, lest at any time your hearts be overcharged with surfeiting, and drunkenness" (Luke 21:34). And those who are monks, and are zealous to achieve the full measure of sanctity and purity, should take particular care always to keep themselves such that they can say with the Apostle, "I keep under my body, and bring it into subjection" (1 Corinthians 9:27).

The third movement comes from the evil spirits, who thus tempt us out of envy and try to weaken those who have found purity (who are already monks), or to lead astray from the path those who wish to enter into the door of purity (that is, those who are as yet on the threshold of monkhood).

However, if a man arms himself with patience and an unswerving faithfulness to the commandments of God, the Holy Spirit will teach his mind how to purify his soul and body from such movements. But if at any time he weakens in his feeling and permits himself to neglect the commandments and ordinances he has heard, the evil spirits will begin to overpower him, will press upon all parts of the body and will befoul it by this movement, until the tormented soul will not know where to turn, in its despair seeing nowhere whence help could come. Only when sobered, it returns again to the commandments and, shouldering their yoke (or realizing the strength of its obligations), commits itself to the Holy Spirit, it regains a salutary disposition. Then it understands that it should seek peace solely in God, and that only thus is peace possible.   Anthony the Great

---

Satiety in food is the father of fornication; but affliction of the stomach is an agent of purity.   John Climacus

---

According to Gregory the Sinaite there are three degrees in eating: temperance, sufficiency, and satiety. Temperance is when someone wants to eat some more food but abstains, rising from the table still somewhat hungry. Sufficiency is when someone eats what is needed and sufficient for normal nourishment. Satiety is when someone eats more than enough and is more than satisfied.

Now if you cannot keep the first two degrees and you proceed to the third, then, at least, do not become a glutton, remembering the words of the Lord: "Woe to you that are full now, for you shall hunger" (Lk 6:25). Remember also that rich man who ate in this present life sumptuously every day, but who was deprived of the desired bosom of Abraham in the next life, simply because of this sumptuous eating. Remember how he longed to refresh his tongue with a drop of water.

Basil not only did not forgive the young people who ate to satiety but also those who ate until satisfied; he preferred that all eat temperately. He said, "Nothing subdues and controls the body as does the practice of temperance. It is this temperance that serves as a control to those youthful passions and desires.'"

Gregory the Theologian has also noted in his poetry: "No satiety has brought forth prudent behavior; for it is in the nature of fire to consume matter. And a filled stomach expels refined thoughts; it is the tendency of opposites to oppose each other."

Job, too, assuming that one could fall into sin through eating, offered sacrifice to God for his sons who were feasting among themselves. "And when the days of the feast had run their course, Job would send and sanctify them, and he would rise early in the morning and offer burnt offerings according to the number of them all; for Job said: 'It may be that my sons have sinned, and cursed God in their hearts'" (Jb 1:5-8). In interpreting this passage Olympiodoros wrote: "We learn from this that we ought to avoid such feasts which can bring on sinfulness. We must also purify ourselves after they have been concluded, even if these are conducted for the sake of concord and brotherly love as in the case of the sons of Job."

Surely then, if the sons of Job were not at a feast but in prayer or some other spiritual activity, the devil would not have dared to destroy the house and them, as Origen interpreted the passage: "The devil was looking for an opportunity to destroy them. Had he found them reading, he would not have touched the house, having no reason to put them to death. Had he found them in prayer, he would not have had any power to do anything against them. But when he found an opportune time, he was powerful. What was the opportune time? It was the time of feasting and drinking." Do you see then, dear reader, how many evils are brought forth by luxurious foods and feasting in general?

Nicodemos

The heart of gluttons dreams only of food and eatables, but the heart of those who weep dreams of judgment and castigation.   John Climacus

The prince of demons is the fallen Lucifer, and the prince of passions is gluttony.   Ibid

When heavy with over-eating, the body makes the intellect spiritless and sluggish; likewise, when weakened by excessive abstinence, the body makes the contemplative faculty of the soul dejected and disinclined to concentrate. We should therefore regulate our food according to the condition of the body, so that it is appropriately disciplined when in good health and adequately nourished when weak. The body of one pursuing the spiritual way must not be enfeebled; he must have enough strength for his labors, so that the soul may be suitably purified through bodily exertion as well.

Diadochos of Photiki

It is just as shameful for lovers of the flesh and the belly to search out spiritual things as it is for a harlot to discourse on chastity.   Isaac of Syria

God

'Blessed be the God and Father of our Lord Jesus Christ'(2 Cor. 1:3). Blessed also be His Only-begotten Son. For with the thought of 'God' let the thought of 'Father' at once be joined, that the ascription of glory to the Father and the Son may be made indivisible. For the Father has not one glory, and the Son another, but one and the same, since He is the Father's Only-begotten Son; and when the Father is glorified, the Son also shares the glory with Him, because the glory of the Son flows from His Father's honor: and again, when the Son is glorified, the Father of so great a blessing is highly honored.

Cyril of Jerusalem

To participate in these deifying energies are intelligible creatures, i.e., the angels - pure images, to whom the soul is likened. But God remains unknown in Himself, incomprehensible in His nature.   Gregory of Nyssa

God is the only Being that truly is - the only eternal and immutable Being - who neither receives being from non-being nor returns to non-being; who is Tri-hypostatic and Almighty.   Gregory Palamas

Concerning God we speak not all we ought (for that is known to Him only), but so much as the capacity of human nature has received, and so much as our weakness can bear. For we explain not what God is but candidly confess that we have not exact knowledge concerning Him. For in what concerns God to confess our ignorance is the best knowledge.   Cyril of Jerusalem

...though a thing be all heavenly, or above heaven, and far higher in nature and nearer to God than we, yet it is farther distant from God, and from the complete comprehension of His Nature, than it is lifted above our complex and lowly and earthward-sinking composition.   Gregory Nazianzen

To say that God turns away from the wicked is the same as to say that the sun hides itself from those who lose their sight.   Antony the Great

---

A man standing on the seashore sees the immense expanse of water, but his eye can embrace only a small part and cannot reach its limit. In the same way a man who, through contemplation, is given to see the limitless ocean of Divine glory and to see God Himself with the eyes of his mind, sees God and the infinite vastness of His Glory, though not the whole as it really is, but only as much as is possible for him.   Symeon the New Theologian

---

Abraham passed through all the reasoning that is possible to human nature about the divine attributes, and after he had purified his mind of all such concepts, he took hold of a faith that was unmixed and pure of any concept, and he fashioned for himself this token of knowledge of God that is completely clear and free of error, namely the belief that God completely transcends any knowable symbol. And so, after this ecstasy which came upon him as a result of these lofty visions, Abraham returned one more to his human frailty: `I am,' he admits (Gen. 18:27), `dust and ashes,' mute, inert, incapable of explaining rationally the Godhead that my mind has seen.

Gregory of Nyssa

According to the Apostle, God has both goodness and severity (cf. Rom. 11:22): His goodness addresses those who rest firmly in the Faith, the severity in those who distance themselves from it. And since the saint has been confirmed in the Faith, he says: `You have dealt graciously with Your servant.'   Didymus the Blind

---

But some one will say, If the Divine substance is incomprehensible, why then do you discourse on these things? So then, because I cannot drink up all the river, an I not even to take in moderation what is expedient for me? Because with eyes so constituted as mine I cannot take in all the sun, am I not even to look upon him enough to satisfy my wants? Or again, because I have entered into a great garden, and cannot eat all the supply of fruits, would you have me go away altogether hungry? I praise and glorify Him Who made us; for it is a divine command, which says, 'Let every breath praise the Lord' (Ps. 150:6). I am attempting now to glorify the Lord, but not to describe Him, knowing nevertheless that I shall fall short of glorifying Him worthily, yet deeming it a work of piety even to attempt it at all.

Cyril of Jerusalem

By nature [essence] God is above being and knowledge. What we say of God affirmatively does not indicate His nature, but His attributes [or energies]."

John Damascene

Even a whisper of the Divine is glory beyond compare to all the content of life lived apart from God.   Archimandrite Sophrony

For devotion it suffices us simply to know that we have a God; a God who is One, a living, an ever-living God; always like unto Himself; who has no Father, none mightier than Himself, no successor to thrust Him out from His kingdom: Who in name is manifold, in power infinite, in substance uniform. For though He is called Good, and Just, and Almighty and Sabaoth, He is not on that account diverse and various; but being one and the same, He sends forth countless operations of His Godhead, not exceeding here and deficient there, but being in all things like unto Himself. Cyril of Jerusalem

God Himself and naught else is light for eternal beings...God...is the primal and supreme light illumining all intelligent nature.　　　Gregory Palamas

God belongs to all free beings. He is the life of all, the salvation of all faithful and unfaithful, just and unjust, pious and impious, passionate and dispassionate, monks and laymen, wise and simple, healthy and sick, young and old just as the effusion of light, the sight of the sun, and the changes of the seasons are for all alike; 'for there is no respect of persons with God.'

John Climacus

God belongs to all free beings. He is the life of all, the salvation of all – faithful and unfaithful, just and unjust, pious and impious, passionate and dispassionate, monks and laymen, wise and simple, healthy and sick, young and old – just as the effusion of light, the sight of the sun, and the changes of the seasons are for all alike; "for there is no respect of persons with God."

Ibid

God is a fire that warms and kindles the heart and inward parts. Hence, if we feel in our hearts the cold, which comes from the devil - for the devil, is cold - let us call on the Lord. He will come to warm our hearts with perfect love, not only for Him but also for our neighbor, and the cold of him who hates the good will flee before the heat of His countenance.　　　Seraphim of Sarov

God is a fire that warms and kindles the heart and inward parts. Hence, if we feel in our hearts the cold which comes from the devil - for the devil is cold - let us call on the Lord. He will come to warm our hearts with perfect love, not only for Him but also for our neighbor, and the cold of him who hates the good will flee before the heat of His countenance.   Seraphim of Sarov

God is comprehensible in our contemplation of His attributes [or divine energies], but God is incomprehensible in our contemplation of His divine essence."   Maximus the Confessor

God is fire that warms and kindles the heart and inward parts. And so, if we feel in our hearts coldness, which is from the devil for the devil is cold then let us call upon the Lord and He will come and warm our hearts with perfect love not only for Him but for our neighbor as well.   Seraphim of Sarov

God is invisible because he is immeasurably manifest.
                                                    Dionysius the Areopagite

God is praised as "Logos" [word] by the sacred scriptures not only as the leader of word, mind, and wisdom, but because He also initially carries within His own unity the causes of all things and because He penetrates all things, reaching, as scripture says, to the very end of all things. But the title is used especially because the divine Logos is simpler than any simplicity and, in its utter transcendence, is independent of everything. This Word is simple total truth. Divine faith revolves around it because it is pure and unwavering knowledge of all. It is the one sure foundation for those who believe, binding them to the truth, building the truth in them as something unshakably firm so that they have an uncomplicated knowledge of the truth of what they believe.
                                                    Dionysius the Areopagite

God then is in an improper sense the Father of many, but by nature and in truth of One only, the Only-begotten Son, our Lord Jesus Christ; not having attained in course of time to being a Father, but being ever the Father of the Only-begotten. Not that being without a Son before, He has since by change of purpose become a Father: but before every substance and every intelligence, before times and all ages, God has the dignity of Father, magnifying Himself in this more than in His other dignities; and having become a Father, not by passion, or union, not in ignorance, not by effluence, not by diminution, not by alteration, for 'every good gift and every perfect gift is from above, coming down from the Father of lights, with Whom can be no variation, neither shadow of turning' (James 1:17). Perfect Father, He begat a perfect Son, and delivered all things to Him Who is begotten.

Cyril of Jerusalem

God then is infinite and incomprehensible: and all that is comprehensible about Him is His infinity and incomprehensibility. But all that we can affirm concerning God does not show forth God's nature, but only the qualities of His nature. For when you speak of Him as good, and just, and wise, and so forth, you do not tell God's nature but only the qualities of His nature. Further there are some affirmations which we make concerning God which have the force of absolute negation: for example, when we use the term darkness, in reference to God, we do not mean darkness itself, but that He is not light but above light: and when we speak of Him as light, we mean that He is not darkness.

John of Damascus

God works in our body, in its natural function, supporting it, feeding it, and rearing it. He also acts in the grass, or in the trees, or in the animals, clothing the grass, rearing the tree and adorning it with leaves and fruit, feeding the animals and rearing their bodies. Of ourselves, we cannot do or create anything in our body, not one jot, as it is said. "You canst not make one hair white or black." God is equally in the infinitely great and in the infinitely small, not being limited either by the one or the other, but is wholly present in everything, being indivisible and above all.

John of Kronstadt

Hence when a man suffers the loss of that Good, how are we to represent the magnitude of that catastrophe? The great David rightly shows us how impossible this is. Lifted out of himself by the Spirit, he glimpsed in that blessed ecstasy God's infinite and incomprehensible beauty. He saw as much as a mere mortal can see, leaving the covering of the flesh, and by thought alone entering into contemplation of that immaterial and spiritual realm. And though yearning to say something which would do justice to his vision, he can only cry out (in words that all can echo after him): `Every man is a liar" (Ps. 115:11). And this I take to mean that anyone who attempts to portray that ineffable Light in language is truly a liar - not because of any abhorrence of the truth, but merely because of the infirmity of his explanations.

Gregory of Nyssa

Honor God and you will know the incorporeal; serve Him and He will show you the understanding of the ages.   Abbot Evagrius

I was running to lay hold on God, and thus I went up into the Mount, and drew aside the curtain of the Cloud, and entered away from matter and material things, and as far as I could I withdrew within myself. And then when I looked up, I scarce saw the back parts of God (Ex. 33:23); although I was sheltered by the Rock, the Word that was made flesh for us. And when I looked a little closer, I saw, not the First and unmingled Nature, known to Itself - to the Trinity, I mean; not That which abides within the first veil, and is hidden by the Cherubim; but only that Nature, which at last even reaches to us. And that is, as far as I can learn, the Majesty, or as holy David calls it, the Glory (Ps. 8:1) which is manifested among the creatures which It has produced and governs. For these are the Back Parts of God, which He leaves behind Him, as tokens of Himself like the shadows and reflection of the sun in the water, which show the sun to our weak eyes, because we cannot look at the sun himself, for by his unmixed light he is too strong for our power of perception.   Gregory Nazianzen

In the case of the Godhead, what created being is able to investigate Him? For there is a great chasm between him and the Creator. In the case of the Godhead, it is not that He is distant from His possessions, for there exists love between Him and creation. None of those who try to investigate God has ever drawn near to Him -- yet He is extremely close to those who have discernment.   Ephraim the Syrian

---

It is difficult to conceive God but to define Him in words is an impossibility.
                                                    Gregory Nazianzen

---

Now the beauty of God, being unified, good, and the Source of all perfection, is wholly free from dissimilarity, and bestows its own Light upon each according to his merit; and in the most divine Mysteries perfects them in accordance with the unchangeable fashioning of those who are being perfected harmoniously to Itself.   Dionysius the Areopagite

---

One of the elders said to the brethren at Kellia, "Nothing is greater than God; nothing is equal to Him; nothing is only a little inferior to Him. What then is stronger or more blessed than someone who has the help of God?" And again: "Let us gather together the cures of the soul: piety, righteousness, humility, submission. The greatest physician of souls, Christ our God, is near to us and is willing to heal us: let us not underestimate Him." John Moschus

---

The Divine Nature then it is impossible to see with eyes of flesh: but from the works, which are Divine, it is possible to attain to some conception of His power, according to Solomon, who says, 'For by the greatness and beauty of the creatures proportionably the Maker of them is seen'   Cyril of Jerusalem

The anger of God is not a disturbing emotion of His mind, but a judgment by which punishment is inflicted upon sin. His thought and reconsideration also are the unchangeable reason, which changes things; for He does not, like man, repent of anything He has done, because in all matters His decision is as inflexible as His prescience is certain. But if Scripture were not to use such expressions as the above, it would not familiarly insinuate itself into the minds of all classes of men, whom it seeks access to for their good, that it may alarm the proud, arouse the careless, exercise the inquisitive, and satisfy the intelligent; and this it could not do, did it not first stoop, and in a manner descend, to them where they lie.   Augustine

The divine nature [essence] surpasses intelligence, and though they may contemplate the Trinity, though they may receive the plenitude of His light [energy], human intellects cannot know God in His nature [essence]."

Gregory of Naziansus

The light of the sun is inseparable from the sun's rays and from the heat which they dispense; yet for those who receive the rays but have no eyes the light is imperceptible and they sense only the heat coming from the rays. For those bereft of eyes cannot possibly perceive light. In the same way, but to a greater extent, no one who enjoys the divine radiance can participate in the essence of the Creator. For there is absolutely no creature that possesses the capacity to perceive the Creator's nature.   Gregory Palamas

The transcendently and absolutely perfect Goodness is Intellect; thus what else could the which proceeds from It as from a source be except Intelligence-content or Logos? But the divine Logos is not to be understood in the same way as the human thought-form that we express orally, for that proceeds not from the intellect but from a body activated by the intellect...Thus the supreme Logos is the Son, and is so described by us, in order that we may recognize Him to be perfect in a perfect and individual hypostasis, since He comes from the Father and is in no way inferior to the Father's essence, but is indistinguishably identical with Him, although not according to hypostasis; for His distinction as hypostasis is manifest in the fact that the Logos is begotten in a divinely fitting manner from the Father.

Ibid

Three realities pertain to God: essence, energy, and the triad of divine hypostases. As we have seen, those privileged to be united to God so as to become one spirit with Him - as Paul said, 'He who cleaves to the Lord is one spirit with Him' (1 Cor. 6:17) - are not united to God with respect to His essence, since all theologians testify that with respect to His essence God suffers no participation.

Moreover, the hypostatic union is fulfilled only in the case of the Logos, the God-man.

Thus those privileged to attain union with God are united to Him with respect to His energy; and the 'spirit', according to which they who cleave to God are one with Him, is and is called the uncreated energy of the Holy Spirit, but not the essence of God.   Ibid

We do not know God from His essence. We know Him rather from the grandeur of His creation and from His providential care for all creatures.

Maximos the Confessor

We in accordance with the true doctrine speak of the Son as neither like, nor unlike the Father. Each of these terms is equally impossible, for like and

146

unlike are predicated in relation to quality, and the divine is free from
quality.   Pachomius

We know our God in His energies. For although His energies descend to us,
His essence remains inaccessible.   Basil the Great

When the intellect is established in God, it at first ardently longs to discover
the principles of His essence. But God's inmost nature does not admit of such
investigation, which is indeed beyond the capacity of everything created. The
qualities that appertain to His nature, however, are accessible to the intellect's
longing: I mean the qualities of eternity, infinity, indeterminateness,
goodness, wisdom, and the power of creating, preserving and judging
creatures. Yet of these, only infinity may be grasped fully; and the very fact
of knowing nothing is knowledge surpassing the intellect, as the theologians
Gregory of Nazianzos and Dionysius have said.   Maximos the Confessor

---

Who can make an imitation of the invisible, incorporeal, uncircumscribed,
formless God? Therefore to give form to the Deity is the height of folly and
impiety. And hence it is that in the Old Testament the use of images was not
common, but after God in His bowels of pity became in truth man for our
salvation, not as He was seen by Abraham in the semblance of a man, nor as
He was seen by the prophets, but in being truly man, and after He lived upon
the earth and dwelt among men, worked miracles, suffered, was crucified,
rose again and was taken back to Heaven, since all these things actually took
place and were seen by men, they were all written for the remembrance and
instruction of us who were not alive at that time in order that though we saw
not, we may still, hearing and believing, obtain the blessing of the Lord.

John of Damascus

"Rich is the Lord, and enriching; powerful is He, and He gives unconquerable power; wise is He, and He gives wisdom; holy is He and He hallows. For every gift is good and every gift is perfect that comes from Him to those who strive to follow Him."   Theophan the Recluse

There is not a fraction of a moment during which He, as the All-perfect, Most-wise, All-merciful, Omniscient, Omnipresent, Almighty Spirit, does not shower benefits and wisdom upon His creatures. There is not a fraction of a moment during which He does not apply His wisdom and omnipotence, for God is a Self-acting Being, infinitely productive. Thus you look upon the world, but look upon it and observe everywhere in it its Author - God, everywhere present in it, filling everything, moving in everything, and ordering everything.   John of Kronstadt

Every created nature is far removed from and completely foreign to the divine nature. For if God is nature, other things are not nature; but if every other thing is nature, He is not a nature, just as He is not a being if all other things are beings. And if He is a being, then all other things are not beings. And if you accept this as true also for wisdom, goodness, and in general all things that pertain to God or are ascribed to Him, then your theology will be correct and in accordance with the saints.   Gregory Palamas

Far be it that we should ever think such an iniquity that God could become unmerciful. For the property of Divinity does not change as do mortals. God does not acquire something which He does not has, or lose what He has, or supplement what He has, as do created beings. But what God has from the beginning, He will have and has forever.   Isaac the Syrian

God both is and is said to be the nature of all beings, in so far as all partake of Him and subsist by means of this participation: not, however, by participation in His nature - far from it - but by participation in His energy. In this sense He is the Being of all beings, the Form that is in all forms as the author of form, the Wisdom of the wise and, simply, the All of all things.

Gregory Palamas

"To God pertains both incomprehensibility and comprehensibility, though He Himself is one. The same God is incomprehensible in His essence, but comprehensible from what He creates according to His divine energies: according, that is, to His pre-eternal wisdom with regard to us, and - to use the words of Maximos - His infinite power, wisdom and goodness."   Ibid

---

Good

Since to the highest possible degree He [God] loves, knows and is able to effect what is profitable for us, everything that comes to us from Him, even though it is without our wanting it, will certainly prove to be to our profit.

Ibid

Gossip

...do not take pleasure in listening to gossip or criticisms, or the calumnies, which some people spread about their brethren; but either stop them, if you can, or withdraw, so as not to hear them.   Lorenzo Scupoli

---

Do not listen gleefully to gossip at your neighbors expense or chatter to a person who likes finding fault.   Maximos the Confessor

---

Do not listen gleefully to gossip at your neighbor's expense or chatter to a person who likes finding fault.   Ibid

---

Give no ear to the slanderer's talk nor let your talk run on in the fault-finder's hearing, by readily speaking and listening to things against your neighbor; otherwise you will fall from divine charity [love] and be found a foreigner to eternal life.   Ibid

---

We should shun loose speech like an asp's venom...for it can plunge us into total forgetfulness of the inner struggle.   Hesychios

---

Grace

"For truly the assistance which God gives to our nature is provided to those who correctly live the life of virtue. This assistance was already there at our birth, but it is manifested and made known whenever we apply ourselves to diligent training in the higher life and strip ourselves for the more vigorous contests."   Gregory of Nyssa.

At the start of the spiritual way, the soul usually has the conscious experience of being illumined with its own light through the action of grace. But, as it advances further in its struggle to attain theology, grace works its mysteries within the soul for the most part without its knowledge.

Diadochos of Photiki

"The law of grace directly teaches those who are led by it to imitate God Himself. For it is permitted to speak in this way despite the fact that because of sin we were His enemies.

God loved us so much more than Himself that, although He is beyond every being, He entered without changing into our being, supra-essentially took on human nature, became man and, wishing to reveal Himself as a man among men, did not refuse to make His own the penalty we pay.

And as in His providence He became man, so He deified us by grace, in this way teaching us not only to cleave to one another naturally and to love others spiritually as ourselves, but also, like God, to be more concerned for others than for ourselves, and as proof of our love for each other readily to choose, as virtue enjoins, to die for others. For as Scripture tells us, there is no greater love than to lay down one's life for a friend" (cf. John 15: 13).

'The pure of heart will see God,' according to the Lord's infallible word (Mt. 5:8), according to his capacity, receiving as much as his mind can sustain; yet the infinite and incomprehensible nature of the Godhead remains beyond all understanding.

For 'the magnificence of His glory,' as the Prophet says (Ps. 144-5), has no end, and as we contemplate Him He remains ever the same, at the same distance above us.

The Great David enjoyed in his heart those glorious elevations as he progressed from strength to strength; and yet he cried to God: Lord, 'You are the most High,' forever and ever (Ps. 82:19). And by this I think he means that in all the infinite eternity of centuries, the man who runs towards You constantly becomes greater as he rises higher, ever growing in proportion to his increase in grace. 'You,' indeed, 'are the most High,' abiding forever, and canst never seem smaller to those who approach You, for You are always to the same degree higher and loftier than the faculties of those who are rising.

Gregory of Nyssa

At the start of the spiritual way, the soul usually has the conscious experience of being illumined with its own light through the action of grace. But, as it advances further in its struggle to attain theology, grace works its mysteries within the soul for the most part without its knowledge. Grace acts in these two ways so that it may first set us rejoicing on the path of contemplation, calling us from ignorance to spiritual knowledge, and so that in the midst of our struggle it may then keep this knowledge free from arrogance.

Diadochos of Photiki

Every good work, which we perform through our own natural power, causes us to refrain from the corresponding sin; but without grace it cannot contribute to our sanctification.

Mark the Ascetic

God also acted through cattle before the Ark, when he wanted to save His people (1 Samuel 6). Could a priest's life or virtues accomplish something like that? The Gifts of God are not such that they depend upon the virtue of the priest. Everything comes from Grace. It is for the priest to open his lips, and everything is performed by God, while the priest performs the visible actions.

John Chrysostom

Grace has been given mystically to those who have been baptized into Christ; and it becomes active within them to the extent that they actively observe the commandments. Grace never ceases to help us secretly; but to do good - as far as lies in our power - depends on us.   Mark the Ascetic

---

Grace has been given mystically to those who have been baptized into Christ; and it becomes active within them to the extent that they actively observe the commandments. Grace never ceases to help us secretly; but to do good - as far as lies in our power - depends on us   Ibid

---

Grace operates as well through the unworthy, so that we are sanctified as well thought unworthy priests.   Theophylact of Bulgaria

---

In the Divine womb, that is, in the holy font, we freely receive perfect Divine grace. If after this we cover it over with the fog of passions, either through abuse of temporal things, or though excess of cares for worldly activities, it is possible, even after this, to regain possession of it, to restore its supernatural brightness and to see quite vividly its manifestation, by repentance and the fulfillment of commandments whose action is Divine. Grace manifests in proportion to each man's zeal in remaining faithful to faith, but above all through the help and benevolence of our Lord Jesus Christ.
                                                  Callistus and Ignatius

---

It may happen that for a certain time a man is illumined and refreshed by God's grace, and then this grace is withdrawn. This makes him inwardly confused and he starts to grumble; instead of seeking through steadfast prayer to recover his assurance of salvation, he loses patience and gives up.

He is like a beggar who receives alms from the palace, and feels put out because he was not asked inside to dine with the king.   John of Karpathos

---

The grace of the priesthood is one thing, the grace of the great schema is another, the grace of the Mysteries is different, and the action of grace in ascesis is also different. They all spring from the same source, but each one differs from the other in eminence and glory. The grace of repentance, which acts in those who struggle, is a patristic inheritance. It is a divine transaction and exchange in which we give dust and receive heaven. We exchange matter for the Spirit. Every drop of sweat, every pain, every ascesis for God is an exchange.   Joseph the Hesychast

---

The roof of any house stands upon the foundations and the rest of the structure. The foundations themselves are laid in order to carry the roof. This is both useful and necessary, for the roof cannot stand without the foundations and the foundations are absolutely useless without the roof - no help to any living creature. In the same way the grace of God is preserved by the practice of the commandments, and the observance of these commandments is laid down like foundations through the gift of God. The grace of the Spirit cannot remain with us without the practice of the commandments, but the practice of the commandments is of no help or advantage to us without the grace of God.   Symeon the New Theologian

---

The roof of any house stands upon the foundations and the rest of the structure. The foundations themselves are laid in order to carry the roof. This is both useful and necessary, for the roof cannot stand without the foundations and the foundations are absolutely useless without the roof - no help to any living creature. In the same way the grace of God is preserved by the practice of the commandments, and the observance of these commandments is laid down like foundations through the gift of God. The grace of the Spirit cannot remain with us without the practice of the commandments, but the practice of the commandments is of no help or advantage to us without the grace of God.   Ibid

154

The signs accompanying grace are much joy, peace, love, and truth. Such truth impels man to seek truth. But the signs of sin are accompanied by turmoil, not joy and love toward God."   Macarius

To God always belongs Grace, as does the Mystery, while to man, the performer of the Mystery, belongs only service. If he is good, then he is in concert with God and acts in harmony with Him; if bad, then God performs the visible form of the Mystery through him, but Himself endows it with invisible Grace:. Do not imagine that Divine Mysteries depend upon human morality and actions. They are holy because of the One to Whom they belong.   Augustine

What is grace? It is the blessed power of God. . the power that cleanses, sanctifies, enlightens, that helps in doing good and withdraws from evil, that comforts and gives courage in misfortunes, sorrows, and sickness; that is a pledge of receiving the everlasting blessings, prepared by God in heaven for His chosen ones.   John of Kronstadt

When through self-control we have purified our body, and when through divine love we have made our incensive power and our desire incentives for virtue, and when we offer to God our intellect cleansed by prayer, then we will possess and see within ourselves the grace promised to the pure in heart (cf. Matt. 5:8).   Gregory Palamas

In order to live spiritually and draw breath from grace, we must continually exhale the ashes of sin.   Ignaty Brianchaninov

At the start of the spiritual way, the soul usually has the conscious experience of being illumined with its own light through the action of grace. But, as it advances further in its struggle to attain theology, grace works its mysteries within the soul for the most part without its knowledge. <u>Diadochos of Photiki</u>

Every good work, which we perform through our own natural powers, causes us to refrain from the corresponding sin; but without grace it cannot contribute to our sanctification. <u>Kosmas Aitolos</u>

Grace has been given mystically to those who have been baptized into Christ; and it becomes active within them to the extent that they actively observe the commandments. Grace never ceases to help us secretly; but to do good- as far as lies in our power- depends on us . <u>Ibid</u>

Initially grace arouses the conscience in a divine manner. That is how even sinners have come to repent and so to conform to God's will.

<u>Kosmas Aitolos</u>

Again, grace may be bidden in advice given by a neighbor. Sometimes it also accompanies our understanding during reading, and as a natural result teaches our intellect the truth about itself. If, then, we do not hide the talent given to us in this way, we shall enter actively into the joy of the Lord.

<u>Kosmas Aitolos</u>

Everyone baptized in the orthodox manner has received mystically the fullness of grace; but he becomes conscious of this grace only to the extent that he actively observes the commandments.   Ibid

---

The grace of the Spirit is one and unchanging, but energizes in each one of us as He wills (cf. 1Co 12:11).   Ibid

---

When rain falls upon the earth, it gives life to the quality inherent in each plant: sweetness in the sweet, astringency in the astringent; similarly, when grace falls upon the hearts of the faithful, it gives to each the energies appropriate to the different virtues without itself changing.   Ibid

---

To him who hungers after Christ grace is food; to him who is thirsty, a reviving drink; to him who is cold, a garment; to him who is weary, rest; to him who prays, assurance; to him who mourns, consolation.   Ibid

Gratitude

Let us not grieve that One Who showed us unceasing love and affection with transgressions, murmuring, disobedience and various forms of sin, but as grateful servants let us strive to give rest to the bowels of His mercy, so that He be consoled, as the psalmist said: "He will comfort Himself concerning His servants" (Ps. 134/5:14 LXX).   Ephraim of Philotheou

He who has received a gift from God, and is ungrateful for it, is already on the way to losing it.   Peter of Damaskos

---

When God is thanked, He gives us still further blessings, while we, by receiving His gifts, love Him all the more and through this love attain that divine wisdom whose beginning is the fear of God (cf. Prov. 1:7).   Ibid

---

Gratitude is a form of intercession. Only it must not be like the gratitude of the Pharisee, who condemned others and justified himself (cf. Luke 18:11). On the contrary, it must make one regard oneself as a greater debtor than all other men; one gives thanks in astonished bewilderment because one understands God's unutterable restraint and forbearance.   Ibid

---

Gratitude from the receiver incites the giver to bestow gifts greater than before. He who is ungrateful in lesser things, is false and unjust in greater.
                                                          Callistus and Ignatius

---

When evening comes, collect your thoughts and ponder over the entire course of the day: observe God's providential care for you; consider the grace He has wrought in you throughout the whole span of the day; consider the rising of the moon, the joy of daylight, all the hours and moments, the divisions of time, the sight of different colors, the beautiful adornment of creation, the course of the sun, the growth of your own stature, how your own person has been protected, consider the blowing of the winds, the ripe and varied fruits, how the elements minister to your comfort, how you have been preserved from accidents, and all the other activities of grace. When you have pondered on all this, wonder of God's love toward you will well up within you, and gratitude for his acts of grace will bubble up inside you.

John the Solitary

reat Passion of Jesus Christ

Today the Master of the creation and the Lord of glory is nailed to the Cross and His side is pierced; and He who is the sweetness of the Church tastes gall and vinegar. A crown of thorns is put upon Him who covers the heaven with clouds. He is clothed in a cloak of mockery, and He who formed man with His hands is struck by a hand of clay. He who wraps the heaven in clouds is smitten upon His back. He accepts spitting and scourging, reproach and buffeting; and all these things my Deliverer and God endures for me that am condemned, that in His compassion He may save the world from error.

Aposticha

---

reed

There was in Alexandria a virgin of humble appearance but of overbearing disposition. She was exceedingly rich, but never gave an obol to a stranger, virgin, church, or poor man. Despite the many rebukes of the fathers, she did not turn herself away from material wealth. Now she had some relatives and she adopted one of them, her sister's daughter, and night and day without any longing for heaven she kept promising her all her wealth. For this is one way the devil deceives us, by contriving to make us fight to excess in the guise of loving one's relatives .

Now they say that the blessed Macarius wished to tap a vein of this virgin to alleviate her greed. This Macarius, priest and superior of the poorhouse for cripples, devised the following ruse. In his younger days he had been a worker in stones, what they call a gem engraver. He went to her and said: "Some precious stones, emeralds, and hyacinths, have come into my possession; whether they are simply a find or stolen property, I cannot say. Their value has not been ascertained, since they are priceless, but they can be had by anyone who has five hundred coins. If you take them, you will get your five hundred coins back from one stone; the rest you can use to pretty up your niece."

Intent on his every word, the maiden took the bait and fell at his feet, "I beseech you," she exclaimed, "do not let anyone else have them." Then he invited her, "Come to my dwelling and see them." She was not willing to wait, however, but threw down the five hundred coins for him, saying, "Take them as you wish, for I do not want to see the man who put them up for sale."

He took the five hundred coins and gave them for the needs of the hospital. Some time elapsed, and since the man seemed to have a very great reputation in Alexandria, and a love of God, and was charitable -- he was active until he was a hundred; we spent some time with him ourselves -- well, she was discreet about reminding him. Eventually she found him in the church and asked him, "I beg you, what did you decide about those stones for which I gave you the five hundred coins?"

He said in reply, "Just as soon as you gave me the money I put it down for the price of the stones. If you wish, come and see them in the hospital, for they are there. Come and see if they please you; if they do not, take your money back."

Now the hospital had the women on the upper floor and the men on the ground floor. And leading her he brought her up to the entrance and asked: "What do you want to see first, the hyacinths or the emeralds?" She replied: "As you please." He took her to the upper floor, pointed out the crippled and inflamed women, and said: "Look, here are your hyacinths!" And he led her back down again and showed her the men: "Behold your emeralds! If they do not please you, take your money back!"   Palladius Hist

---

Grief

Do you see what grief arises in a humble soul and the consolation that ensues: Indeed, self-reproach on its own, when lying for a protracted time upon the soul's thoughts like some intellectual weight, crushes and presses and squeezes out the saving wine that gladdens the heart of man (Cf.. Ps. 104:15), that is to say, our inner self. This wine is compunction. Together with grief compunction crushes the passions and, having freed the soul from the weight that oppresses it, fills it with blessed joy. That is the reason why Christ says, 'Blessed are those who grieve, for they will be consoled' (Mt. 5:4).   Gregory Palamas

---

A man who craves esteem cannot be rid of the causes of grief. Isaac of Syria

Grumbling

One should fear and beware of grumbling at God, for while the Lord God, according to His great mercy, is long-suffering and patient with our sins, His mercy does not extend to the tendency to complain.   Antony of Optina

Guardian Angel

Do not be surprised that you fall every day, do not give up, but stand your ground courageously. And assuredly, the angel who guards you will honor your patience. While a wound is still fresh and warm, it is easy to heal; but old, neglected and festering ones are hard to cure, and require for their care much treatment, cutting, plastering and cauterization. Many from long neglect become incurable, but with God all things are possible.
                                                                             John Climacus

---

Do not be surprised that you fall every day; do not give up, but stand your ground courageously. And assuredly, the angel who guards you will honor your patience.   Mark the Ascetic

If you feel sweetness or compunction at some word of your prayer, dwell on it; for then our guardian angel is praying with us. John Climacus

In the presence of an invisible spirit, the body becomes afraid; but in the presence of an angel, the soul of the humble is filled with joy. Therefore, when we recognize the presence from the effect, let us quickly hasten to prayer, for our good guardian has come to pray with us. Ibid

The angel who is always near us is by nothing so distressed and made indignant as when, without being constrained by some necessity, we deprive ourselves of the ministration of the Holy Mysteries and of reception of Holy Communion, which grants remission of sins. For at that hour the priest offers up the sacrifice of the Body of Him Who gives us life, and the Holy Spirit descends and consecrates the Body and Blood and grants remission to creation. The Cherubim, the Seraphim, and the angels stand with great awe, fear, and joy. They rejoice over the Holy Mysteries while experiencing inexpressible astonishment. The angel who is always by us is consoled, because he also partakes in that dread spectacle and is not deprived of that perfect intercourse. Isaac the Syrian

When you close the doors to your dwelling and are alone you should know that there is present with you the angel whom God has appointed for each man...This angel, who is sleepless and cannot be deceived, is always present with you; he sees all things and is not hindered by darkness. You should know, too, that with him is God, who is in every place; for there is no place and nothing material in which God is not, since He is greater than all things and holds all men in His hand. Antony the Great

Guile

Guile is a perversion of honesty, a deluded way of thinking, a lying disposition, false oaths, ambiguous words, a dark secrecy of heart, an abyss of cunning, deceit that has become habit, conceit turned into nature, a foe to humility, a pretence of repentance, an estrangement from mourning, hostility to confession, a teacher of willfulness, a cause of falls, a hindrance to resurrection, a smiling at offences, affected frowning, sham reverence, diabolical life.   John Climacus

Guilt

But nothing causes such exceeding grief as when anyone, lying under the captivity of sin, calls to mind from where he has fallen, because he turned aside to carnal and earthly things, instead of directing his mind in the beautiful ways of the knowledge of God. So you find Adam concealing himself, when he knew that God was present and wishing to be hidden when called by God with that voice which wounded the soul of him yourself? Why are you concealed? Why do you avoid Him Whom you once longed to see? A guilty conscience is so burdensome that it punishes itself without a judge, and wishes for covering, and yet is bare before God.   Ambrose Milan

Habits

An illness that has become chronic, like the habit of wrong-doing that has become ingrained is very hard to heal. If after that, as very often happens, the habit turns into second nature, a cure is out of the question.

So the ideal would be to have no contact with evil. But there is another possibility: to distance yourself from evil, to run away from it as from a poisonous snake, once you have experienced it.

I have known some unfortunate people who in their youth let themselves slide into evil habits, which have held them, enslaved all their lives. Like pigs wallowing continually in the mire and becoming increasingly filthy, such sinners as these multiply their shame every day with fresh sins.

So blessed is the one who has never thought of evil. However, if through his wiles, the suggestions of the Enemy have found a foothold in your heart, do not remain inactive in the toils of sin.

Be careful not to be utterly overcome by it. If the sin is already weighing you down, if the dust of riches has already settled on you, if your soul has been dragged right down by attachment to material things, then before you fall into utter ruin get rid of the heavy burden. Before the ship sinks, follow the example of sailors and cast overboard the possessions you have accumulated overmuch.   Basil

---

"Allow the Spirit of God to dwell within you; then in His love He will come and make a habitation with you; He will reside in you and live in you. If your heart is pure you will see Him and He will sow in you the good seed of reflection upon His actions and wonder at His majesty. This will happen if you take the trouble to weed out from your soul the undergrowth of desires, along with the thorns and tares of bad habits."   Evagrius

---

Happiness

Happy is the Christian who studies and follows the teaching of Christ. He is happy in this temporary life and in the life after death. Yes, he will be happy after death, because the soul does not vanish after death, is not perishable like the body, but continues to live, to exist. Through death, it is simply separated from the perishable body.   Raphael, Nicholas and Irene of Lesvos

---

Happy is the Christian who studies and follows the teaching of Christ. He is happy in this temporary life and in the life after death. Yes, he will be happy after death, because the soul does not vanish after death, is not perishable like the body, but continues to live, to exist. Through death, it is simply separated from the perishable body."   Raphael

---

In answer to your question as to what constitutes a happy life, whether splendor, fame and wealth, or a quiet, peaceful, family life, I will say that I agree with the latter, but will add the following: A life lived in humility and with an irreproachable conscience brings peace, tranquility, and true happiness. But wealth, honor, glory and exalted position often serve as the cause of a multitude of sins, and such happiness is not one on which to rely.

Makary of Optina

Hate

Again I entreat you, brethren, since God is love, he is not well-pleased by things that take place without love. How would God accept prayer, or gifts, or first fruits, or offering from a murderer, unless they first repented in accordance with God's word? But you will no doubt say to me, 'I am not a murderer.' And I will prove to you that you are, or rather John the Theologian will convict you, when he says, 'Every one who hates their brother is a homicide.'   Ephrem the Syrian

---

If somebody regards you with rancor, be pleasant to him, be humble and agreeable in his company, and you will deliver him from his passion.

Maximos the Confessor

If you feel that hatred has overwhelmed you, remain silent. Say nothing until, by ceaseless prayer and self-recrimination, you have calmed your heart.

Hilarion of Optina

If you harbor rancor against anybody, pray for him and you will prevent the passion from being aroused; for by means of prayer you will separate your resentment from the thought of the wrong he has done you. When you have become loving and compassionate towards him, you will wipe the passion completely from your soul.

Maximos the Confessor

My children, desire to purify your hearts from envy and from anger with each other, lest death should overcome you, and you will be counted among the murderers. For whosoever hates his brother, kills a soul.

Anthony the Great

Stop pleasing yourself and you will not hate your brother; stop loving yourself and you will love God."

Maximos the Confessor

Heart

Whoever has God in his heart, has all goods. And he cannot bear to do sin! Whoever does not have God in his heart, has the devil. And he does all evils, and all sins.

Kosmas Aitolos

Always keep your mind collected in your heart.

Theofan the Recluse

Do you not notice that our heart acts first in our life and in nearly all our knowledge? The heart sees certain truths (ideas) before the mind knows them. When knowledge is acquired, it happens thus: the heart sees at once, indivisibly, instantaneously; afterwards this single action of the sight of the heart is transmitted to the intellect and subdivided in the intellect into parts or sections, preceding and subsequent; the sight of the heart is analyzed in the intellect. The idea belongs to the heart and not to the intellect; that is, to the inner man, and not to the outer one. Therefore, to have the eyes of their understanding enlightened (Eph. 1:18) is a very important matter in acquiring all knowledge, but especially in that of the truths of faith and of the laws of morality."

John of Kronstadt

God is at all times nearer to us than any man, nearer than garments, than air or light. . . I live through him in body and soul, I breathe through Him, I think, reason, purpose, talk, venture and act through Him. . . We must condition ourselves in such a way that nothing can displace Him in our thoughts and hearts, nothing, no obstacle of any sort, can obstruct His presence. . . But, when I sin, or when I have a predilection for something, then I am far away from Him, not in distance but in my heart ... then I am left without His grace.

John of Kronstadt

God the Holy Spirit has many abodes in this vast universe, but a pure human heart is the place in which He most delights to dwell. This is His true abode; all others are only His workshop.

Nicolai Velimirovich

Our heart constantly craves and seeks comforts and pleasures. It should find them in the inner order of things, by keeping and bearing in itself Him, in Whose image man has been created, Who is the very source of every comfort. But in our downfall, we fell away from God, preferring ourselves, we lost also our foothold in ourselves, and fell into the flesh; thereby we went outside ourselves and began to seek for joys and comforts there. Our senses became our guides and intermediaries in this. Through them the soul goes outside and tastes the things experienced by each sense. It then delights in the things, which delight the senses; and out of all these together it builds the circle of comforts and pleasures, whose enjoyment it considers as its primary good. So the order of things has become inverted: instead of God within, the heart seeks for pleasures without and is content with them. Those who have listened to the voice of God...repent and lay down for themselves the law of re-establishing the original order of life, that is, of returning from without to within, and from within to God, in order to live in Him and by Him, and to have this as their first good, bearing within themselves the source of every comfort.   Lorenzo Scupoli

---

Our heart is like a mirror; as the objects of the outer world are reflected in an ordinary mirror, so ought the truth to be reflected with all exactitude in our hearts.   John of Kronstadt

---

Our heart is like the darkened earth; the Gospel is like the sun, enlightening and giving life to our hearts. May the true sun of Your righteousness shine in our hearts, Oh Lord!   Ibid

---

Seat yourself before the Lord continually, keeping the memory of Him in your heart, lest having lingered outside His memory, you are unable to speak boldly when you enter in before Him, because boldness with God comes from constant conversing with Him and from much prayer. Our connection and continuance with men is through the body; but our connection and continuance with God is through the soul's recollection [Syriac: meditation] and the vigilance and sacred offering of frequent prayer. From long continuance in His recollection, a man is transported at times to astonishment and wonder. For, "The heart of them that seek the Lord shall rejoice."
                                    Isaac the Syrian

The Savior commanded: Enter your closet and pray there to God your Father, which is in secret. This closet, according to the interpretation of Dimitri of Restov, signifies the heart. Consequently, the Lord's command obliges us to pray to God secretly, with the mind in the heart. This command extends to all Christians.   Theopha the Recluse

The heart can change several times in one moment - to good or evil, to faith or unbelief, to simplicity or cunning, to love or hatred, to benevolence or envy, to generosity or avarice, to chastity or fornication. Oh, what inconstancy! Oh, how many dangers! Oh, how sober and watchful we must be!   John of Kronstadt

The intellectual activity consisting of thought and intuition is called intellect, and the power that activates thought and intuition is likewise the intellect; and this power Scripture also calls the heart."   Gregory Palamas

The most important work in spiritual struggle is to enter the heart and there to wage war with Satan; to hate Satan, and to fight him by opposing his thoughts. If a man keeps his body outwardly free from lust and corruption, and yet inwardly commits adultery before God, by fornication in his thoughts, then is there no profit whatever in keeping the body pure.
                                               Nicephorus the Solitary

When we strive with diligent sobriety to keep watch over our rational faculties, to control and correct them, how else can we succeed in this task except by collecting our mind, which is dispersed abroad through the senses, and bringing it back into the world within, into the heart itself, which is the storehouse of all our thoughts?   Gregory Palamas

Whoever has God in his heart, has all goods. And he cannot bear to do sin! Whoever does not have God in his heart, has the devil. And he does all evils, and all sins.   Kosmas Aitolos

Heedfulness

He who is traveling the path of heedfulness should not trust only his own heart, but should verify the workings of his heart and his life with the law of God and with the active life of ascetics of piety who have passed through such endeavor. By this means one may the more easily both save oneself from the evil one and more clearly behold the truth.   Seraphim of Sarov

Hell

When you hear that at that time the Lord freed the souls from hell and the regions of darkness and that He descended into hell and did an amazing work, do not think that this does not have any personal meaning for you. Man, indeed, can readily accept the evil one. Death has its grip on the children of Adam and their thoughts are imprisoned in darkness. And when you hear mention made of tombs, do not at once think only of visible ones. For your heart is a tomb and a sepulcher. When the prince of evil and his angels have built their nest there and have built roads and highways on which the powers of Satan walk about inside your mind and in your thoughts, then really, are you not a hell and a sepulcher and a tomb dead to God? ... But the Lord descends into the souls of those who seek Him. He goes into the depths of the hellish heart and there He commands death, saying, "Release those captive souls that seek after me, those that you hold by force in bondage." He breaks through the heavy stones that cover the soul. He opens the tombs. He truly raises to life the dead person and leads that captive soul forth out of the dark prison.   Macarius

Heresy

Anyone who is able to speak the truth and does not do so will be condemned by God.   Justin the Philosopher

---

As for all those who pretend to confess the sound Orthodox Faith, but are in communion with people who hold a different opinion, if they are forewarned and still remain stubborn, you must not only not be in communion with them, but you must not even call them brothers.   Basil

---

But what a thing it is, to assert and contend that they who are not born in the Church can be the sons of God! For the blessed apostle sets forth and proves that baptism is that wherein the old man dies and the new man is born, saying, 'He saved us by the washing of regeneration.' But if regeneration is in the washing, that is, in baptism, how can heresy, which is not the spouse of Christ, generate sons to God by Christ?"   Cyprian of Carthage

---

Caecilius of Bilta said: I know only one baptism in the Church, and none out of the Church. This one will be here, where there is the true hope and the certain faith. For thus it is written: 'One faith, one hope, one baptism;' not among heretics, where there is no hope, and the faith is false, where all things are carried on by lying.   The Seventh Council of Carthage Under Cyprian

---

Chrysostomos loudly declares not only heretics, but also those who have communion with them, to be enemies of God.   Theodore the Studite

---

Contentions," he means, with heretics, in which he would not have us labor to no purpose, where nothing is to be gained, for they end in nothing. For when a man is perverted and predetermined not to change his mind, whatever may happen, why should you labor in vain, sowing upon a rock, when you should spend your honorable toil upon your own people, in discoursing with them upon almsgiving and every other virtue?

How then does he elsewhere say, "If God peradventure will give them repentance" (2 Tim. ii.25); but here, "A man that is an heretic after the first and second admonition reject, knowing that he that is such is subverted and sins, being condemned of himself"? In the former passage he speaks of the correction of those of whom he had hope, and who had simply made opposition. But when he is known and manifest to all, why do you contend in vain? why do you beat the air? What means, "being condemned of himself"? Because he cannot say that no one has told him, no one admonished him; since therefore after admonition he continues the same, he is self-condemned.   John Chrysostom

---

Even if one should give away all his possessions in the world, and yet be in communion with heresy, he cannot be a friend of God, but is rather an enemy.   Theodore the Studite

---

Felix of Bagai said: As, when the blind leads the blind, they fall together into the ditch; so, when the heretic baptizes a heretic, they fall together into death. And therefore a heretic must be baptized and made alive, lest we who are alive should hold communion with the dead.

The 7th Council of Carthage Under Cyprian

Guard yourselves from soul-destroying heresy, communion with which is alienation from Christ.   Theodore the Studite

Is it permissible to harshly treat those heretics who sincerely believe that they are right ? We should never idealize heretics, since in the roots of their apostasy lies not piety, but passions and sins of pride, obstinacy and anger. Harsh treatment of heretics is beneficial not only for preserving (other) people from their influence, but also for their own sake. The Holy Fathers considered the most stubborn schismatics equal to heretics. Therefore, is it really right to be gentle with them as it oftentimes happens with us. And all that for the sake of pernicious, false peace.   Anthony Khrapovitsky

Just as the fishermen hide the hook with bait and covertly hook the fish, similarly, the crafty allies of the heresies cover their evil teachings and corrupt understanding with pietism and hook the more simple, bringing them to spiritual death.   Isidore of Pelusium

Marcellus of Zama said: Since sins are not remitted saved in the baptism of the Church, he who does not baptize a heretic holds communion with a sinner."   The Seventh Council of Carthage Under Cyprian

Nicomedes of Segermae said: My opinion is this, that heretics coming to the Church should be baptized, for the reason that among sinners without they can obtain no remission of sins.   The 7th Council of Carthage Under Cyprian

Not only if one posses rank or knowledge is one obliged to strive to speak and teach the doctrines of the orthodoxy ,but even if one be a disciple in rank ,one is obliged to speak truth boldly and openly.   Theodore the Studite

Novatus of Thamugada said: Although we know that all the Scriptures give witness concerning the saving baptism, still we ought to declare our faith, that heretics and schismatics who come to the Church, and appear to have been falsely baptized, ought to be baptized in the everlasting fountain; and therefore, according to the testimony of the Scriptures, and according to the decree of our colleagues, men of most holy memory, that all schismatics and heretics who are converted to the Church must be baptized; and moreover, that those who appeared to have been ordained must be received among lay people.   The Seventh Council of Carthage Under Cyprian

Some have suffered final shipwreck with regard to the faith. Others, though they have not drowned in their thoughts, are nevertheless perishing through communion with heresy.   Theodore the Studite

Some have suffered final shipwreck with regard to the faith. Others, though they have not drowned in their thoughts, are nevertheless perishing through communion with heresy.   Theodore the Studite

Maximus the Confessor said: "Even if the whole universe holds communion with the [heretical] patriarch, I will not communicate with him. For I know from the writings of the holy Apostle Paul: the Holy Spirit declares that even the angels would be anathema if they should begin to preach another Gospel, introducing some new teaching.   Maximus the Confessor

The desire to rule is the mother of heresies.   John Chrysostom

---

Victor of Gor said: Since sins are not remitted save in the baptism of the Church, he who admits a heretic to communion without baptism does two things against reason: he does not cleanse the heretics, and he befouls the Christians."   The Seventh Council of Carthage Under Cyprian

---

Victoricus of Thabraca said: If heretics are allowed to baptize and to give remission of sins, wherefore do we brand them with infamy and call them heretics?"   Ibid

---

We have excised and cut them [the Papists] off from the common body of the Church, we have, therefore, rejected them as heretics, and for this reason we are separated from them"; they are, therefore, heretics, and we have cut them off as heretics.   Mark of Ephesus

---

Beware of reading the doctrines of heretics for they, more than anything else, can equip the spirit of blasphemy against you.   Isaac of Syria

---

"The poison of heresy is not too dangerous when it is preached only from outside the Church. Many times more perilous is that poison which is gradually introduced into the organism in larger and larger doses by those who, in virtue of their position, should not be poisoners but spiritual physicians."   Metropolitan Philaret

Heresy of Arianism

"On one occasion, some Arians went to Abbot Sisoes, on the mountain of Abbot Anthony, and immediately began to denounce the Orthodox. The did not say anything to them; he merely called his disciple and said to him: 'Bring the book by Athanasios and read it.' They remained silent as their heresy was disclosed, and Abbot Sisoes subsequently dismissed them, after wishing them a good journey."   Seraphim Rose

Heterodoxy

Our differences with someone who is not Orthodox, that is, "issues of faith," must in no way diminish "the feeling of love."   Nectarios of Aegina

Holiness

After this [in the Divine Liturgy] the Priest says, 'Holy things to holy men.' Holy are the gifts presented, having received the visitation of the Holy Spirit; holy are you also, having been deemed worthy of the Holy Spirit; the holy things therefore correspond to the holy persons. Then you say, 'One is Holy, One is the Lord, Jesus Christ.' For One is truly holy, by nature holy; we too are holy, but not by nature, only by participation, and discipline, and prayer.
                                                    Cyril of Jerusalem

"If but ten of us lead a holy life, we shall kindle a fire which shall light up the entire city."   John Chrysostom

Holy Communion

I say that the ineffable speech, which Paul heard spoken in Paradise were the eternal good things which eye has not seen, nor ear heard, nor the heart of man conceived.

These things, which God has prepared for those who love Him, are not protected by heights, nor enclosed in some secret place, nor hidden in the depths, nor kept at the ends of the earth or sea.

They are right in front of you, before your very eyes. So, what are they?

Together with the good things stored up in heaven, these are the Body and Blood of our Lord Jesus Christ, which we see every day, and eat and drink. These, we avow, are those good things.

Outside of these you will not be able to find one of the things spoken of, even if you were to traverse the whole of creation.

If you do want to know the truth of my words, become holy by practicing God's commandments and then partake of the holy things, and you will know precisely the force of what I am telling you."   Symeon the New Theologian

---

For all has been restored to us. What things, bodily or spiritual, perishable or imperishable, do we lack? Nothing. For as He gives us each day His deified Body and Blood, what is higher than these? Certainly nothing. In what mysteries does God count man, made of earth, worthy to serve! Oh heavenly, inestimable love; one drop of divine love surpasses all the bodily, worldly love under the sun.   Ephraim of Philotheou

---

The greatest charity, the greatest good, that which more than anything else relieves the soul that finds itself in the other world, is the sacrifice of the divine Lamb upon the Holy Table in the Holy Liturgy.

In the Old Testament it is written that the blood of goats and bulls and the ashes of a heifer cleansed sinners from their transgressions of the Law; how much more will the Blood of Christ, says the Apostle Paul, cleanse us from all sin (Heb. 9:13).

Great, therefore, is the benefit, and this is because the innocent Lamb of God is sacrificed in order to purify men from their sins and to unbind them from the diverse bonds of captivity to the passions.   bid

---

5. "As Moses lifted up the serpent in the wilderness, so must the Son of Man be lifted up" (John 3:14). And just exactly as all who were bitten by the serpents looked upon the bronze serpent which was suspended and were healed, thus also every Christian who believes in our Christ and has recourse to His life-bearing wounds, who eats His Flesh and drinks His all-holy Blood, is cured of the bits of the spiritual serpent of sin and by this most holy nourishment is made to live unto the renewal of a new creation, that is, new life in harmony with His life-giving commandments.   Ibid

---

Oh, how indispensable must and ought we in all ways to approach this heavenly communal feast, which grants us this lofty mystery of the Holy Table!

The angels are present invisibly; in great reverence the priests, who in this moment of mystery are honored above the angels, sacrifice the blameless Lamb.

The angels minister and faithful approach to eat and drink the Body and Blood of Christ: "receive the Body of Christ, taste the fountain of immortality," in order thus to live in Christ and not die through sin.   Ibid

---

So "let a man examine himself, and so eat of the bread and drink of the cup"(1 Cor. 11:28), according to the divine Apostle, for "he who eats and drinks unworthily, eats and drinks judgment upon himself" (1 Cor. 11:29). "For if we judged ourselves truly, we would not be judged; but when we are judged by the Lord we are chastened" (1 Cor. 11:31-32).   Ibid

Whenever someone wants to be presented to the king, he prepares himself for days that is, through general preparation, preparation as to cleanliness, word, manner, character, etc., so as to attract the royal sympathy and thus obtain the desired request. Likewise, every Christian also ought to prepare for Divine Communion in a manner befitting the incomparable difference between the two kings, in order to obtain mercy and forgiveness.   Ibid

Try to receive Communion as often as possible -- you have the freedom -- for divine Communion is the best help for one struggling against sin.   Ibid

7. May you approach the divine mystery with much compunction, contrition and consciousness of your sins. Great is the mercy of God, Who condescends to enter within you, not abhorring the multitude of your sins. But from a boundless love and affection He comes to sanctify you, counting you worthy to be His child and co-heir of His kingdom.   Ibid

' I have received of the Lord that which I also delivered unto you, that the Lord Jesus, the same night in which He was betrayed, took bread, etc. [1 Cor. 11:23]'. This teaching of the Blessed Paul is alone sufficient to give you a full assurance concerning those Divine Mysteries, which when you are vouchsafed, you are of (the same body) [Eph 3:6] and blood with Christ. For he has just distinctly said, (That our Lord Jesus Christ the same night in which He was betrayed, took bread, and when He had given thanks He brake it, and said, Take, eat, this is My Body: and having taken the cup and given thanks, He said, Take, drink, this is My Blood.) [1 Cor. 2:23-25] Since then

He Himself has declared and said of the Bread, (This is My Body), who shall dare to doubt any longer? And since He has affirmed and said, (This is My Blood), who shall ever hesitate, saying, that it is not His blood?

Cyril of Jerusalem

' The cup of blessing which we bless, is it not communion of the Blood of Christ?' Very trustworthily and awesomely does he say it. For what he is saying is this: 'What is in the cup is that which flowed from His side, and we partake of it.' He called it a cup of blessing because when we hold it in our hands that is how we praise Him in song, wondering and astonished at His indescribable Gift, blessing Him because of His having poured out this very Gift so that we might not remain in error, and not only for His having poured out It out, but also for His sharing It with all of us."

John Chrysostom

'And your floors shall be filled with wheat, and the presses shall overflow equally with wine and oil.' . . . This has been fulfilled mystically by Christ, who gave to the people whom He had redeemed, that is, to His Church, wheat and wine and oil in a mystic manner. For the wheat is the mystery of His sacred Body; and the wine His saving Blood; and again, the oil is the sweet unguent with which those who are baptized are signed, being clothed in the armaments of the Holy Spirit."

Ephraim of Syria

'The great Athanasius in his sermon to the newly baptized says this:' You shall see the Levites bringing loaves and a cup of wine, and placing them on the table. So long as the prayers of supplication and entreaties have not been made, there is only bread and wine. But after the great and wonderful prayers have been completed, then the bread is become the Body, and the wine the Blood, of our Lord Jesus Christ. 'And again:' Let us approach the celebration of the mysteries. This bread and this wine, so long as the prayers and supplications have not taken place, remain simply what they are. But after the great prayers and holy supplications have been sent forth, the Word comes down into the bread and wine - and thus His Body is confected."

Athanasius

...with full assurance let us partake of the Body and Blood of Christ: for in the figure of Bread is given to you His Body, and in the figure of Wine His Blood; that you by partaking of the Body and Blood of Christ, may be made of the same body and the same blood with Him. For thus we come to bear Christ in us, because His Body and Blood are distributed through our members; thus it is that, according to the blessed Peter, 'we become partakers of the divine nature' (2 Peter 1:4).   Cyril of Jerusalem

After the disciples had eaten the new and holy Bread, and when they understood by faith that they had eaten of Christ's body, Christ went on to explain and to give them the whole Sacrament. He took and mixed a cup of wine. The He blessed it, and signed it, and made it holy, declaring that it was His own Blood, which was about to be poured out. ...Christ commanded them to drink, and He explained to them that the cup, which they were drinking, was His own Blood: 'This is truly My Blood, which is shed for all of you. Take, all of you, drink of this, because it is a new covenant in My Blood, As you have seen Me do, do you also in My memory. Whenever you are gathered together in My name in Churches everywhere, do what I have done, in memory of Me. Eat My Body, and drink My Blood, a covenant new and old."   Ephraim of Syria

After the type had been fulfilled by the Passover celebration and He had eaten the flesh of the lamb with His Apostles, He takes bread which strengthens the heart of man, and goes on to the true Sacrament of the Passover, so that just as Melchisedech, the priest of the Most High God, in prefiguring Him, made bread and wine an offering, He too makes Himself manifest in the reality of His own Body and Blood."   Jerome

After this you hear the singing which invites you with a divine melody to the

Communion of the Holy Mysteries, and which says, 'Taste and see that the Lord is good.' Do not trust to the judgment of the bodily palate - no, but to unwavering faith. For they who are urged to taste do not taste of bread and wine, but to the antitype, of the Body and Blood of Christ."

Cyril of Jerusalem

And extending His hand, He gave them the Bread, which His right hand had made holy: 'Take, all of you eat of this; which My word has made holy. Do not now regard as bread that which I have given you; but take, eat this Bread, and do not scatter the crumbs; for what I have called My Body, that it is indeed. One particle from its crumbs is able to sanctify thousands and thousands, and is sufficient to afford life to those who eat of it. Take, eat, entertaining no doubt of faith, because this is My Body, and whoever eats it in belief eats in it Fire and Spirit. But if any doubter eat of it, for him it will be only bread. And whoever eats in belief the Bread made holy in My name, if he be pure, he will be preserved in his purity; and if he be a sinner, he will be forgiven.' But if anyone despise it or reject it or treat it with ignominy, it may be taken as certainty that he treats with ignominy the Son, who called it and actually made it to be His Body."

Ephraim of Syria

As the bread which is from the earth, after receiving the invocation of God upon it, is no longer common bread, but the Eucharist, consisting of two things, an earthly and a heavenly, so our bodies after partaking of the Eucharist are no longer destructible, having hope of the resurrection that is forever.

Irenaeus

As the prayer proceeds, we ask and say: 'Give us this day our daily bread.' This can be understood both spiritually and simply, because either understanding is of profit in divine usefulness for salvation.

For Christ is the bread of life and the bread here is of all, but is ours. And as we say 'Our Father,' because He is the Father of those who understand and

---

believe, so too we say 'our Bread,' because Christ is the bread of those of us who attain to His body.

Moreover, we ask that this bread be given daily, lest we, who are in Christ and receive the Eucharist daily as food of salvation, with the intervention of some more grievous sin, while we are shut off and as non-communicants are kept from the heavenly bread, be separated from the body of Christ as He Himself declares, saying: 'I am the bread of life which came down from heaven. If any man eat of my bread he shall live forever. Moreover, the bread that I shall give is my flesh for the life of the world.'

Since then! He says that, if anyone eats of His bread, he lives forever, as it is manifest that they live who attain to His body and receive the Eucharist by right of communion, so on the other hand we must fear and pray lest anyone, while he is cut off and separated from the body of Christ, remain apart from salvation, as He Himself threatens, saying: 'Unless you eat the flesh of the Son of man and drink His blood, you shall not have life in you.' And so we petition that our bread, that is Christ, be given us daily, so that we, who abide and live in Christ, may not withdraw from His sanctification and body.",

Cyprian of Carthage

But every Lord's day, do you gather yourselves together, and break bread, and give thanksgiving after having confessed your transgressions, that your sacrifice may be pure. But let no one that is at variance with his fellow come together with you, until they be reconciled, that your sacrifice may not be profaned. For this is that which was spoken by the Lord... [Matt. 5:23-24]

The Teaching of the Twelve Apostles

But look at the men who have those perverted notions about the grace of Jesus Christ...They will not admit the Eucharist is the self same body of our Savior Jesus Christ which suffered for our sins, and which the Father in His goodness afterwards raised up again.

Ignatius

But, in fact, the one who prays to receive this super-substantial bread does not receive it altogether as this bread is in itself, but as he is able to receive it. For the Bread of Life, out of His love for men, gives Himself to all who ask Him but not in the same manner to everyone: to those who have done great works, He gives Himself more fully, to those who have done smaller ones, less; to each, then, according to the spiritual dignity enabling him to receive it.   Maximos the Confessor

---

Cease not to pray and plead for me when you draw down the Word by your word, when in an unbloody cutting you cut the Body and Blood of the Lord, using your voice for a sword."   Gregory Nanzianzen

---

Christ said indicating (the bread and wine): 'This is My Body,' and "This is My Blood," in order that you might not judge what you see to be a mere figure. The offerings, by the hidden power of God Almighty, are changed into Christ's Body and Blood, and by receiving these we come to share in the life-giving and sanctifying efficacy of Christ."   Cyril of Alexandria

---

Come together in common, one and all without exception in charity, in one faith and in one Jesus Christ, who is of the race of David according to the flesh, the son of man, and the Son of God, so that with undivided mind you may obey the bishop and the priests, and break one Bread which is the medicine of immortality and the antidote against death, enabling us to live forever in Jesus Christ."   Ignatius of Antioch

---

Consider how contrary to the mind of God are the heterodox in regard to the grace of God which has come to us ... They abstain from the Eucharist and from prayer, because they do not admit that the Eucharist is the flesh of our

Savior Jesus Christ, the flesh which suffered for our sins and which the Father, in His graciousness, raised from the dead."   Ignatius of Antioch

---

Contemplate therefore the Bread and Wine not as bare elements, for they are, according to the Lord's declaration, the Body and Blood of Christ; for though sense suggests this to you, let faith establish you. Judge not the matter from taste, but from faith be fully assured without misgiving, that you have been vouchsafed the Body and Blood of Christ."   Cyril of Jerusalem

---

Do not err, my brethren: if anyone follow a schismatic, he will not inherit the Kingdom of God. If any man walk about with strange doctrine, he cannot lie down with the passion. Take care, then, to use one Eucharist, so that whatever you do, you do according to God: for there is one Flesh of our Lord Jesus Christ, and one cup in the union of His Blood; one altar, as there is one bishop with the presbytery and my fellow servants, the deacons."

Ignatius of Antioch

For just as the bread which comes from the earth, having received the invocation of God, is no longer ordinary bread, but the Eucharist, consisting of two realities, earthly and heavenly, so our bodies, having received the Eucharist, are no longer corruptible, because they have the hope of the resurrection."   Irenaeus of Lyons

---

For the whole Church observes this practice which was handed down by the Fathers: that it prayers for those who have died in the communion of the Body and Blood of Christ, when they are commemorated in their own place in the sacrifice itself; and the sacrifice is offered also in memory of them on their behalf.   Augustine

Having...been fully assured that the seeming bread is not bread, though sensible to taste, but the Body of Christ; and that the seeming wine is not wine, though taste will have it so, but the Blood of Christ; and that of this David sang of old, saying, 'And bread strengthens man's heart, to make his face to shine with oil' (Ps. 104:15), 'strengthen then your heart,' by partaking thereof as spiritual, and 'make the face of your soul to shine.' And so having it unveiled with a pure conscience, may you 'reflect as a mirror the glory of the Lord' (2 Cor. 3:18), and proceed from 'glory to glory', in Christ Jesus our Lord: - To Whom be honor, and might, and glory, forever and ever. Amen.

<u>Cyril of Jerusalem</u>

He offered Himself for us, Victim and Sacrifice, and Priest as well, and 'Lamb of God, who takes away the sin of the world.' When did He do this? When He made His own Body food and His own Blood drink for His disciples; for this much is clear enough to anyone, that a sheep cannot be eaten by a man unless its being eaten be preceded by its being slaughtered. This giving of His own Body to His disciples for eating clearly indicates that the sacrifice of the Lamb has now been completed."   <u>Gregory of Nyssa</u>

He, therefore, who approaches the Body and Blood of Christ in commemoration of Him who died for us and rose again must be free not only from defilement of flesh and spirit, in order that he may not eat drink unto judgment, but he must actively manifest the remembrance of Him who died for us and rose again, by being dead to sin, to the world, and to himself, and alive unto God in Christ Jesus, our Lord."   <u>Basil</u>

His poverty enriches, the fringe of His garment heals, His hunger satisfies, His death gives life, His burial gives resurrection. Therefore, He is a rich

treasure, for His bread is rich. And 'rich' is apt for one who has eaten this bread will be unable to feel hunger. He gave it to the Apostles to distribute to a believing people, and today He gives it to us, for He, as a priest, daily consecrates it with His own words. Therefore, this bread has become the food of the saints."
Ambrose of Milan

I have no taste for the food that perishes nor for the pleasures of this life. I want the Bread of God which is the Flesh of Christ, who was the seed of David; and for drink I desire His Blood which is love that cannot be destroyed."
Ignatius of Antioch

I said to (Onnophrius), "My good father, did you suffer when you first came to this place in the desert?" The blessed old man said, "I suffered a great deal, my son. Believe me, my beloved son, I came close to dying many times on account of hunger and thirst and on account of the burning fire during the day and the frost at night. My members were soaked by the dew of the sky.

When God saw me, that I patiently endured in the fight of fasting and that I devoted myself to ascetic practice, He had the holy angels serve me my daily food, giving it to me every night and a little water every night in order to strengthen my body. And this one palm tree produced for me twelve bunches of dates each year, one each month, and I would eat it.

He made the other plants that grow in the desert places sweet in my mouth, sweeter than honey in my mouth. For it is written, 'A person shall not live by bread alone, but he will live by every word that proceeds from the mouth of God.'

For if you do the will of God, wherever you are, He will care for you, because your Father in heaven knows what all your needs are, what you will eat or what you will drink. But rather seek first His kingdom and His righteousness, and all these things will be added unto you.'" Now when I heard these thins from him I was greatly amazed.

I said to him, "My sweet and good father, where do you receive the Eucharist on the Sabbath and the Lord's Day?" He said to me, "Every Sabbath and every Lord's Day, and angel comes to me and gives me the Eucharist. And blessed is everyone who lives as a citizen in the desert on account of God and sees no human being -- He brings the Eucharist to them and comforts them. If they desire to see anyone, they are taken up to heavenly heights and they see them. They greet them and the hearts are filled with light. They rejoice in the Spirit and are glad in the good things they will never lack. When they see them, they are comforted, and they completely forget the afflictions that have been theirs. Afterwards they return to their places, and they are comforted for a long time, as though they had been removed to another world. Because of the great joy they have seen, they do not remember that this world even exists."   Paphnutius

---

I wish to add something that is plainly awe-inspiring, but do not be astonished or upset. This Sacrifice, no matter who offers it, be it Peter or Paul, is always the same as that which Christ gave His disciples and which priests now offer: The offering of today is in no way inferior to that which Christ offered, because it is not men who sanctify the offering of today; it is the same Christ who sanctified His own. For just as the words which God spoke are the very same as those which the priest now speaks, so too the oblation is the very same."   John Chrysostom

---

In the Old Testament also there was show-bread; but this, as it belonged to the Old Testament, has come to an end; but in the New Testament there is Bread of heaven, and a Cup of salvation, sanctifying soul and body; for as the Bread corresponds to our body, so is the Word appropriate to our soul. Consider therefore the Bread and the Wine not as bare elements, for they are, according to the Lord's declaration, the Body and Blood of Christ; for even though sense suggests this to you, yet let faith establish you. Judge not the matter from the taste, but from faith be fully assured without misgiving, that the Body and Blood of Christ have been given to you.

Cyril of Jerusalem

In the sacred Mysteries, then, we depict His burial and proclaim His death. By them we are begotten and formed and wondrously united to the Savior, for they are the means by which, as Paul says, "in Him we live, and move, and have our being" (Acts 17:28). Baptism confers being and, in short, existence according to Christ. It receives us when we are dead and corrupted and first leads us into life. The anointing with chrism perfects him who has received [new] birth by infusing into him the energy that befits such a life. The Holy Eucharist preserves and continues this life and health, since the Bread of life enables us to preserve that which has been acquired and to continue in life. It is therefore by this Bread that we live and by the chrism that we are moved, once we have received being from the baptismal washing. In this way we live in God.   Nicholas Cabasilas

In the sacred Mysteries, then, we depict His burial and proclaim His death. By them we are begotten and formed and wondrously united to the Savior, for they are the means by which, as Paul says, "in Him we live, and move, and have our being" (Acts 17:28). Baptism confers being and in short, existence according to Christ. It receives us when we are dead and corrupted and first leads us into life. The anointing with chrism perfects him who has received [new] birth by infusing in to him the energy that befits such a life. The Holy Eucharist preserves and continues this life and health, since the Bread of life enables us to preserve that which has been acquired and to continue in life. It is therefore by this Bread that we live and by the chrism that we are moved, once we have received being from the baptismal washing. In this way we live in God.   Ibid

Indeed, who was ever able to grasp Christ or His Spirit perfectly without first purifying himself? Chastity is the exercise, which from childhood prepares the soul for glory by making it attractive and lovable, and with ease, brings this adornment for her to the next world untried. It holds up great expectations as the reward for small toil and renders our bodies immortal. It is only fitting then that all should gladly praise and esteem chastity above all other things; some, because by practicing virginity been emancipated from that condemnation, `Earth you are, and unto earth you shall return.'

`The cup of blessing which we bless, is it not a participation in the blood of Christ?' Paul's words are thoroughly persuasive and flowed from Christ's side; that is what we share in.' He has called it a cup of blessing, because when we have it in our hands we praise Christ in wonder and astonishment at His unspeakable gift, by blessing Him for pouring out this very cup to free us from error; and not only for pouring it out but also for allowing us all to share in it. So Christ is saying to of irrational beasts; let is be My altar with My Blood.' What could be more awesome, what more profoundly loving that that?   John Chrysostom

---

It is certainly a finer and more wonderful thing to change the mind of enemies and bring them to another way of thinking than to kill them, especially when we recall that the [disciples] were only twelve and the whole world was full of wolves. . . . We ought then to be ashamed of ourselves, we who act so very differently and rush like wolves upon our foes. So long as we are sheep we have the victory; but if we are like wolves we are beaten, for then the help of the shepherd is withdrawn from us, for he feeds sheep not wolves. . . . This mystery [of the Eucharist] requires that we should be innocent not only of violence but of all enmity, however slight, for it is the mystery of peace.   Ibid

---

It is not the power of man, which makes what is put before us the Body and Blood of Christ, but the power of Christ Himself who was crucified for us. The priest standing there in the place of Christ says these words but their power and grace are from God. 'This is My Body,' he says, and these words transform what lies before him."   Ibid

---

Let us be assured that this is not what nature formed, but what the blessing consecrated, and that greater efficacy resides in the blessing than in nature, for by the blessing nature is changed. . . . Surely the word of Christ, which could make out of nothing that which did not exist, can change things already in existence into what they were not. For it is no less extraordinary to give things new natures than to change their natures. . . . Christ is in that Sacrament, because it is the Body of Christ; yet, it is not on that account corporeal food, but spiritual. Whence also His Apostle says of the type: `For our fathers ate spiritual food and drink spiritual drink.' [1 Cor. 10:2-4] For the body of God is a spiritual body."   Ambrose of Milan

Make an effort, then, to meet more frequently to celebrate God's Eucharist and to offer praise. For when you meet frequently in the same place, the forces of Satan are overthrown, and his baneful influence is neutralized by the unanimity of your faith. Peace is a precious thing: it puts an end to every war waged by heavenly or earthly enemies.   Ignatius of Antioch

Not as common bread or common drink do we receive these, but since Jesus Christ our savior was made incarnate by the word of God and had both flesh and blood for our salvation, so too as we have been taught, the food which has been made into the Eucharist by the Eucharistic prayer set down by Him, and by the change of which our blood and flesh is nourished, is both the flesh and the blood of that incarnated Jesus.   Justin Martyr

Our Lord Jesus took in His hands what in the beginning was only bread; and He blessed it, and signed it, and made it holy in the name of the Father and in the name of the Spirit; and He broke it and in His gracious kindness He distributed it to all His disciples one by one. He called the bread His living Body, and did Himself fill it with Himself and the Spirit.   Ephraim of Syria

Reverence with all the powers of your soul all the sacraments, and say to yourself in respect to every sacrament before the celebration or the communion of it: `This is God's mystery. I myself am only the unworthy witness or partaker of it.' Otherwise our proud intellect even wishes to search out God's mystery, and, if unable to penetrate it, rejects it as not coming under the small measure of our intellect.   John of Kronstadt

---

Rightly then, do we believe that the bread consecrated by the word of God has been made over into the Body of God the Word. For that Body was, as to its potency bread; but it has been consecrated by the lodging there of the Word, who pitched His tent in the flesh."   Gregory of Nyssa

---

So perfect is this Mystery [the Eucharist], so far does it excel every other sacred rite that it leads to the very summit of good things. Here also is the final goal of every human endeavor. For in it we obtain God Himself, and God is united with us in the most perfect union, for what attachment can be more complete than to become one spirit with God?   Nicholas Cabasilas

---

So then, if the mixed cup and the manufactured bread receive the Word of God and become the Eucharist, that is to say, the Blood and Body of Christ, which fortify and build up the substance of our flesh, how can these people claim that the flesh is incapable of receiving God's gift of eternal life, when it is nourished by Christ's Blood and Body and is His member? As the blessed apostle says in his letter to the Ephesians, 'For we are members of His Body, of His flesh and of His bones' Eph. 5:30

He is not talking about some kind of 'spiritual' and 'invisible' man, 'for a spirit does not have flesh an bones' (Lk. 24:39). No, he is talking of the organism possessed by a real human being, composed of flesh and nerves and bones. It is this, which is nourished by the cup, which is His Blood, and is fortified by the bread, which is His Body.

The stem of the vine takes root in the earth and eventually bears fruit, and 'the grain of wheat falls into the earth' (Jn. 12:24), dissolves, rises again, multiplied by the all-containing Spirit of God, and finally after skilled processing, is put to human use.

These two then receive the Word of God and become the Eucharist, which is the Body and Blood of Christ.   Irenaeus of Lyons

---

The Blood of the Lord, indeed, is twofold. There is His corporeal Blood, by which we are redeemed from corruption; and His spiritual Blood, that with which we are anointed. That is to say, to drink the Blood of Jesus is to share in His immortality. The strength of the Word is the Spirit just as the blood is the strength of the body. Similarly, as wine is blended with water, so is the Spirit with man. The one, the Watered Wine, nourishes in faith, while the other, the Spirit, leads us on to immortality. The union of both, however, - of the drink and of the Word, - is called the Eucharist, a praiseworthy and excellent gift. Those who partake of it in faith are sanctified in body and in soul. By the will of the Father, the divine mixture, man, is mystically united to the Spirit and to the Word."   Clement of Alexandria

---

The Christian receives great benefit from the Divine Mysteries, both in his soul and in his body. . . . Before he communes, he must make the necessary preparation, that is, he must confess to his spiritual father, correct himself, feel compunction, acquire inner attention, guard himself from passionate thoughts as far as possible, and also from every other vice. Similarly, he must exercise self-restraint, pray, be inwardly awake, become more devout, and do every other kind of good deed, reflecting what awesome King he is about to receive within himself; especially if he considers that the grace which is given to him from Communion is proportionate to his preparation. It is evident that the more one makes such preparation, the more benefit he receives."   Macarius of Corinth

The Church is the Body of Christ; the Eucharist is the Body of Christ. This is a fundamental identity: the Church in the Eucharist and the Eucharist in the Church."   Justin Popovich

---

The Holy Eucharist is the first, most important, and greatest miracle of Christ. All the other Gospel miracles are secondary. How could we not call the greatest miracle the fact that simple bread and wine were once transformed by the Lord into His very Body and His very Blood, and then have continued to be transformed for nearly two thousand years by the prayers of priests, who are but simple human beings? And what is more, this mystery has continued to effect a miraculous change in those people who communicate of the Divine Mysteries with faith and humility. Abbot Cronius

---

The Lord rose up from the place where He had made the Passover and had given His Body as food and His Blood as drink, and He went with His disciples to the place where He was to be arrested ... With His own hands the Lord presented His own Body to be eaten, and before he was crucified He gave His blood as drink; and He was taken at night and was judged until the sixth hour; and at the sixth hour they condemned Him and raised Him on the cross."   Aphraates, the Persian Sage

---

The Seraph could not touch the fire's coal with his fingers, but just brought it close to Isaiah's mouth: the Seraph did not hold it, Isaiah did not consume it, but us our Lord has allowed to do both.   Isaac the Syrian

---

The angel who is always near us is by nothing so distressed and made indignant as when, without being constrained by some necessity, we deprive ourselves of the ministration of the Holy Mysteries and of reception of Holy

---

Communion, which grants remission of sins. For at that hour the priest offers up the sacrifice of the Body of Him Who gives us life, and the Holy Spirit descends and consecrates the Body and Blood and grants remission to creation. The Cherubim, the Seraphim, and the angels stand with great awe, fear, and joy. They rejoice over the Holy Mysteries while experiencing inexpressible astonishment. The angel who is always by us is consoled, because he also partakes in that dread spectacle and is not deprived of that perfect intercourse.   Ibid

The Word is everything to a child: both Father and Mother, both Instructor and Nurse. 'Eat My Flesh,' He says, 'and drink My Blood.' The Lord supplies us with these intimate nutrients. He delivers over His Flesh, and pours out His Blood; and nothing is lacking for the growth of His children. Oh incredible mystery!"   Clement of Alexandria

The bread is at first common bread; but when the mystery sanctifies it, it is called and actually becomes the Body of Christ."   Gregory of Nyssa

The gates of Paradise were opened for Adam, but it was fitting that they be closed when he fell from the state in which he ought to have remained. These gates Christ Himself opened, "Who committed no sin" (1Pet. 2:22) and cannot sin, for as it says, "His righteousness remained for ever" (Ps. 111:3). Wherefore they must of necessity remain open and lead to life, but without providing a way out of life, for "I came," says the Savior, "that they might have life" (Jn. 10:10). This is the life, which the Lord came to bring, that those who come through these Mysteries should be partakers of His death and share in His passion. Apart from this it is impossible to escape death. It is not possible for him who has not been "baptized in water and the Spirit" (Jn. 3:5) to enter into life, nor can those who have not eaten the Flesh of the Son of man and drunk His Blood have life in themselves (Jn. 6:24).

The means to confirm and strengthen Christian hope are prayer, especially frequent and sincere prayer, confession of our sins, frequent reading of the Word of God, and, above all, frequent communion of the holy and life-giving sacraments of the Body and Blood of Christ.   John of Kronstadt

---

The mystery of the Eucharist is called 'participation' for by it we participate in Christ's divinity. It is also called 'Communion' which it indeed is, for through it we are brought into fellowship with Christ ... we are also, through it, in fellowship and unity with one another ... We should, therefore, be on our guard not to accept participation from heretics or give it to them ... lest we become sharers in their false faith. But if there is true union with Christ and with one another, then we indeed willingly unite with those with whom we participate.   John of Damascus

---

The peace and plenteousness of life in the heart after Communion is the greatest, the most inestimable gift of our Lord Jesus Christ, surpassing all the gifts relating to the body which are received at the same time. Without peace of the soul - when the heart is straitened and tormented - man cannot avail himself of any blessings, either material or spiritual; at that time the delights that come from the feeling of truth, goodness and beauty do not exist for him, because the very center of his life - the heart, or the inner man himself - is crushed, slain.   John of Kronstadt

---

There is nothing impossible unto those who believe; lively and unshaken faith can accomplish great miracles in the twinkling of an eye. Besides, even without our sincere and firm faith, miracles are accomplished, such as the miracles of the sacraments; for God's Mystery is always accomplished, even though we were incredulous or unbelieving at the time of this celebration.

John of Kronstadt

Therefore with fullest assurance let us partake as of the Body and Blood of Christ: for in the figure of Bread is given to you His Body, and in the figure of Wine His Blood; that you by partaking of the Body and Blood of Christ, might be made of the same body and the same blood with Him. For thus we come to bear Christ in us, because His Body and Blood are diffused through our members; thus it is that, according to the blessed Peter, (we become partaker of the divine nature.) [2 Peter 1:4] "   Cyril of Jerusalem

---

Therefore, in order that we may become of His Body, not in desire only, but also in very fact, let us become commingled with that Body. This, in truth, takes place by means of the food, which He has given us as a gift, because He desire to prove the love which He has for us. It is for this reason that He shared Himself with us and has brought His Body down to our level, namely, that we might be one with Him as the body is joined with the head. This, in truth is characteristic of those who greatly love. Job, indeed, was implying this when he said of his servants--by whom he was loved with such an excess of love--that they desired to cleave to his flesh. In giving expression to the great love, which they possessed, they said: `Who will give us of his flesh that we may be filled?' Moreover, Christ has done even this to spur us on to even greater love. And to show the love He has for us He has made it possible for those who desire, not merely to look upon Him,! but even to touch Him and to consume Him and to fix their teeth in His Flesh and to be commingled with Him; in short, to fulfill all their love. Let us, then, come back from that table like lions breathing out fire, thus becoming terrifying to the Devil, and remaining mindful of our Head and of the love which He has shown for us.   John Chrysostom

These things having learnt, and being fully persuaded that what seems bread is not bread, though bread by taste, but the Body of Christ; and that what seems wine is not wine, though the taste will have it so, but the Blood of Christ; and that of this David sung of old, saying, (And bread which strengthened man's heart, and oil to make his face to shine) [Ps. 104:15], `strengthen your heart', partaking thereof as spiritual, and `make the face of your soul to shine'. And so having it unveiled by a pure conscience, may you behold as in a glass the glory of the Lord, and proceed from glory to glory [2 Cor. 3:18], in Christ Jesus our Lord:--To whom be honor, and might, and glory, for ever and ever. Amen."   Cyril of Jerusalem

This food we call the Eucharist, of which no one is allowed to partake except one who believes that the things we teach are true, and has received the washing for forgiveness of sins and for rebirth, and who lives as Christ handed down to us. For we do not receive these things as common bread or common drink; but as Jesus Christ our Savior being incarnate by God's Word took flesh and blood for our salvation, so also we have been taught that the food consecrated by the Word of prayer which comes from him, from which our flesh and blood are nourished by transformation, is the flesh and blood of that incarnate Jesus."   Justin Martyr

Thus, every soul which receives the bread which comes down from heaven is a house of bread, the bread of Christ, being nourished and having its heart strengthened by the support of the heavenly bread which dwells within it."

Ambrose of Milan

To communicate each day and to partake of the holy Body and Blood of Christ is good and beneficial; for He says quite plainly: 'He that eats My Flesh and drinks My Blood has eternal life.' Who can doubt that to share continually in life is the same thing as having life abundantly? We ourselves communicate four times each week, on Sunday, Wednesday, Friday, and Saturday; and on other days if there is a commemoration of any saint."

Basil

We have been instructed in these matters and filled with an unshakable faith, that that which seems to be bread, is not bread, though it tastes like it, but the Body of Christ, and that which seems to be wine, is not wine, though it too tastes as such, but the Blood of Christ . . . draw inner strength by receiving this bread as spiritual food and your soul will rejoice."   Cyril of Alexandria

We see that the Savior took [something] in His hands, as it is in the Gospel, when He was reclining at the supper; and He took this, and giving thanks, He said: 'This is really Me.' And He gave to His disciples and said: 'This is really Me.' And we see that It is not equal nor similar, not to the incarnate image, not to the invisible divinity, not to the outline of His limbs. For It is round of shape, and devoid of feeling. As to Its power, He means to say even of Its grace, 'This is really Me.'; and none disbelieves His word. For anyone who does not believe the truth in what He says is deprived of grace and of a Savior."   Epiphanius of Salamis 374 A.D.

What is the mark of a Christian? That he be purified of all defilement of the flesh and of the spirit in the Blood of Christ, perfecting sanctification in the fear of God and the love of Christ, and that he have no blemish nor spot nor any such thing; that he be holy and blameless and so eat the Body of Christ and drink His Blood; for 'he that eats and drinks unworthily, eats and drinks judgment to himself.' What is the mark of those who eat the Bread and drink the Cup of Christ? That they keep in perpetual remembrance Him who died for us and rose again."   Basil

When the word says, 'This is My Body,' be convinced of it and believe it, and look at it with the eyes of the mind. For Christ did not give us something tangible, but even in His tangible things all is intellectual. So too with Baptism: the gift is bestowed through what is a tangible thing, water; but what is accomplished is intellectually perceived: the birth and the renewal. If you were incorporeal He would have given you those incorporeal gifts naked; but since the soul is intertwined with the body, He hands over to you in tangible things that which is perceived intellectually. How many now say, 'I wish I could see His shape, His appearance, His garments, His sandals.' Only look! You see Him! You touch Him! You eat Him!"   John Chrysostom

---

When we speak of the reality of Christ's nature being in us, we would be speaking foolishly and impiously - had we not learned it from Him. For He Himself says: 'My Flesh is truly Food, and My Blood is truly Drink. He that eats My Flesh and drinks My Blood will remain in Me and I in him.' As to the reality of His Flesh and Blood, there is no room left for doubt, because now, both by the declaration of the Lord Himself and by our own faith, it is truly the Flesh and it is truly Blood. And These Elements bring it about, when taken and consumed, that we are in Christ and Christ is in us. Is this not true? Let those who deny that Jesus Christ is true God be free to find these things untrue. But He Himself is in us through the flesh and we are in Him, while that which we are with Him is in God."   Hilary of Poiters

---

You ought to know what you have received, what you are going to receive, and what you ought to receive daily. That Bread which you see on the altar, having been sanctified by the word of God, is the Body of Christ. The chalice, or rather, what is in that chalice, having been sanctified by the word of God, is the Blood of Christ."   Augustine

---

You perhaps say: 'My bread is usual.' But the bread is bread before the words of the sacraments; when consecration has been added, from bread it becomes the flesh of Christ. So let us confirm this, how it is possible that what is bread

200

is the body of Christ. By what words, then, is the consecration and by whose expressions? By those of the Lord Jesus. For all the rest that are said in the preceding are said by the priest: praise to God, prayer is offered, there is a petition for the people, for kings, for the rest. When it comes to performing a venerable sacrament, then the priest uses not his own expressions, but he uses the expressions of Christ. Thus the expression of Christ performs this sacrament."   Ambrose of Milan

[Christ] has declared the cup, a part of creation, to be his own Blood, from which he causes our blood to flow; and the bread, a part of creation, he has established as his own Body, from which he gives increase to our bodies."

Irenaeus of Lyons

[Christ] took the bread and the cup, each in a similar fashion, and said: 'This is My Body and this is My Blood.' Not a figure of His body nor a figure of His blood, as some persons of petrified mind are wont to rhapsodize, but in truth the Body and the Blood of Christ, seeing that His body is from the earth, and the bread and wine are likewise from the earth."

Marcarius the Magnesian

[How the Eucharist enables us to worship "in spirit and in truth"] Yet we are such wretched material that the seal cannot remain unaffected, "for we have this treasure in earthen vessels" (2 Cor. 4:7). We therefore partake of the remedy, not once for all, but constantly. The potter must constantly sit by the clay and repeatedly restore the shape, which is being blurred. We must continually experience the Physician's hand as He heals the decaying matter and raises up the failing will, lest death creep in unawares. For it says, "even when we were dead through trespasses He made us alive together with Christ" (Eph.2:5), and "the blood of Christ shall purify your conscience from dead works to serve the living God" (Heb. 9:14). The power of the holy table draws to us the true life from that blessed Body, and there we become able to worship God purely.   Nicholas Cabasilas

------

`The cup of blessing which we bless, is it not a participation in the blood of Christ?' Paul's words are thoroughly persuasive and awe-inspiring. What he is saying is this: `What is in the cup is what flowed from Christ's side; that is what we share in.' He has called it a cup of blessing, because when we have it in our hands we praise Christ in wonder and astonishment at His unspeakable gift, by blessing Him for pouring out this very cup to free us from error; and not only for pouring it out but also for allowing us all to share in it. So Christ is saying to us: `If you want blood, do not make the altar of idols red with the blood of irrational beasts; let is be My altar with My Blood.' What could be more awesome, what more profoundly loving that that?   John Chrysostom

------

...the Lord in His life-giving Mysteries - wherever they are offered - is eternally the sole, indivisible, Creator 'and has made of one blood all nations of men' (Acts 17:26). Through His one Spirit, living in the Holy Sacrament of the Body and Blood, celebrated in all the churches of the world, He wishes to unite us to Himself - we who have fallen from union with Him through sin and obedience to the Devil - and to cut off and cleanse that which in all of us prevents union with Him and with each other, 'that they all may be one; as You, Father, are in Me, and I in You, that they also may be one in Us' (John 17:21). Such is the object of the mystery of the Communion.

John of Kronstadt

Holy Communion causes great progress in the life according to Christ. For what the external accidents of bread and wine effect in the body, the same is effected in the immaterial soul mystically and invisibly by the Body of Christ. And just as bread sustains and nourishes the body, so the Body of Christ sustains and nourishes our soul; and again, just as we are regenerated through Holy Baptism and receive the being of grace, in place of the being of sin which we had, so, as we are nourished by Holy Communion we grow in the grace of God and make progress. Macarios of Corinth

When in fear, trembling and unworthiness we are yet permitted to receive the divine, undefiled Mysteries of Christ, our King and Lord, we should then display even greater watchfulness, strictness and guard over our hearts, so that the divine fire, the body of our Lord Jesus Christ, may consume our sins and stains, great and small. For when that fire enters into us, it at once drives the evil spirits from our heart and remits the sins we have previously committed, leaving the intellect free from the turbulence of wicked thoughts. And if after this, standing at the entrance to our heart, we keep strict watch over the intellect, when we are again permitted to receive those Mysteries the divine body will illumine our intellect still more and make it shine like a star.

Hesychios the Priest

Holy Communion causes great progress in the life according to Christ. For what the external accidents of bread and wine effect in the body, the same is effected in the immaterial soul mystically and invisibly by the Body of Christ. And just as bread sustains and nourishes the body, so the Body of Christ sustains and nourishes our soul; and again, just as we are regenerated through Holy Baptism and receive the being of grace, in place of the being of sin which we had, so, as we are nourished by Holy Communion we grow in the grace of God and make progress. Macarios of Corinth

I have no taste for corruptible food nor for the pleasures of this life. I desire the Bread of God, which is the flesh of Jesus Christ, who was of the seed of David; and for drink I desire His blood, which is love incorruptible. (Letter to Romans 7:3) Take care, then, to use one Eucharist, so that whatever you do, you do according to God: For there is one flesh of our Lord Jesus Christ, and one cup in the union of His blood; one altar, as there is one bishop with the presbytery. Ignatius of Antioch

They [i.e. the Gnostics] abstain from the Eucharist and from prayer, because they do not confess that the Eucharist is the flesh of our Savior Jesus Christ, flesh which suffered for our sins and which the Father, in his goodness, raised up again.   Ibid

We call this food Eucharist; and no one else is permitted to partake of it, except one who believes our teaching to be true and who has been washed in the washing which is for the remission of sins and for regeneration [Baptism], and is thereby living as Christ has enjoined. For not as common bread nor common drink do we receive these; but since Jesus Christ our Savior was made incarnate by the word of God and had both flesh and blood for our salvation, so too, as we have been taught, the food which has been made into the Eucharist by the Eucharistic prayer set down by Him, and by the change of which our blood and flesh is nourished, is both the flesh and blood of that incarnate Jesus.   Justin Martyr

Moreover, as I said before, concerning the sacrifices which you at that time offered, God speaks through Malachi [1:10-12]...It is of the sacrifices offered to Him in every place by us, the Gentiles, that is, of the bread of the Eucharist and likewise of the cup of the Eucharist, that He speaks at that time; and He says that we glorify His name, while you profane it.   Ibid

He took from among creation that which is bread, and gave thanks, saying This is My body." The cup likewise, which is from among the creation to which we belong, He confessed to be His blood. (Against Heresies 4:17:5) But what consistency is there in those who hold that the bread over which thanks have been given is the body of their Lord, and the cup His blood, if they do not acknowledge that He is the Son of the Creator... How can they say that the flesh, which has been nourished by the body of the Lord and by

His blood, gives way to corruption and does not partake of life? ...For as the bread from the earth, receiving the invocation of God, is no longer common bread but the Eucharist, consisting of two elements, earthly and heavenly.

Irenaeus

If the body be not saved, then, in fact, neither did the Lord redeem us with His BLOOD; and neither is the cup of the Eucharist the partaking of His blood nor is the bread which we break the partaking of His body... He has declared the cup, a part of creation, to be His own blood, from which He causes our blood to flow; and the bread, a part of creation, He has established us as His own body, from which He gives increase to our bodies. When, therefore, the mixed cup and the baked bread receives the Word of God and becomes the Eucharist, the body of Christ, and from these the substance of our flesh is increased and supported, how can they say that the flesh is not capable of receiving the gift of God, which is eternal life -- flesh which is nourished by the body and blood of the Lord...receiving the Word of God, becomes the Eucharist, which is the body and blood of Christ.

Ibid

The flesh feeds on the body and blood of Christ, so that the soul too may fatten on God.

Tertullian

The Sacrament of the Eucharist, which the Lord commanded to be taken at meal times and by all, we take even before daybreak in congregations... We take anxious care lest something of our Cup or Bread should fall upon the ground.

Ibid

We give thanks to the Creator of all, and, along with thanksgiving and prayer for the blessings we have received, we also eat the bread presented to us; and this bread becomes by prayer a sacred body, which sanctifies those who sincerely partake of it. <u>Origen</u>

You are accustomed to take part in the divine mysteries, so you know how, when you have received the body of the Lord, you reverently exercise every care lest a particle of it fall, and lest anything of the consecrated gift perish... how is it that you think neglecting the word of God a lesser crime than neglecting His body? <u>Ibid</u>

...now, however, in full view, there is the true food, the flesh of the Word of God, as He Himself says: "My flesh is real food, and My blood is real drink."

<u>bid</u>

Calling her children about her, she [the Church] nourishes them with holy milk, that is, with the Infant Word...The Word is everything to a child: both Father and Mother, both Instructor and Nurse. "Eat My flesh," He says, "and drink My blood." The Lord supplies us with these intimate nutriments. He delivers over His flesh and pours out His blood; and nothing is lacking for the growth of His children. Oh incredible mystery! <u>Clemet of Alexandria</u>

He Himself warns us, saying, "Unless you eat the flesh of the Son of Man and drink His blood you shall not have life in you." Therefore do we ask that our Bread, which is Christ, be given to us daily, so that we who abide and live in Christ may not withdraw from His sanctification and from His Body.

<u>Cyprian of Carthage</u>

After having spoken thus ["This is My body...This is My blood"], the Lord rose up from the place where He had made the Passover and had given His Body as food and His Blood as drink, and He went with His disciples to the place where He was to be arrested. But He ate of His own Body and drank of His own Blood, while He was pondering on the dead. With His own hands the Lord presented His own Body to be eaten, and before He was crucified He gave His blood as drink.   Aprahat

Our Lord Jesus took in His hands what in the beginning was only bread; and He blessed it, and signed it, and made it holy in the name of the Father and in the name of the Spirit; and He broke it and in His gracious kindness He distributed it to all His disciples one by one. He called the bread His living Body, and did Himself fill it with Himself and the Spirit. And extending His hand, He gave them the Bread, which His right hand had made holy: "Take, all of you eat of this, which My word has made holy. Do not now regard as bread that which I have given you; but take, eat this Bread [of life], and do not scatter the crumbs; for what I have called My Body, that it is indeed. One particle from its crumbs is able to sanctify thousands and thousands, and is sufficient to afford life to those who eat of it. Take, eat, entertaining no doubt of faith, because this is My Body, and whoever eats it in belief eats in it Fire and Spirit. But if any doubter eat of it, for him it will be only bread. And whoever eats in belief the Bread made holy in My name, if he be pure, he will be preserved in his purity; and if he be a sinner, he will be forgiven." But if anyone despise it or reject it or treat it with ignominy, it may be taken as a certainty that he treats with ignominy the Son, who called it and actually made it to be His Body. After the disciples had eaten the new and holy Bread, and when they understood by faith that they had eaten of Christ's body, Christ went on to explain and to give them the whole Sacrament. He took and mixed a cup of wine. Then He blessed it, and signed it, and made it holy, declaring that it was His own Blood, which was about to be poured out...Christ commanded them to drink, and He explained to them that the cup which they were drinking was His own Blood: "This is truly My Blood, which is shed for all of you. Take, all of you, drink of this, because it is a new covenant in My Blood. As you have seen Me do, do you also in My memory. Whenever you are gathered together in My name in Churches everywhere, do what I have done, in memory of Me. Eat My Body, and drink My Blood, a covenant new and old."   Ephraim the Syrian

You shall see the Levites bringing loaves and a cup of wine, and placing them on the table. So long as the prayers of supplication and entreaties have not been made, there is only bread and wine. But after the great and wonderful prayers have been completed, then the bread is become the Body, and the wine the Blood, of our Lord Jesus Christ... Let us approach the celebration of the mysteries. This bread and this wine, so long as the prayers and supplications have not taken place, remain simply what they are. But after the great prayers and holy supplications have been sent forth, the Word comes down into the bread and wine -- and thus is His Body confected.

Thanasius

For just as the bread and the wine of the Eucharist before the holy invocation of the adorable Trinity were simple bread and wine, but the invocation having been made, the bread becomes the Body of Christ and the wine the Blood of Christ.   Cyril of Jerusalem

This one teaching of the blessed Paul is enough to give you complete certainty about the Divine Mysteries, by your having been deemed worthy of which, you have become united in body and blood with Christ. For Paul proclaimed clearly that: "On the night in which He was betrayed, our Lord Jesus Christ, taking bread and giving thanks, broke it and gave it to His disciples, saying: 'Take, eat, This is My Body.' And taking the cup and giving thanks, He said, 'Take, drink, This is My Blood.'" He Himself, therefore, having declared and said of the Bread, "This is My Body," who will dare any longer to doubt? And when He Himself has affirmed and said, "This is My Blood," who can ever hesitate and say it is not His Blood?   Ibid

Do not, therefore, regard the Bread and the Wine as simply that; for they are, according to the Master's declaration, the Body and Blood of Christ. Even though the senses suggest to you the other, let faith make you firm. Do not judge in this matter by taste, but -- be fully assured by the faith, not doubting that you have been deemed worthy of the Body and Blood of Christ.   Ibid

---

Then, having sanctified ourselves by these spiritual songs, we call upon the benevolent God to send out the Holy Spirit upon the gifts, which have been laid out: that He may make the bread the Body of Christ, and the wine the Blood of Christ; for whatsoever the Holy Spirit touches, that is sanctified and changed.   Ibid

---

When we speak of the reality of Christ's nature being in us, we would be speaking foolishly and impiously -- had we not learned it from Him. For He Himself says: "My Flesh is truly Food, and My Blood is truly Drink. He that eats My Flesh and drinks My Blood will remain in Me and I in Him." As to the reality of His Flesh and Blood, there is no room left for doubt, because now, both by the declaration of the Lord Himself and by our own faith, it is truly Flesh and it is truly Blood. And These Elements bring it about, when taken and consumed, that we are in Christ and Christ is in us. Is this not true? Let those who deny that Jesus Christ is true God be free to find these things untrue. But He Himself is in us through the flesh and we are in Him, while that which we are with Him is in God.   Hilary of Poitiers

This Body, by the indwelling of God the Word, has been made over to divine dignity. Rightly then, do we believe that the bread consecrated by the word of God has been made over into the Body of God the Word. For that Body was, as to its potency, bread; but it has been consecrated by the lodging there of the Word, who pitched His tent in the flesh. From the same cause, therefore, by which the bread that was made over into that Body is made to change into divine strength, a similar result now takes place. As in the former case, in which the grace of the Word made holy that body the substance of which is from bread, and in a certain manner is itself bread, so in this case too, the bread, as the Apostle says, "is consecrated by God's word and by prayer"; not through its being eaten does it advance to become the Body of the Word, but it is made over immediately into the Body by means of the word, just as was stated by the Word, "This is My Body!" ...In the plan of His grace He spreads Himself to every believer by means of that Flesh, the substance of which is from wine and bread, blending Himself with the bodies of believers, so that by this union with the Immortal, man, too, may become a participant in incorruption.   Gregory of Nyssa

---

Holy Friday

What thing is this? Today there is great silence upon the earth, great silence and stillness, verily great silence, for the King sleeps. The earth was frightened and became still, for God fell asleep in the flesh and raised up those who from ages past were sleeping. God died in the flesh and Hades shuddered. God slumbered briefly, and those in Hades He awoke.

                                                      Epiphanios of Cyprus

---

When you hear that at that time the Lord freed the souls from hell and the regions of darkness and that He descended into hell and did an amazing work, do not think that this does not have any personal meaning for you. Man, indeed, can readily accept the evil one. Death has its grip on the children of Adam and their thoughts are imprisoned in darkness. And when you hear mention made of tombs, do not at once think only of visible ones. For your heart is a tomb and a sepulcher. When the prince of evil and his angels have built their nest there and have built roads and highways on which the powers of Satan walk about inside your mind and in your thoughts, then really, are you not a hell and a sepulcher and a tomb dead to God? ... But the Lord descends into the souls of those who seek Him. He goes into the depths of the hellish heart and there He commands death, saying, "Release those captive souls that seek after me, those that you hold by force in bondage." He breaks through the heavy stones that cover the soul. He opens the tombs. He truly raises to life the dead person and leads that captive soul forth out of the dark prison.   Macarius

Holy Monday

Let those of us who have wisely finished the course of fasting And who celebrate with love the beginning of the suffering of the Passion of the Lord, Let us all, my brothers, zealously imitate the purity of self-controlled Joseph; Let us fear the sterility of the fig tree; Let us dry up through almsgiving the sweetness of passion. In order that we may joyously anticipate the Resurrection, Let us procure like myrrh pardon from on high Because the Eye that never sleeps observes all things.

Oh Savior, consider those of us who have appeared at the season of Your passion, worthy to worship also Your Resurrection, oh Eye that does not sleep.   Romanos the Melodist

Holy Spirit

...the Holy Spirit, being one, and of one nature, and indivisible, divides to each His grace, 'according as He wills' (1 Cor. 12:11) and as the dry tree, after partaking of water, puts forth shoots, so also the soul in sin, when it has been through repentance made worthy of the Holy Spirit, brings forth clusters of righteousness.   Cyril of Jerusalem

...though remission of sins is given equally to all, the communion of the Holy Spirit is bestowed in proportion to each man's faith. If you have labored little, you receive little; but if you have wrought much, the reward is great. You are running for yourself, see to your own interest   Ibid

A house roof is held up by the foundations and the rest of the building, and the foundation and the rest of the building are laid to hold the roof - since both are necessary and useful - and neither is the roof built without the foundations and the rest of the house, nor can foundations and walls without roof make a building fit to live in. So it is with the soul: the grace of the Holy Spirit is preserved by keeping the commandments, and the keeping of the commandments is the foundation laid for receiving the gifts of God's grace. Neither does the grace of the Holy Spirit remain in us without our obeying the commandments, nor can obeying the commandments be useful and salutary without Divine grace.   Simeon the New Theologian

---

A man ... wrestles with many ... demons; and often the demon, whom many men could not master with iron bands, has been mastered by the man himself with words of prayer, which is in him of the Holy Spirit; and the mere breathing of the Exorcist becomes as fire to that unseen foe. A mighty ally and protector, therefore, have we from God; a great Teacher of the Church, a mighty Champion on our behalf. Let us not be afraid of the demons, nor of the devil; for mightier is He who fights for us.   Cyril of Jerusalem

---

As it is written, it is clear the Spirit is not a creature, but takes part in the act of creation. The Father creates all things through the Word in the Spirit; for where the Word is, there is the Spirit also, and it is out of the Spirit from the Word that the things, which are created through the Word, have their power to exist. Thus it is written in the thirty-second psalm: `By the Word of the Lord the heavens were established, and by the Spirit of his mouth is all their might' (Ps. 32:6).   Athanasius the Great

---

But when the Holy Spirit dwells in the heart of a person, He shows him all his inner poverty and weakness, and the corruption of his heart and soul, and his separation from God; and with all his virtues and righteousness. He shows him his sins, his sloth and indifference regarding the salvation and good of people his self-seeking in his apparently most disinterested virtues,

212

his coarse selfishness even where he does not suspect it. To be brief, the Holy Spirit shows him everything as it really is. Then a person begins to have true humility, begins to lose hope in his own powers and virtues, and regards himself as the worst of men. And when a person humbles himself before Jesus Christ Who alone is Holy in the glory of God the Father, he begins to repent truly, and resolves never again to sin but to live more carefully. And if he really has some virtues, then he sees clearly that he practiced and practices them only with the help of God, and therefore he begins to put his trust only in God.   Innocent of Irkutsk

Faith and love, which are gifts of the Holy Spirit, are such great and powerful means that a person who has them can easily, and with joy and consolation, go the way Jesus Christ went. Besides this, the Holy Spirit gives man the power to resist the delusions of the world so that although he makes use of earthly good, yet he uses them as a temporary visitor, without attaching his heart to them. But a man who has not got the Holy Spirit, despite all his learning and prudence, is always more or less a slave and worshipper of the world.   Ibid

If we are illumined by divine power, and fix our eyes on the beauty of the image of the invisible God, and through the image are let up to the indescribably beauty of its source, it is because we have been inseparably joined to the Spirit of knowledge. He gives those who love the vision of truth the power that enables them to see the image, and this power is Himself. He does not reveal it to them from outside sources, but leads them to knowledge personally. `No one knows the Father except the Son.'   Basil

In my opinion the grace of the Holy Spirit most readily fills those who undertake spiritual work wholeheartedly and determine from the very beginning to stand firm and never to give ground to the enemy in no matter what battle, until they conquer him. However, the Holy Spirit, Who has called them, at first makes all things easy for them, in order thus to sweeten the beginning of the work of repentance, and only later shows them its ways in their full truth (arduousness). Helping them in all things, He impresses on them what works of repentance they should undertake, and lays down the form and limits both as regards the body and the soul, until He brings them to complete conversion to God, their Creator. For this purpose He constantly urges them to give exertion to body and soul in order that both alike, being equally sanctified, should equally become worthy heirs of eternal life; to exert the body in constant fasting, work and frequent vigils, and the soul, in spiritual exercises and diligence in all forms of service (and obedience) performed through the body. This (to do nothing carelessly, but always with care and the fear of God) should be zealously observed in all work done with the body, if we wish it to bear fruit.   Anthony

----

It was said that a person who has not the Holy Spirit within him cannot pray true prayer. This is perfectly true. We need to make considerable use of toil and suffering in order to be able to pray holy prayer. We cannot suddenly or quickly attain to such a state as to be able to raise our thoughts and hearts to God. Not only with us ordinary people, but even with many who have consecrated their whole life to prayer, it happens that you go to turn your thoughts to God and you find them distracted in different directions and taken up with various matters; you want to have God in your thoughts, and something quite different comes to you, and sometimes it is even something terrible.   Innocent of Alaska

----

Leading the repentant man to undertake spiritual work, the Holy Spirit, Who called him to repentance, also grants him His comforts and teaches him not to turn back nor be attached to anything of this world. To this end, He opens the eyes of the soul and gives her to see the beauty of the purity reached through the works of repentance. In this way He kindles in it zeal for complete purification both of itself and of the body, that the two may be one in purity. For this is the aim of the teaching and guidance of the Holy Spirit - to purify them completely and bring them back to their original state, in which they were before the Fall, by destroying in them all adulterations introduced by the devil's envy, so that nothing of the enemy should remain therein. Then the body will become obedient to the dictates of the mind in all things, and the mind will masterfully determine its food and drink, its sleep and its every other action, constantly learning from the Holy Spirit to "keep under" the "body, and bring it into subjection" (1 Corinthians 9:27) as did Apostle Paul.   Anthony

---

Let us therefore make use of this great benefit, and seek for personal experience of this most needful Gift. For the Apostle says, in words I have already cited, `But we have not received the spirit of this world, but the Spirit which is of God, that we may know the things that are given unto us by God.' We receive Him, then, that we may know. Faculties of the human body, if denied their exercise, will lie dormant. The eye without light, natural or artificial, cannot fulfill its office; the ear will be ignorant of its function unless some voice or sound be heard; the nostrils unconscious of their purpose unless some scent be breathed. Not that the faculty will be absent, because it is never called into use, but that there will be no experience of its existence. So, too, the soul of man, unless through faith it have appropriated the gift of the Spirit, will have the innate faculty of apprehending God, but be destitute of the light of knowledge. That Gift, which is in Christ, is One, yet offered, and offered fully, to all; denied to none, and given to each according to the measure of his willingness to receive; its stores the richer, the more earnest the desire to earn them. This gift is with us unto the end of the world, the solace of our waiting, the assurance, by the favors, which He bestows, of the hope that shall be ours, the light of our minds, and the sun of our souls. This Holy Spirit we must seek and must earn, and then hold fast by faith and obedience to the commands of God.   Hilary of Poitiers

---

Peace is liberation from passions, which cannot be attained without the action of the Holy Spirit.   Mark the Ascetic

---

Some brethren came one day to test him to see whether he would let his thoughts get dissipated and speak of the things of this world. They said to him, "We give thanks to God that this year there has been much rain and the palm trees have been able to drink, and their shoots have grown, and the brethren have found manual work." Abbot John said to them, "So it is when the Holy Spirit descends into the hearts of men; they are renewed and they put forth leaves in the fear of God."   Desert Fathers

---

Some say that we can do nothing good until we actively receive the grace of the Holy Spirit. This is not true.   Mark the Ascetic

---

That is the reason why the Holy Spirit comes in the form of a dove: it is a simple joyous creature, not bitter with gall, not biting savagely, without vicious rearing claws; it loves to dwell with humankind, it keeps to one house for assembling; when they mate they hatch their young together, when they fly anywhere they keep their formation, the resorts they live in are shared in common, by their billing too they pay tribute to concord and peace, in all things they fulfill the law of unanimity. The same is the simplicity of the Church, which we need to learn, this is the charity we must acquire, that we may imitate the doves in our love for the brethren, and rival lambs and sheep in their meekness and gentleness.   Cyprian

---

The Comforter, the Holy Spirit, Who fills the whole universe, passes through all believing, meek, humble, good and simple human souls, dwelling in them, vivifying and strengthening them. He becomes one spirit with them and everything to them - light, strength, peace, joy, success in their undertakings, especially to a pious life, and everything good."   John of Kronstadt

---

The Holy Spirit accomplishes all wonders and miracles. By the same Spirit power is given to one, and to another works of power. You have only to speak with faith, and need have no anxiety as to the fulfillment of the word; the Holy Spirit will care for this.   John of Kronstadt

---

The Holy Spirit comes when we are receptive. He does not compel. He approaches so meekly that we may not even notice. If we would know the Holy Spirit we need to examine ourselves in the light of the Gospel teaching, to detect any other presence, which may prevent the Holy Spirit from entering into our souls. We must not wait for God to force Himself on us without our consent. God respects and does not constrain man. It is amazing how God humbles Himself before us. He loves us with a tender love, not haughtily, not with condescension. And when we open our hearts to Him we are overwhelmed by the conviction that He is indeed our Father. The soul then worships in love."   Archimandrite Sophrony

The Holy Spirit often visits us; but if He does not find rest how can He remain? He departs. Joy is in the hearts of those who are cleansed and who are able to maintain within themselves the grace of the Holy Spirit of the All-holy Trinity. There is no greater joy and happiness for man. I am not able to describe to you how one feels then.   Nil Sorsky

The Lord has assigned the Spirit His proper place; why should we forsake it to invent another place? He is always described as united with the Godhead; why should He be deprived of His glory? We hear His name in the creed, at saving baptism, in the working of miracles. He takes up His abode in the saints; He bestows grace on the obedient. No gift can be bestowed on creation unless the Holy Spirit gives it; not even a single word can be spoken in defense of Christ unless the Holy Spirit inspires it - as we have learned in the Gospels from our Lord and Savior (Mt. 10:19-20).   Basil

The Spirit does not take up His abode in someone's life through a physical approach; how could a corporeal being approach the Bodiless one? Instead, the Spirit comes to us when we withdraw ourselves from evil passions, which have crept into the soul through its friendship with the flesh, alienating us from a close relationship with God. Only when a man has been cleansed from the shame of his evil, and has returned to his natural beauty, and the original form of the Royal Image has been restored in him, is it possible for him to approach the Paraclete. Then, like the sun, He will show you in Himself the image of the invisible, and with purified eyes you will see in this blessed image the unspeakable beauty of its prototype.   Ibid

---

The deifying gift of the Spirit is a mysterious light, and transforms into light those who receive its richness. He does not only fill them with eternal light, but grants them a knowledge and a life appropriate to God. Thus, as Maximus teaches, Paul lived no longer a created life, but "the eternal life of Him Who indwelt him." Similarly, the prophets contemplated the future as if it were the present.   Gregory Palamas

---

The glory that shone from the face of Moses was a prefiguring of the true glory of the Holy Spirit. Just as it was impossible then for anyone to gaze at it, so now the darkness of the passions cannot bear the same glory shining in the souls of Christians, but is put to flight, repulsed by its brilliance.

Macarios of Egypt

The power to bear Mysteries, which the humble man has received, which makes him perfect in every virtue without toil, this is the very power which the blessed apostles received in the form of fire. For its sake the Savior commanded them not to leave Jerusalem until they should receive power from on high, that is to say, the Paraclete, which, being interpreted, is the Spirit of consolation. And this is the Spirit of divine visions. Concerning this it is said in divine Scripture: 'Mysteries are revealed to the humble' [Ecclus 3:19]. The humble are accounted worthy of receiving in themselves this Spirit of revelations Who teaches mysteries   Isaac the Syrian

---

Through the Holy Spirit comes our restoration to Paradise, our ascension to the Kingdom of heaven, our adoption as God's sons, our freedom to call God our Father, our becoming partakers of the grace of Christ, in a word, our inheritance of the fullness of blessings, both in this world and the world to come. Even while we wait for the full enjoyment of the good things in store for us, by the Holy Spirit we are able to rejoice through faith in the promise of the graces to come. If the promise itself is so glorious, what must its fulfillment be like? We are also able to distinguish between the grace that comes from the Spirit and mere baptism in water. John baptized in water for repentance, but our Lord Jesus Christ baptized in the Holy Spirit.   Basil

Thus the deifying gift of the Spirit is a mysterious light, and transforms into light those who receive its richness; He does not only fill them with eternal light, but grants them a knowledge and a life appropriate to God. Thus, as Maximus teaches, Paul lived no longer a created life, but "the eternal life of Him Who indwelt him." Similarly, the prophets contemplated the future as if it were the present.   Gregory Palamas

What, then, is more divine than the working of the Holy Spirit, since God Himself teaches that the Holy Spirit presides over His blessings, saying: "I will put My Spirit upon your seed and My blessings upon your children." For no blessing can be full except through the inspiration of the Holy Spirit. Wherefore, too, the Apostle found nothing better to wish us than this, as He himself said: "We cease not to pray and make request for you that you may be filled with the knowledge of His will, in all wisdom and spiritual understanding walking worthily of God." (Col 1:9) He taught, then, that this was the will of God, that rather by walking in good works and words and affections, we should be filled with the will of God, Who puts His Holy Spirit in our hearts.   Ambrose of Milan

"Creation is a slave; the Spirit sets free. Creation stands in need of life; the

Spirit is the Life-Giver. Creation needs instruction; the Spirit is the Teacher. Creation is sanctified; the Spirit is the Sanctifier."   Basil

---

You ask what is the procession of the Holy Spirit? Do you tell me first what is the unbegottenness of the Father, and I will then explain to you the physiology of the generation of the Son, and the procession of the Spirit, and we shall both of us be stricken with madness for prying into the mystery of God.   Gregory the Theologian

---

We have learned that there is a difference between generation [begetting] and procession, but the nature of the difference we in no wise understand.

John of Damascus

"Creation is a slave; the Spirit sets free. Creation stands in need of life; the Spirit is the Life-Giver. Creation needs instruction; the Spirit is the Teacher. Creation is sanctified; the Spirit is the Sanctifier."   Basil

---

There are those who claim that we cannot do good unless we actively receive the grace of the Spirit.   Kosmas Aitolos

---

He who can without strain keep vigil, be long-suffering and pray is manifestly a partaker of the Holy Spirit. But he who feels strain while doing these things, yet willingly endures it, also quickly receives help.   Ibid

The grace of the Spirit is one and unchanging, but energizes in each one of us as He wills (cf. 1Co 12:11).   Ibid

When you hear Scripture saying of the Holy Spirit that He 'rested upon each' of the Apostles (Ac 2:3), or 'came upon' the Prophet (1Sm 11:6), or 'energizes' (1Co 12:11), or is 'grieved' (Ep. 4:30), or is 'quenched' (1Th 5:19), or is 'vexed' (Is 63:10), and again, that some 'have the first fruits' (Rm 8:23), and that others are 'filled with the Holy Spirit' (Ac 2:4), do not suppose that the Spirit is subject to some kind of division, variation or change; but be sure that, in the way we have described, He is unvarying, unchanging and all-powerful. Therefore in all His energies He remains what He is, and in a divine manner He gives to each person what is needful. On those who have been baptized He pours Himself out in His fullness like the sun. Each of us is illumined by Him to the extent to which we hate the passions that darken us and get rid of them. But in so far as we have a love for them and dwell on them, we remain in darkness.   Ibid

Holy Tradition

But as for you, continue in what you have learned and have firmly believed, knowing from whom you learned it and how from childhood you have been acquainted with the sacred writings which are able to instruct you for salvation through faith in Christ Jesus. All scripture is inspired by God and profitable for teaching, for reproof, for correction, and for training in righteousness, that the man of God may be complete, equipped for every good work. 2 Timothy 3:14-17 (RSV)

Suppose that for some reason the Church were to be bereft of all her liturgical books, of the Old and New Testaments, the works of the Holy Fathers—what would happen? Sacred Tradition would restore the Scriptures, not word for word, perhaps—the verbal form might be different but in essence the new Scriptures would be the expression of that same 'faith which was once delivered unto the saints.' They would be the expression of the one and only Holy Spirit continuously active in the Church, her foundation and her very substance..   Archimandrite Sophrony

---

An eagle was flying in the heights and delighting in the beauty of the word, and he thought: "I cover great expanses, and I see valleys and mountains, seas and rivers, meadows and forests. I see towns and settlements, and how men live; while here a village rooster knows nothing except his own yard. I shall fly to him and tell him about the life of the world."

The eagle flew onto the roof of the country house and saw how gallantly and merrily the rooster was strolling amidst his hens. And the eagle began to speak to the rooster of the world's beauty and wealth. At first, the rooster listened with attention, but did not understand anything. The eagle, seeing that the rooster did not understand anything, was saddened, and it became hard for him to speak with the rooster; while the rooster, not understanding what the eagle was saying, began to be bored, and it became hard for him to listen to the eagle.

Thus it happens when a learned man speaks with an unlearned man, but even more when a spiritual man speaks with an unspiritual man. A spiritual man is like the eagle, while an unspiritual man is like the rooster; the mind of a spiritual man meditates on the law of the Lord day and night and by prayer ascends to God, while the mind of an unspiritual man is attached to the earth or occupied with thoughts. And when a spiritual man meets an unspiritual man, intercourse for them both is boring and difficult.   Seraphim Rose

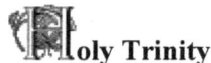

Holy Trinity

... we know according to godliness One Father, who sent His Son to be our Savior; we know One Son, who promised that He would send the Comforter from the Father; we know the Holy Spirit, who spoke in the Prophets, and who on the day of Pentecost descended upon the Apostles in the form of fiery tongues, here, in Jerusalem, in the Upper Church of the Apostles.

According to the Scriptures, to know the One God is the root of immortality, and to know the dominion of the Three-in-One is the whole and entire truth. The word of the Gospel on this subject can be understood thus: 'This is life eternal, that they might know You, the only true God' in three hypostases, 'and Jesus Christ Whom You have sent' in two natures and two wills (John 17:3).
Gregory of Sinai

God is known and understood in everything in three hypostases. He holds all things and provides for all things through His Son in the Holy Spirit; and no one of Them, wherever He is invoked, is named or thought of as existing apart or separately from the two others.
Gregory of Sinai

It is the Father to Whom all existence owes its origin. In Christ and through Christ He is the source of all. In contrast to all else He is self-existent. He does not draw His being from without, but possesses it from Himself and in Himself. He is infinite, for nothing contains Him and He contains all things; He is eternally unconditioned by space, for He is illimitable; eternally anterior to time, for time is His creation. Let imagination range to what you may suppose is God's utmost limit, and you will find Him present there; strain as you will there is always a further horizon towards which to strain. Infinity is His property, just as the power of making such effort is yours. Words will l fail you, but His being will not be circumscribed.

Hilary of Poitiers

Just in the same way, man has mind, word and spirit; and the mind cannot be without the word, nor the word without the spirit, but the three are always in one another, yet exist in themselves. The mind speaks by means of words, and the word is manifested through the spirit. This example shows that man bears in himself a feeble image of the ineffable prototype, the Trinity, thus demonstrating that he has been made in God's image.   <u>Gregory of Sinai</u>

The Father through the Son, with the Holy Spirit, is the giver of all grace; the gifts of the Father are none other than those of the Son, and those of the Holy Spirit; for there is one salvation, one Power, one Faith; One God, the Father; One Lord, His only-begotten Son; One Holy Spirit, the Comforter. And it is enough for us to know these things; but inquire not curiously into His nature or substance: for had it been written, we would have spoken of it; what is not written, let us not venture on; it is sufficient for our salvation to know that there is Father, and Son, and Holy Spirit.   <u>Cyril of Jerusalem</u>

The Spirit of the supreme Logos is a kind of ineffable yet intense longing or 'eros' experienced by the Begetter for the Logos born ineffably from Him, a longing experienced also by the beloved Logos and Son of the Father for His Begetter; but the Logos possesses this love by virtue of the fact that it comes from the Father in the very act through which He comes from the Father, and it resides co-naturally in Him.

It is from the Logos's discourse with us through His incarnation that we have learned what is the name of the Spirit's distinct mode of coming to be from the Father and that the Spirit belongs not only to the Father but also to the Logos. For He says 'the Spirit of Truth, who proceeds from the Father' (John 15:26), so that we may know that from the Father comes not solely the Logos - who is begotten from the Father - but also the Spirit who proceeds from the Father. Yet the Spirit belongs also to the Son, who receives Him from the Father as the Spirit of Truth, Wisdom and Logos. For Truth and Wisdom constitute a Logos that befits His Begetter, a Logos that rejoices with the Father as the Father rejoices in Him.

This accords with the words that He spoke through Solomon: 'I was She who rejoiced together with Him' (Prov. 8:30). Solomon did not say simply 'rejoiced' but 'rejoiced together with'. This pre-eternal rejoicing of the Father and the Son is the Holy Spirit who, as I said, is common to both, which explains why He is sent from both to those who are worthy. Yet the Spirit has His existence from the Father alone, and hence He proceeds as regards His existence only from the Father. Our intellect, because created in God's image, possesses likewise the image of this sublime Eros or intense longing - an image expressed in the love experienced by the intellect for the spiritual knowledge that originates from it and continually abides in it."

Gregory Palamas

The final end of Orthodoxy is pure knowledge of the two dogmas of faith - the Trinity and the Duality; to contemplate and know the Trinity as indivisible and yet not merged together; to know the Duality as the two natures of Christ joined in one person - that is, to know and to profess one's faith in the Son of God both before incarnation, and after incarnation, to praise Him in His two natures and wills unmerged, the one Divine and the other human.   <u>Gregory of Sinai</u>

The kingdom of God is knowledge of the Holy Trinity, extending as far as the state of one's mind permits, and filling it with an endlessly blessed life.

Evagrius the Monk

There is One God, the Father, Lord of the Old and the New Testament: and One Lord, Jesus Christ, who was prophesied of in the Old Testament and came in the new; and One Holy Spirit, who through the prophets preached of Christ, and when Christ was come, descended, and manifested Him.

Cyril of Jerusalem

Three realities pertain to God: essence, energy, and the triad of divine hypostases. As we have seen, those privileged to be united to God so as to become one spirit with Him - as Paul said, 'He who cleaves to the Lord is one spirit with Him' (1 Cor. 6:17) - are not united to God with respect to His essence, since all theologians testify that with respect to His essence God suffers no participation.

Moreover, the hypostatic union is fulfilled only in the case of the Logos, the God-man.

Thus those privileged to attain union with God are united to Him with respect to His energy; and the 'spirit', according to which they who cleave to God are one with Him, is and is called the uncreated energy of the Holy Spirit, but not the essence of God.   Gregory Palamas

---

Trinity is simple unity; it is not merged together - it is three in one. The One three-hypostatical God has the three hypostases perfectly distinct in Himself.

Gregory of Sinai

We sin in thought, word, and deed. In order to become pure images of the Most Holy Trinity, we must strive that our thoughts, words, and deeds may be holy. Thought corresponds, in God, to the Father, the word to the Son, and the deed to the all-accomplishing Holy Spirit.   John of Kronstadt

---

Where, then, the grace of the Spirit is asserted, is that of God the Father of the Only-Begotten Son denied? By no means; for as the Father is in the Son, and the Son in the Father, so, too, "the love of God is shed abroad in our hearts by the Holy Spirit, Who has been given us" (Rom. 5:5). And as he who is blessed in Christ is blessed in the Name of the Father, and of the Son, and of the Holy Spirit, because the Name is one and the Power one; so, too, when any divine operation, whether of the Father, or of the Son, or of the Holy Spirit, is treated of it is not referred only to the Holy Spirit, but also to the Father and the Son, and not only to the Father, but also to the Son and the Spirit.   Ambrose of Milan

Who then is that Father Who had no beginning? One Whose very Existence had no beginning; for one whose existence had a beginning must also have begun to be a Father. He did not then become a Father after He began to be, for His being had no beginning. And He is Father in the absolute sense, for He is not also Son; just as the Son is Son in the absolute sense, because He is not also Father. These names do not belong to us in the absolute sense, because we are both, and not one more than the other; and we are of both, and not of one only.   Gregory Nazianzen

Holy Wednesday

And indeed, if He had been making a law, He would not have brought in the woman [who had anointed His feet with ointment], but that you might learn that for her sake these things were said, that they might not mar her budding faith, but rather cherish it, therefore He says it, teaching us whatever good thing may be done by any man, though it be not quire perfect, to receive it, and encourage it, and advance it, and not to seek all perfection at the beginning.   John Chrysostom

Lo, the day has dawned which I longed to see, A time favorable for me. My God is lodged in the house of Simon. I shall hasten to Him and weep, just as Anna did about her sterility. Simon may consider me drunk, Just as Elias then considered Anna. I shall keep on praying And saying, 'Lord, I do not ask for a child. I seek my very own soul, which I have lost! Oh Emmanuel, born of a virgin, just as You have removed the stigma of sterility when Samuel was born Of the childless woman, so deliver me, a harlot, From the slime of my deeds'."   Romanos the Melodist

Holy Week

Let those of us who have wisely finished the course of fasting And who celebrate with love the beginning of the suffering of the Passion of the Lord, Let us all, my brothers, zealously imitate the purity of self-controlled Joseph; Let us fear the sterility of the fig tree; Let us dry up through almsgiving the sweetness of passion. In order that we may joyously anticipate the Resurrection, Let us procure like myrrh pardon from on high because the eye that never sleeps observes all things.   Ibid

Lo, the day has dawned which I longed to see, A time favorable for me. My God is lodged in the house of Simon, I shall hasten to him and weep, just as Anna did about her sterility. Simon may consider me drunk, Just as Elias then considered Anna. I shall keep on praying And saying, `Lord, I do not ask for a child. I seek my very own soul, which I have lost! Oh Emmanuel, born of a Virgin, just as You has removed the stigma of sterility when Samuel was born of the childless woman, so deliver me, a harlot From the slime of my deeds.'   Ibid

Honesty

If you wish that God should speedily give you hearty faith in prayer, strive with all your heart to speak and to do everything in regard to other people sincerely, and never be deceitful in your dealings with them. If you are straightforward and truthful with others, then God will give you straightforwardness and sincere faith also in reference to Himself."

John of Kronstadt

Hope

A man cannot acquire hope in God unless he first does His will with exactness. For hope in God and manliness of heart are born of the testimony of the conscience, and by the truthful testimony of the mind we possess confidence in God. The testimony of the mind consists in the fact that a man's conscience does not accuse him of negligence in anything within his power that it is his duty to do.   Isaac the Syrian

---

Man's patience gives birth to hope; good hope will glorify him. "Instructions to Cenobites and Others."   Abbot Evagrius

---

Ample room in the heart denotes hope in God; congestion denotes bodily care.   Kosmas Aitolos

---

Hospitality

...Even if you have only bread or water, with these you can still meet the dues of hospitality. Even if you do not have these, but simply make the stranger welcome and offer him a word of encouragement, you will not be failing in hospitality. Think of the widow mentioned in the Gospel by our Lord: with two mites she surpassed the generous gifts of the wealthy.

Theodoros, the Ascetic

Accepting the task of hospitality, the patriarch [Abraham] used to sit at the entrance to his tent (cf. Gen. 18:1), inviting all who passed by, and his table was laden for all comers including the impious and barbarians, without distinction. Hence he was found worthy of that wonderful banquet when he received angels and the Master of all as guests. We too, then, should actively and eagerly cultivate hospitality, so that we may receive not only angels, but also God Himself. "For inasmuch," says the Lord, "as you have done it to one of the least of these My brethren, you have done it unto Me" (Matt. 25:40). It is good to be generous to all, especially to those who cannot repay you.

Ibid

If your heart has been softened either by repentance before God or by learning the boundless love of God towards you, do not be proud with those whose hearts are still hard. Remember how long your heart was hard and incorrigible.

Seven brothers were ill in one hospital. One recovered from his illness and got up and rushed to serve his other brothers with brotherly love, to speed their recovery. Be like this brother. Consider all men to be your brothers, and sick brothers at that. And if you come to feel that God has given you better health than others, know that it is given through mercy, so in health you may serve your frailer brothers   Nikolai Velimirovic

---

Lift up and stretch out your hands, not to heaven but to the poor; for if you stretch out your hands to the poor, you have reached the summit of heaven. But if you lift up your hands in prayer without sharing with the poor, it is worth nothing ... Every family should have a room where Christ is welcomed in the person of the hungry and thirsty stranger. The poor are a greater temple than the sanctuary; this altar the poor, you can raise up anywhere, on any street, and offer the liturgy at any hour."   John Chrysostom

---

Lift up and stretch out your hands, not to heaven but to the poor; for if you stretch out your hands to the poor, you have reached the summit of heaven. But if you lift up your hands in prayer without sharing with the poor, it is worth nothing ... Every family should have a room where Christ is welcomed in the person of the hungry and thirsty stranger. The poor are a greater temple than the sanctuary; this alter the poor, you can raise up anywhere, on any street, and offer the liturgy at any hour."   John Chrysostom

---

Look at all the earth supplies in summer and in autumn! Every Christian, especially the priest, ought to imitate God's bountifulness. Let your table be open to everybody, like the table of the Lord. The avaricious is God's enemy."   John of Kronstadt

---

On a cold night two, two under the same blanket gain warmth from each other. Ecclesiastes 4:11

When Abbot Agathon went down to the city to sell some of his baskets and to procure a little bread, he found near the market place an old, poor cripple.

"For the love of God, Abbot," the cripple began to plead on seeing the , "don't you, too, leave this poor wretch unaided. Bring me near to you."

Abbot Agathon picked the man up and sat him next to him in the place where he had set up his baskets to sell them.

'How much money did you make, Abbot?' the cripple would ask each time that the sold a basket.

"Such and such," the would tell him.

"That's good enough," the cripple finally said. "Won't you buy me a little pie, Abbot? That would be good of you, since I have not eaten since last evening."

"With pleasure," the told him, immediately fulfilling the cripple's request.

Shortly thereafter, the cripple requested some fruit. And then some sweet. Thus, for each basket that was sold, the spent the proceeds, until, thanks to his patronage, all of the baskets and money were gone, without his having kept even two pennies for himself. More importantly, he did this all with great eagerness, even though he knew that he would thus go perhaps two weeks without any bread for himself.

Since he had sold his last basket, the got ready to leave the marketplace.

"So you're going?" the cripple asked him.

"Yes, I have completed all of my work."

"Uh, do me the favor of taking me as far as the crossroads, and you can leave for the desert from there," the strange old man again pleadingly said.

The good Agathon took the cripple on his back and carried him to the place where he wanted to go, though with great difficulty, since he was exhausted from his day's work.

As soon as he reached the crossroads and started to put down his living burden, he heard a sweet voice say to him:

"May you be blessed, Agathon, by God, both on earth and in Heaven."

The raised up his eyes to see who it was who had spoken with him. The would-be old man had completely disappeared, since he was an Angel sent by God to test the 's love. <u>The Desert Fathers</u>

Love giving hospitality, my child, for it opens the gates of Paradise. In this you also offer hospitality to angels. "Entertain strangers so that you won't be a stranger to God." <u>Amphilochios</u>

Hospitality... the greatest of virtues. It draws the grace of the Holy Spirit towards us. In every stranger's face, my child, I see Christ himself.   Ibid

How to live

What are the rules for living a good life? In the first place to love the Lord with all one's heart, with all one's soul and with all one's strength. Then, to love one's neighbor as oneself.   Benedict of Nursia

Human Nature

...it is a property of human nature not to possess any trace of the heavenly graces of its own will or, as it were, by its own nature. 'For what have you that you did not receive?' it is asked (1 Cor. 4:7). Rather, it was enriched from outside and by acquisition, that is, from God, with that which transcends its own nature. It was necessary that the only-begotten Word of God who brought Himself down to the level of self-emptying, should not repudiate the low estate arising from that self-emptying, but should accept what is full by nature on account of the humanity, not for His own sake, but for ours, who lack every good thing.   Cyril of Alexandria

Humiliation

A little fire softens a large piece of wax. So, too, a small indignity often softens, sweetens and wipes away suddenly all the fierceness, insensibility and hardness of our heart.   John Climacus

Humility

The most easy, brief and safe path to heaven is humility. This is the only safe and undangerous path. <u>Joseph the Hesychast</u>

All Saints through humility were elevated, honored, glorified, made wondrous and sanctified by God. If you take away humility no one would be.

<u>bid</u>

... Inner and real humility is for one to feel, that whatever he has, life, health, wealth, wisdom all are foreign, are gifts of God. <u>bid</u>

...The only hope of salvation from the delusions and the heresies, the innovations and the traps of wicked people and of the devil is prayer, repentance and humility. <u>Ibid</u>

"The Lord does not forbid us to desire to become His favorites, for He wants us to desire advancement in the spiritual life. But He does not want us to grasp for honors and privileges, but rather to acquire the heights by humility." <u>Theophylact</u>

Paul writes, 'I know of nothing against myself, yet I am not justified by this' (1 Cor. 4:4). You see he does not exalt himself, but humbles and abases himself in every way, and that just when he had reached the summit. And the Three Children were in the fire, in the midst of the furnace, and what did they say? 'For we have sinned and transgressed by departing from You; and we have done evil in every way' (Dan. 3:29). This is what it is to have a contrite heart.   John Chrysostom

---

If the grace of God comes, everyone and everything changes; however, in order for it to come, we must humble ourselves first.   Porphyrios

---

God gives us His Grace, when we are humble.   Ibid

If you are enclosed within yourself through prayer, humility, and mourning, you will find a spiritual treasure -- only let pride and criticism be far from you.   Ephraim of Philotheou

---

6. May you love one another and not be embittered by reason of egotism. Humility is a sure guide; it does not allow the one who has it to strike against the reefs of carelessness and be crushed, but as a luminous guide it leads faultlessly to safety.   Ibid

---

I think the quality needed is a certain deep humility of mind that enables one to accept other ways of looking at things, other emphases, as equally Orthodox with one's own.   Seraphim Rose

---

'Know yourself': this is true humility, the humility that teaches us to be inwardly humble and makes our heart contrite. Such humility you must cultivate and guard. For if you do not yet know yourself you cannot know what humility is, and have not yet embarked truly on the task of cultivating and guarding. To know oneself is the goal of the practice of the virtues.

Nikitas Stithatos

Reading and spiritual knowledge are good, but only when they lead to greater humility.   Peter of Damaskos

A single raising of your mind to God, and a single humble genuflexion to His glory and in His honor has infinitely more value than all the treasures of the world.   Lorenzo Scupoli

The more a man is found worthy to receive God's gifts, the more he ought to consider himself a debtor to God, who has raised him from the earth and bestowed on dust the privilege of imitating to some degree its Creator and God. For to endure injustice with joy, patiently to do good to one's enemies, to lay down one's own life for one's neighbor, and so on, are gifts from God, bestowed on those who are resolved to receive them from Him through their solicitude in cultivating and protecting what has been entrusted to them, as Adam was commanded to do (cf. Gen. 2:15)."   Peter of Damascus

True humility does not say humble words, nor does it assume humble looks, it does not force oneself either to think humbly of oneself, or to abuse oneself in self-belittlement. Although all such things are the beginning, the manifestations and the various aspects of humility, humility itself is grace, given from above. There are two kinds of humility, as the holy fathers teach: to deem oneself the lowest of all beings and to ascribe to God all one's good actions. The first is the beginning, the second the end.   Gregory of Sinai

We have never achieved anything good on our own, but all good things are ours from God by grace, and come as it were from nothingness into being. For 'what do you have which you did not receive?' asks Paul - receive, that is, freely from God; 'and if you received it, why do you boast as if you had not received it' (1 Cor. 4:7), but had achieved it by yourself? Yet by yourself you cannot achieve anything, for the Lord has said: 'Without Me, you can do nothing' (John 15:5).   Peter of Damascus

A brother from Abbot Poemen's neighborhood left to go to another country one day. There he met an anchorite. The latter was very charitable and many came to see him. The brother told him about Abbot Poemen. When he heard of his virtue, the anchorite wanted to see him. Some times afterwards when the brother had returned to Egypt the anchorite went there to see the brother who had formerly paid him a visit. He had told him where he lived.

When he saw him, the brother was astonished and very pleased. The anchorite said to him, "Please, will you be so kind as to take me to Abbot Poemen?" So he brought him to the old man and presented him, saying, "This is a great man, full of charity, who is held in high estimation in his district. I have spoken to him about you, and he has come because he wants to see you." So Abbot Poemen received him with joy. They greeted one another and sat down.

The visitor began to speak of the Scriptures, of spiritual and of heavenly things. But Abbot Poemen turned his face away and answered nothing. Seeing that he did not speak to him, the other went away deeply grieved and said to the brother who had brought him, "I have made this long journey in vain. For I have come to see the old man, and he does not wish to speak to me."

Then the brother went inside to Abbot Poemen and said to him, "Abbot, this great man who has so great a reputation in his own country has come here because of you. Why did you not speak to him?" The old man said, "He is great and speaks of heavenly things and I am lowly and speak of earthly things. If he had spoken of the passions of the soul, I should have replied, but he speaks to me of spiritual things and I know nothing about that."

Then the brother came outside and said to the visitor, "The old man does not readily speak of the Scriptures, but if anyone consults him about the passions of the soul, he replies." Filled with compunction, the visitor returned to the old man and said to him, "What should I do, Abbot, for the passions of the soul master me?"

The old man turned towards him and replied joyfully, "This time, you come as you should. Now open your mouth concerning this and I will fill it with good things." Greatly edified, the other said to him, "Truly, this is the right way!"

He returned to his own country giving thanks to God that he had been counted worthy to meet so great a saint.   The Desert Fathers

---

A brother questioned Abbot Motius, saying, "If I go to dwell somewhere, how do you want me to live?" The old man said to him, "If you live somewhere, do not seek to be known for anything special {i.e. by setting oneself apart from the common practice of Christians}... For these things make an empty reputation and later you will be troubled because of this. For men rush there where they find these {special} practices." The brother said to him, "What shall I do, then?" The old man said, "Wherever you live, follow the same manner of life as everyone else and if you see devout men, whom you trust doing something, do the same and you will be at peace. For this is humility: to see yourself to be the same as the rest. When men see you do not go beyond the limits, they will consider you to be the same as everyone else and no-one will trouble you."   Abbot Motius

---

A brother questioned Abbot Poemen saying, "Give me a word." And he said to him, "The fathers put compunction as the beginning of every action." The brother said again, "Give me another word." The old man replied, "As far as you can, do some manual work so as to be able to give alms, for it is written that alms and faith purify from sin." The brother said, "What is faith?" The old man said, "Faith is to live humbly and to give alms."   The Desert Fathers

---

A brother questioned an old man, "Tell me something which I can do, so that I may live by it", and the old man said, "If you can bear to be despised, that is a great thing, more than all the other virtues."   Apophthegmata Patrum

---

A characteristic of those who are still progressing in blessed mourning is temperance and silence of the lips; and of those who have made progress – freedom from anger and patient endurance of injuries; and of the perfect – humility, thirst for dishonors, voluntary craving for involuntary afflictions, non- condemnation of sinners, compassion even beyond one's strength. The first are acceptable, the second laudable; but blessed are those who hunger for hardship and thirst for dishonor, for they shall be filled with the food whereof there can be no satiety.   John Climacus

---

A man who is truly humble is not troubled when he is wronged and he says nothing to justify himself against the injustice, but he accepts slander as truth; he does not attempt to persuade men that he is calumniated, but he begs forgiveness.   Isaac the Syrian

---

A person who suffers bitterly when slighted or insulted should recognize from this that he still harbors the ancient serpent in his breast. If he quietly endures the insult or responds with great humility, he weakens the serpent and lessens its hold. But if he replies acrimoniously or brazenly, he gives it strength to pour its venom into his heart and to feed mercilessly on his guts.

In this way the serpent becomes increasingly powerful; it destroys his soul's strength and his attempts to set himself right, compelling him to live for sin and to be completely dead to righteousness.   Symeon the New Theologian

---

Abbot Anthony said, "I saw the snares the enemy spreads out over the world and I said groaning, "What can escape from such snares?" Then I heard a voice saying to me, "Humility."   Anthony the Great

---

Abbot Cronius said that Abbot Joseph of Pelusium told him the following story

When I was living in Sinai, there was a brother who was good, ascetic, and handsome. He came to church for the Liturgy dressed in a little old mafort patched and darned all over. Once when I saw him coming to the Liturgy I said to him, "Brother, do you not see the brothers, looking like angels for the Liturgy in church? How can you always come here in that garb?" He said to me, "Forgive me, Abba, but I have nothing else." So I took him in to my cell and gave him a tunic and whatever else he needed.

After that he wore them like the other brethren and was like an angel to look at. Now once it was necessary for the fathers to send ten brethren to the emperor about something or other, and he was chosen as one of the group to go. When he heard this, the brother made a prostration before his Abba saying, "In the Lord's name, excuse me, for I am the slave of a great man there, and if he recognizes me, he will deprive me of my habit and force me to serve him again." The brothers were convinced and left him behind. But later, they learned from someone who had had known him well when he was in the world that he had been the head of imperial administration and that he had spoken as he did as a ruse, so that no one would know this or bother him about it. So great, amongst the fathers, was their concern to flee from glory and the peace of this world!   The Desert Fathers

Abbot John (the Dwarf) said, "Humility and the fear of God are above all virtues."   Ibid

---

Abbot John (the Dwarf) said, "Who sold Joseph" A brother replied saying, "It was his brethren." The old man said to him, "No, it was his humility which sold him, because he could have said, "I am their brother" and have objected, but, because he kept silence, he sold himself by his humility. It is also his humility which set him up as chief in Egypt."   Desert Fathers

---

Abbot John said, "Who sold Joseph" A brother replied saying, "It was his brethren." The old man said to him, "No, it was his humility which sold him, because he could have said, "I am their brother" and have objected, but, because he kept silence, he sold himself by his humility. It is also his humility, which set him up as chief in Egypt.   Ibid

---

Abbot Or gave this counsel, "Whenever you want to subdue your high and proud thoughts, examine your conscience carefully: Have you kept all the commandments? Have you loved your enemies and been kind to them in their misfortunes? Have you counted yourself to be an unprofitable servant and the worst of all sinners? If you find you have done all this, do not therefore think well of yourself as if you had done everything well but realize that even the thought of such things is totally destructive."   Ibid

---

Abbot Or said, "The crown of the monk is humility."   The Desert Fathers

---

Abbot Poemen said, "As the breath which comes out of his nostrils, so does a man need humility and the fear of God.   <u>bid</u>

Abbot Sisoes asked Abbot Or, "Give me a word," and he said to him, "Do you trust me?" He replied that he did. Then he said to him, "Go, and what you have seen me do, do also." Abbot Sisoes said to him, "Father, what have I seen you do?" The old man said, "In my own opinion, I put myself below all men."   <u>Ibid</u>

Also in this very same city (Ancyra) we found a monk who preferred not to be ordained to the priesthood. He had spent some time in the army and had now spent twenty years as an ascetic. He lived with the bishop of the town. So great was his mercy and so kind was he that he went about at night and had mercy on the needy. He neglected neither the prison nor the hospital, neither the poor nor the rich, but he helped all. To some he gave words of good cheer, being himself stout of heart. Some he encouraged, others he reconciled; to some he gave bodily necessities, to others, clothing.

What is wont to happen in all great cities occurred here, too; for on the church porch there was gathered a crowd of people, some unmarried, others married, lying there for their gifts of daily food. It happened one time in winter that a woman was lying in labor on the church porch at midnight. He heard her crying out in pain. Leaving his customary prayers, he went out and looked at her. He found no midwife, but instead took the midwife's place, not at all squeamish about the unpleasant aspects of childbirth, for the mercy, which worked in him, had rendered him insensible to such things.

Now his clothes are not worth an obol, and his food is about equally cheap. He cannot stand to bend over a writing-table -- his love of humanity drags him away from books. If someone gives him a book as a present, he sells it immediately, saying to the jeering bystanders: "How can I persuade my Teacher that I have mastered His lessons, unless I sell His own Word to practice perfection?"   <u>Palladius</u>

Amma Theodora said that neither asceticism, nor vigils nor any kind of suffering are able to save, only true humility can do that. There was an anchorite who was able to banish the demons; and he asked them, "What makes you go away? Is it fasting?" They replied, "We do not eat or drink." "Is it vigils" They replied, "We do not sleep." "Is it separation from the world?" "We live in the deserts." "What power sends you away then?" They said, "Nothing can overcome us, but only humility." (Amma Theodora said) "Do you see how humility is victorious over the demons?"

The Desert Fathers

An Athonite elder said, "Humility acts like a magnet, drawing to it the grace of God. The humble are granted grace. These things are arranged.

Athonite Gerontikon

An angel fell from heaven without any other passion except pride, and so we may ask whether it is possible to ascend to Heaven by humility alone, without any other of the virtues.   John Climacus

An old man was asked, "What is humility?" and he said in reply, "Humility is a great work, and a work of God. The way of humility is to undertake bodily labor and believe yourself a sinner and make yourself subject to all." Then a brother said, "What does it mean, to be subject to all?" The old man answered, "To be subject to all is not to give your attention to the sins of others but always to give your attention to your own sins and to pray without ceasing to God."   The Desert Fathers

An old man was asked, 'How can I find God?' He said, 'In fasting, in watching, in labors, in devotion, and, above all, in discernment. I tell you, many have injured their bodies without discernment and have gone away from us having achieved nothing. Our mouths smell bad through fasting, we know the Scriptures by heart, we recite all the Psalms of David, but we have not that which God seeks: charity and humility.'   The Desert Fathers

An old man who lived in the desert as a hermit thought that he had attained perfection in the virtues. He prayed to God, saying, "Show me perfection of the soul, and I will do it." God wanted to humble him in his thoughts, and said to him, "Go to this Archimandrite (monastic superior), and do whatever he tells you."

Then God revealed to the Archimandrite, before the other one came to him, "Look, this hermit is coming to you. Tell him to take a whip and go take care of your pigs." When the old man came, he knocked on the door and entered the archimandrite's presence. After they had greeted one another, they sat down. The hermit who had come said to him, "Tell me what to do that I may be saved." The other one said, "You will do whatever I tell you?" And he replied, "Certainly." And he said to him, "Then take a whip and go care for the pigs." Those who had known the hermit or had heard about him, when they saw that he was taking care of the pigs, said, "Have you seen that great hermit about whom we were hearing? He has lost his wits, and is possessed by a demon, and takes care of pigs." When God saw his humility in patiently enduring the taunts of others, he commanded him to return to his home.

Ibid

As in all things to the good, God is prepared to help man acquire humility. Yet man himself must take care of himself. The Holy Fathers say "render up blood and receive spirit." This means, struggle even to the point of giving up your blood, and you will receive a spiritual gift. While you seek after and ask for spiritual gifts, you are unwilling to shed your blood. That is, you want everything, but do not want to be bothered or disturbed by anyone. But can one ever acquire humility living a life of tranquility? Humility consists of seeing oneself as the worst of all, not only of people, but even of dumb beasts, even the evil spirits themselves. Then, when people disturb you, you are aware that you cannot stand it, and that you become angry with people; involuntarily, you then will consider yourself to be a bad person... If in the process you regret being bad, and reproach yourself as incorrigible, if you truly repent of this before God and your spiritual father, then you will already be on the path to humility. Now were no one to bother you, were you live in tranquility, how could you become conscious of your badness? If they are trying to demean you, they want to humble you. You yourself are asking God for humility. Why then should you lament over people?

Amvrossy of Optina

As in all things to the good, God is prepared to help man acquire humility. Yet man himself must take care of himself. The Holy Fathers say "render up blood and receive spirit." This means, struggle even to the point of giving up your blood, and you will receive a spiritual gift. While you seek after and ask for spiritual gifts, you are unwilling to shed your blood. That is, you want everything, but do not want to be bothered or disturbed by anyone. But can one ever acquire humility living a life of tranquility?

Humility consists of seeing oneself as the worst of all, not only of people, but even of dumb beasts, even the evil spirits themselves. And then, when people disturb you, you are aware that you cannot stand it, and that you become angry with people; involuntarily, you then will consider yourself to be a bad person... If in the process you regret being bad, and reproach yourself as incorrigible, if you truly repent of this before God and your spiritual father, then you will already be on the path to humility. But were no one to bother you, were you live in tranquility, how could you become conscious of your badness? If they are trying to demean you, they want to humble you. You yourself are asking God for humility. Why then should you lament over people? Counsels of the   Amvrossy of Optina

As long as you have bad habits do not reject hardship, so that through it you may be humbled and eject your pride.   Maximus the Confessor

As we consider our own selves and come to know our misfortune and wretchedness, we shall have reason enough to be humble. We are born naked and with a cry. We live in calamity, misfortune, and sins. We die with fear, disease, and sighing. We are buried in the earth and return to the earth. There it is not evident where the rich man lies, where the poor, where the noble and where the lowly, where the master and where the servant, where the wise and where the foolish. There they are all made equal, for they all return to the earth. Why, then, should earth and corruption be conceited?

Tikhon of Zadonsk

As with the appearance of light, darkness retreats; so, at the fragrance of humility, all anger and bitterness vanishes.   John Climacus

At the Last Judgment the righteous will be recognized only by their humility and their considering themselves worthless, and not by good deeds, even if they have done them. This is the true attitude.   Peter of Damascus

BROTHER: And what is internal humility?

OLD MAN: The humility of love, peace, friendship, purity, restfulness, tranquility, subjection, faith, remoteness from envy, and a soul which is free from the heat of anger, and is far from the grade of arrogance, and is redeemed from the love of vainglory, and is full of patient endurance like the great deep, and whose motion is drawn after the knowledge of the spirit, and before whose eyes are depicted the fall of the body, and the greatness of the marvel of the Resurrection, and the demand for judgment which shall come after the revivification, and its standing before the awful throne of God. If the soul has these things, redemption shall be unto it. "   The Desert Fathers

Behold, this is the true and the Christian humility. In this you will be able to achieve victory over every vice, by attributing to God rather than to yourself the fact that you have won. <u>John Climacus</u>

Believe that dishonors and reproaches are medicines that heal the pride of your soul, and pray for those who reproach you, as for true physicians of your soul, being assured that he who hates dishonor, hates humility, and he who avoids those who grieve him, flees from meekness. <u>Dorotheos</u>

Now when the Holy Spirit dwells in the heart of a person, He shows him all his inner poverty and weakness, and the corruption of his heart and soul, and his separation from God; and with all his virtues and righteousness. He shows him his sins, his sloth and indifference regarding the salvation and good of people his self-seeking in his apparently most disinterested virtues, his coarse selfishness even where he does not suspect it. To be brief, the Holy Spirit shows him everything as it really is. Then a person begins to have true humility, begins to lose hope in his own powers and virtues, and regards himself as the worst of men. And when a person humbles himself before Jesus Christ Who alone is Holy in the glory of God the Father, he begins to repent truly, and resolves never again to sin but to live more carefully. And if he really has some virtues, then he sees clearly that he practiced and practices them only with the help of God, and therefore he begins to put his trust only in God. <u>Innocent of Irkutsk</u>

Confess yourself to be saved by grace, that He may profess Himself a debtor to you; and not for your good works only, but also for such rightness of mind. For when we do good works, we have Him debtor for our good works only; but when we do not so much as think we have done any good work, then also for this disposition itself; and more for this, than for the other things: so that this is equivalent to our good works.   John Chrysostom

---

Consciously look on yourself as an ant or a worm, so that you can become a man formed by God. If you fail to do the first, the second cannot happen. The lower you descend, the higher you ascend; and when, like the psalmist, you regard yourself as nothing before the Lord (cf. Ps. 39:5), then imperceptibly you will grow great. And when you begin to realize that you have nothing and know nothing, then you will become rich in the Lord through practice of the virtues and spiritual knowledge.   Theognostos

---

Consider well, brethren, how great is the power of humility. Consider how great is the spiritual energy behind saying, 'Pardon me.' Why is the devil called not only 'enemy,' but also 'adversary'? He is called 'enemy' because he is a hater of man, one who hates what is good, a traitor; and 'adversary,' because he always puts obstacles in the way of good. If someone wants to pray he puts obstacles in the way through evil suspicions, shameful thoughts, and spiritual torpor. If a man wants to give alms he obstructs it through avarice or procrastination. If a man wants to keep vigil he obstructs it with hesitations or laziness. In every single thing he is against us when we desire to do good. This is why he is called the enemy and the adversary and why, by lowliness, all his attacks and devices are brought to nothing.

Dorotheos of Gaza

Do not become a disciple of one who praises himself, in case you learn pride instead of Humility.   Mark the Ascetic

---

Even if an angel should indeed appear to you, do not receive him but humiliate yourself, saying, 'I am not worthy to see an angel, for I am a sinner.'   Clement of Rome

---

Extirpate two thoughts within yourself: do not consider yourself worthy of anything great, and do not think that any other man is much lower than you in worth. Learn humble mindedness beforehand, which the Lord commanded in word and showed forth in deed. Hence, do not expect obedience from others, but be ready for obedience yourself.   Basil

---

For nothing is so acceptable to God as to number one's self with the last. This is a first principle of all practical wisdom. For he that is humbled, and bruised in heart, will not be vainglorious, will not be wrathful, will not envy his neighbor, and will not harbor any other passion. For neither when a hand is bruised, though we strive ten thousand times, shall we be able to lift it up on high. If therefore we were thus to bruise our heart likewise, though it were stirred by ten thousand swelling passions, it could not be lifted up, no, not ever so little.   John Chrysostom

---

For this reason the Lord calls blessed those who are opposed to worldly possessions, saying: `Blessed are the poor in spirit, for theirs is the kingdom of heaven.' Why to the words, `Blessed are the poor,' does He add, `in spirit'? So that by this would be shown that He considers blessedness to be the humility of the soul. Why did He not say, blessed are the poor-spirited - and thus would be demonstrated the humility of thinking - but rather He says, `poor in spirit'? By this He wants to teach us that bodily poverty is also a blessedness, in that through this one can receive the kingdom of heaven, when it is done for the sake of the humility of the soul. This is the case when bodily poverty is united with the humility of the soul and when it is for the person the principle of the humility of the soul. Having called blessed `those poor in spirit,' He demonstrated in a wonderful way what are the root and cause of the visible poverty of the saints - that is, their spirit.

Gregory Palamas

God descends to the humble as waters flow down from the hills into the valleys. John of Kronstadt

---

Has someone offended you? Guard your breast with the sign of the Cross; remember what took place on the Cross, and all will be extinguished. Think not of offenses only, but recall also whatever good you have received from the one who has offended you, and at once you shall grow meek. Bring to mind the fear of God, and quickly you shall grow more temperate and calm. Train yourself not to offend another during offenses themselves, and then, when offended, you wilt not feel grief. Think to yourself that he who is offending you is in a frenzy and not in his right mind, and then you wilt not be vexed at the offense. John Chrysostom

---

Having fallen from his heavenly rank through pride, the devil constantly strives to bring down also all those who wholeheartedly wish to approach the Lord; and he uses the same means, which caused his own downfall, that is pride and love of vainglory. These and similar things are the means by which the demons fight us and hope to separate us from God.

Moreover, knowing that he who loves his brother loves also God, they put into our hearts hatred of one another - and this to such degree that at times a man cannot bear to see his brother or say a word to him. Many have performed truly great labors of virtue, but have ruined themselves through folly. It would not be surprising if the same thing were to happen to you too; if, for example, having cooled towards active work, you begin to imagine that you already possess virtues. For there you have already fallen into that devilish disease (high opinion of yourself), thinking that you are close to God and are in the light, whereas in actual fact you are in darkness.

What made our Lord Jesus Christ lay aside his garments, gird himself with a towel, and, pouring water into a basin, begin to wash the feet of those who were below Him (John 13:4, etc.), if not to teach us humility? For it was humility He showed us by example of what He then did. And indeed those who want to be accepted into the foremost rank cannot achieve this otherwise than through humility; for in the beginning the thing that caused downfall from heaven was a movement of pride. So, if a man lacks extreme humility, if he is not humble with all his heart, all his mind, all his spirit, all his soul and body - he will not inherit the kingdom of God.   Anthony the Great

He who fights this adversary by bodily hardship and sweat is like one who has tied his foe with a string. But he who opposes him by temperance, sleeplessness and vigil is like one who puts a yoke on him. He who opposes him by humility, freedom from irritability and thirst is like one who has killed his enemy and hidden him in the sand. And by sand, I mean humility, because it produces no fodder for the passions, but is mere earth and ashes.

John Climacus

He, therefore, who sets himself to act evilly and yet wishes others to be silent, is a witness against himself, for he wishes himself to be loved more than the truth, which he does not wish to be defended against himself. There is, of course, no man who so lives as not sometimes to sin, but he wishes truth to be loved more than himself, who wills to be spared by no one against the truth. Wherefore, Peter willingly accepted the rebuke of Paul; David willingly hearkened to the reproof of a subject. For good rulers who pay no regard to self-love, , take as a homage to their humility the free and sincere words of subjects. But in this regard the office of ruling must be tempered with such great are of moderation, that the minds of subjects, when demonstrating themselves capable of taking right views in some matters, are given freedom of expression, but freedom that does not issue into pride, otherwise, when liberty of speech is granted too generously, the humility of their own lives will be lost.   Gregory the Great

He, who grieves sorely in his heart when dishonored or offended by others, ought to know from this that he bears within himself the ancient serpent. If he will bear the offense in silence, or will answer the one offending him with deep humility, then he has thereby weakened and crushed this serpent.

Simeon the New Theologian

Hold faith and humility fast within you; for through them you will find mercy, help, and words spoken by God in the heart, along with a protector who stands beside you both secretly and manifestly. Do you wish to obtain these things, which are a fountain of life? From the very onset take hold of simplicity. Walk before God in simplicity and not with knowledge. Simplicity is attended by faith; but subtle and intricate deliberations, by conceit; and conceit is attended by separation from God.   Isaac the Syrian

---

Humility is the only thing we need; one can still fall having virtues other than humility -- but with humility one does not fall.   Benedict of Nusia

---

I have seen pride lead to humility. Also, I remembered him who said: Who has known the mind of the Lord? The pit and offspring of conceit is a fall; but a fall is often an occasion of humility for those who are willing to use it to their advantage.   John Climacus

---

I know a man who kept no long strict fasts, no vigils, did not sleep on bare earth, imposed on himself no other specially arduous tasks; but, recollecting in memory his sins, understood his worthlessness and, having judged himself, became humble - and for this alone the most compassionate Lord saved him; as the divine David says: 'The Lord is nigh unto them that are of a broken heart; and saves such as be of a contrite spirit' (Ps. 34:18). In short, he trusted the words of the Lord and for his faith the Lord received him.

I once caught this mad imposter (pride) as it was rising in my heart, bearing on its shoulders its mother, vainglory. Roping them with the noose of obedience and thrashing them with the whip of humility, I demanded how they got access to me. At last, when flogged, they said: "we have neither beginning nor birth, for we are progenitors and parents of all the passions. Contrition of heart that is born of obedience is our real enemy; we cannot bear to be subject to anyone; that is why we fell from Heaven, though we had authority there.

"In brief, we are the parents of all that opposes humility; for everything which furthers humility, opposes us. We hold sway everywhere, save in Heaven, so where will you run from our presence? We often accompany dishonors, and obedience, and freedom from anger, and lack of resentment, and service. Our offspring are the falls of spiritual men: anger, calumny, spite, irritability, shouting, blasphemy, hypocrisy, hatred, envy, disputation, self-will and disobedience.

There is only one thing in which we have no power to meddle; and we shall tell you this, for we cannot bear your blows: If you keep up a sincere condemnation of yourself before the Lord, you can count us as weak as a cobweb. For pride's saddle horse, as you see, is vainglory, on which I am mounted." But holy humility and self-accusation laugh at both the horse and its rider, happily singing the song of victory: Let us sing to the Lord, for gloriously is He glorified: horse and rider has He hurled into the sea (Exodus 15:1) and into the abyss of humility.   John Climacus

I saw the snares that the enemy spreads out over the world and I said groaning, "What can get through from such snares?" Then I heard a voice saying to me, "Humility."   Anthony the Great

I shall tell you something strange, but do not be surprised by it. Should you fail to attain dispassion because of the predispositions dominating you, but at the time of your death be in the depths of humility, you will be exalted above the clouds no less than the man who is dispassionate.   John Climacus

If the indestructible might of the unfading kingdom is given to the humble and the meek, who would at this point be so deprived of love and desire that the divine gifts as not to tend as much as possible toward humility and meekness to become, to the extent that this is possible for man, the image of God's kingdom by bearing in himself by grace the exact configuration in the Spirit to Christ, Who is truly by nature and essence the Great King?

Maximus the Confessor

If you wilt endure an offensive word, then you have extinguished an ember. But if you wilt think about it, then, like someone kindling a fire, you wilt produce smoke, which is confusion. However, one can conveniently extinguish it too by silence, prayer and a bow from the heart.   Dorotheos

If we are concerned with our salvation, there are many things the intellect can do in order to secure for us the blessed gift of humility. For example, it can recollect the sins we have committed in word, action and thought; and there are many other things which, reviewed in contemplation, contribute to our humility. True humility is also brought about by meditating daily on the achievements of our brethren, by extolling their natural superiorities and by comparing our gifts with theirs. When the intellect sees in this way how worthless we are and how far we fall short of the perfection of our brethren, we will regard ourselves as dust and ashes, and not as men but as some kind of cur, more defective in every aspect and lower than all men on earth.

Hesychius the Priest

If you cannot be merciful, at least speak as though you are a sinner. If you are not a peacemaker, at least do not be a troublemaker. If you cannot be assiduous, at least in your thought be like a sluggard. If you are not victorious, do not exalt yourself over the vanquished. If you cannot close the mouth of a man who disparages his companion at least refrain from joining him in this.   Isaac the Syrian

If, according to the example of Abraham and Job, we think that we are earth and ashes, then we shall never be robbed, but we will always have something to give to others: not gold and silver, but an example of humility, patience, and love toward God. May there be glory to Him forever.

                                                     Barsanuphius & John

In all respects belittle yourself before all men, and you will be raised above the princes of this age.   Isaac the Syrian

In answer to your question as to what constitutes a happy life, whether splendor, fame and wealth, or a quiet, peaceful, family life, I will say that I agree with the latter, but will add the following: A life lived in humility and with an irreproachable conscience brings peace, tranquility, and true happiness. But wealth, honor, glory and exalted position often serve as the cause of a multitude of sins, and such happiness is not one on which to rely.

                                                     Makary of Optina

Increasing self-criticism is the sign of increasing humility. Indeed, there is no clearer sign.   John Climacus

---

It is better for your soul that you confess yourself as guilty in everything and as being the least of all, than to run to self-justification, something that comes from pride. God opposes the proud, and renders grace unto the humble. Counsels of   Hilarion of Optina

---

It is one thing to be humble, another to strive for humility, and another to praise the humble. The first belongs to the perfect, the second to the truly obedient, and the third to all the faithful.   John Climacus

---

It is useless to accuse those around us and those who live with us of somehow interfering with or being an impediment to our salvation and spiritual perfection... Spiritual or emotional dissatisfaction comes from within ourselves, from inexperience and from poorly conceived opinions we do not want to abandon, but which bring on doubt, embarrassment, and misunderstanding. All of this tires and burdens us, and brings us to a sorry state. We would do well to comprehend the Holy Fathers' simple advice: If we will humble ourselves, we will find tranquility anywhere, without having to mentally wander about many other places, where we might have the same, or even worse, experiences. Counsels of the   Amvrossy of Optina

---

It is useless to accuse those around us and those who live with us of somehow interfering with or being an impediment to our salvation and spiritual perfection... Spiritual or emotional dissatisfaction comes from within ourselves, from inexperience and from poorly conceived opinions we do not want to abandon, but which bring on doubt, embarrassment, and misunderstanding. All of this tires and burdens us, and brings us to a sorry state. We would do well to comprehend the Holy Fathers' simple advice: If we will humble ourselves, we will find tranquility anywhere, without having to mentally wander about many other places, where we might have the same, or even worse, experiences.   Amvrossy of Optina

It was said of Abbot Arsenius that once when he was ill at Scetis, the priest came to take him to church and put him on a bed with a small pillow under his head. Now behold, and old man who was coming to see him, saw him lying on a bed with a little pillow under his head and he was shocked and said, "Is this really Abbot Arsenius, this man lying down like this?"

The priest took him aside and said to him, "In the village where you lived, what was your trade?" "I was a shepherd," he replied. "And how did you live?" "I had a very hard life." Then the priest said to him, "And how do you live in your cell now?" The other replied, "I am more comfortable." Then the priest said to him, "Do you see this Abbot Arsenius? When he was in the world he was the guardian of the emperor, surrounded by thousands of slaves with golden girdles, all wearing collars of gold and garments of silk. Beneath him were spread rich coverings. While you were in the world as a shepherd you did not enjoy even the comforts you now have, but he no longer enjoys the delicate life he led in the world. So you are comforted while he is afflicted."

At these words, the old man was filled with compunction and prostrated himself saying, "Father, forgive me, for I have sinned. Truly the way this man follows is the way of truth, for it leads to humility, while mine leads to comfort." So the old man withdrew, edified.   The Desert Fathers

Know that when you do not possess calm, you do not have humility within you. The Lord revealed this in the following words, which indicate as well where to seek after calm. He said: "Learn of me, for I am meek and lowly of heart, and you shall find rest unto your souls" (Matthew 11:29).
                                                                Leo of Optina

Let all who are led by the spirit of God enter with us into this spiritual and wise assembly, holding in their spiritual hands the God-inscribed tablets of knowledge. We have come together, we have investigated, and we have probed the meaning of this precious inscription. And one man said: "It (humility) means constant oblivion of one's achievements." Another: "It is the acknowledgement of oneself as the last of all and the greatest sinner of all." And another: "The mind's recognition of one's weakness and impotence." Another again: "In fits of rage, it means to forestall one's neighbor and be first to stop the quarrel." And again another: "Recognition of Divine grace and divine compassion." And again another: "The feeling of a contrite soul, and the renunciation of one's own will." But when I had listened to all this and had attentively and soberly investigated it, I found that I had not been able to attain to the blessed perception of that virtue from what had been said. Therefore, last of all, having gathered what fell from the lips of those learned and blessed fathers as a dog gathers the crumbs that fall from the table, I too gave my definition of it and said: "Humility is a nameless grace in the soul, its name known only to those who have learned it by experience. It is unspeakable wealth, a name and gift from God, for it is said: "learn not from an angel, nor from man, nor from a book, but from Me, that is, from My indwelling, from My illumination and action in you; for I am meek and humble in heart and in thought and in spirit, and your soul shall find rest from conflicts and relief from thoughts." (Matthew 11:29)

John Climacus

Let our praise be in God, and not of ourselves; for God hates those that commend themselves. Let testimony to our good deeds be borne by others, as it was in the case of our righteous forefathers. Boldness, and arrogance, and audacity belong to those that are accursed of God; but moderation, humility, and meekness to such as are blessed by Him.   Clement

Let us beware therefore of saying anything about ourselves, for this renders us both odious with men and abominable to God. For this reason, the greater the good works we do, the less let us say of ourselves; this being the way to reap the greatest glory both with men and with God. Or rather, not only glory from God, but a reward, yea, a great recompense. Demand not therefore a reward that you may receive a reward. John Chrysostom

Make account that you have done nothing, and then you have done all. For if, being sinners, when we account ourselves to be what we are, we become righteous, as indeed the Publican did; how much more, when being righteous we account ourselves to be sinners. John Chrysostom

Man, as far as his body is concerned, is like a lighted candle. A candle must be consumed; thus also the body must die. But the soul is immortal, and so our care also must be more for the soul than for the body. 'For what shall it profit a man, if he shall gain the whole world, and lose his own soul' (Mk. 8:36). Seraphim of Sarov

Meekness and humility of heart are virtues without which it is impossible to inherit the Heavenly Kingdom, to be happy on earth, or to experience inner calm. Antony of Optina

Never disobey your spiritual teachers and fathers, but obey them willingly in everything, executing their orders quickly and readily, and especially those, which can teach you humility and go against your own will and inclination.

Lorenzo Scupoli

No man, wise in his own opinion, because he has studied all the sciences and is learned in external wisdom, will ever penetrate God's mysteries or see them unless he first humbles himself and becomes foolish in his heart, repudiating his self-opinion together with the acquirements of learning.

Simeon the New Theologian

Nothing else extinguishes passions so much as compassion. On the other hand, if someone struggles as a result of vainglory or with the idea that he is applying himself to virtue, he is not struggling with knowledge. He, though, who abstains with knowledge does not think he is exercising virtue, neither does he want to be commended as an ascetic, but believes that by way of abstinence prudence is obtained and that through this, comes humility.

Dorotheos

Nothing done in humility for the sake of God is bad. But things and pursuits differ. Everything not strictly necessary is a hindrance to salvation - everything, that is to say, that does not contribute to the soul's salvation or to the body's life. For it is not food, but gluttony, that is bad; not money, but attachment to it; not speech, but idle talk; not the world's delights, but dissipation; not love of one's family, but the neglect of God that such love may produce; not the clothes worn only for covering and protection from cold and heat, but those that are excessive and costly; not houses that also protect us from heat and cold, as well as anything human or animal that might harm us, but houses with two or three floors, large and expensive;...not friendship, but the having of friends who are of no benefit to one's soul; not woman, but unchastity; not wealth but avarice; not wine but drunkenness; not anger used in accordance with nature for the chastisement of sin, but its use against one's fellow-men.   Peter of Damaskos

Oh Lord, my heart is not exalted, neither have mine eyes been lifted up."
This Psalm, a short one... teaches us the lesson of humility and meekness.
Now, as we have in a great number of other places spoken about humility,
there is no need to repeat the same things here. Of course we are bound to
bear in mind in how great need our faith stands of humility when we hear the
Prophet thus speaking of it as the equivalent to the performance of the
highest works: "Oh Lord, my heart is not exalted." For a troubled heart is the
noblest sacrifice in the eyes of God. The heart, therefore, must not be lifted
up by prosperity, but humbly kept within the bounds of meekness through the
fear of God.   Hilary of Poitiers

Once a spiritual brother of mine and I visited Zosimas, a Russian hermit at
Karoulia (on Mt. Athos). We found him seated on the ground chopping
firewood. We asked for his blessing, venerated the icons of the small church,
and then asked him to tell us something comforting. Only then did he lift us
his joyful face and utter one word in Russian. It was a word that contains the
entire immense spiritual life of man: "Smirenia, smerenia," he said, which
means humility. Nothing else. He put his head down again and patiently
continued to chop the few bits of firewood he had for the winter.

Athonite Gerontikon

One day Abbot Arsenius consulted an old Egyptian monk about his own
thoughts. Someone noticed this and said to him, "Abbot Arsenius, how is it
that you with such a good Latin and Greek education, ask this peasant about
your thoughts?" He replied, "I have indeed been taught Greek and Latin, but
I do not know even the alphabet of this peasant."   The Desert Fathers

One elder passed seventy weeks in fasting, eating food only twice a week, as
he begged the Lord to reveal to him the meaning of a passage in Holy
Scripture. But God would not reveal it to him. Seeing this, the elder said to

himself, "I have labored long and hard, and I have accomplished nothing. I will go to my brother and ask him."

When he had left his cell and locked the door behind him, an angel from the Lord appeared and said to him: "Seventy weeks of fasting did not bring you nearer to God. Now, however, when you have humbled yourself and resolved to go to your brother with your question, I have been sent to you to explain the meaning of this passage." And fulfilling this, the angel departed.

Paterikon

Our humility is our surest intercessor before the face of the Lord. It is by dint of humility and penance that the last shall be first.　　Macarius of Optina

Our prayer begins to be of value only when grace comes. As long as we have only the natural fruits of prayer, what we achieve is valueless, both in itself and in the judgment of God. For the coming of grace is the sign that God has looked on us in mercy.　　Halassius

Pointing out that man has nothing of which to be proud, the　added "Actually, what does man have to crow about? A ragged, wretched beggar cries out for alms: 'Have Mercy! Have Mercy!' But as to whether he will be shown mercy, who knows?"　　Amvrossy of Optina

Pray Simply. Do not expect to find in your heart any remarkable gift of prayer Consider yourself unworthy of it-then you will find peace. Use the empty, cold dryness of your prayer as food for your humility. Repeat constantly: "I am not worthy, Lord, I am not worthy!" But say it calmly, without agitation. This humble prayer will be acceptable to God.

Pray simply. Do not expect to find in your heart any remarkable gift of prayer. Consider yourself unworthy of it. Then you will find peace. Use the empty cold dryness of your prayer as food for your humility. Repeat constantly: I am not worthy; Lord, I am not worthy! But say it calmly, without agitation.   Macarius of Optina

Q: How can one be saved in the present times?

A: In every time, if a man can cut off his own will in everything, and have a humble heart, and death always before his eyes – he can be saved, by God's grace; and wherever he might be, fear does not take possession of him, for such a one "forgets the things that are behind, and stretches forth to those that are before (Philemon 3:13). Act accordingly, and you will be saved by God without sorrow. "   Barsanuphius and John

Q: Pray that I might place a beginning to salvation.

A: The beginning is humility and the fear of God: "The fear of God is the beginning of wisdom" (Proverbs 1:7). And what is the beginning of wisdom, if it is not to remove oneself from everything hateful to God? Also, how does one remove oneself from this? Do nothing without questioning and counsel; likewise, say nothing unfitting, and at the same time acknowledge oneself to be senseless, unsalted, and degraded, and in general insignificant."   Ibid

Q: When I do something good, how should I humble my thoughts? And how does one reproach oneself after doing something good?

A: For humility of thoughts, even though you might have performed all good deeds and kept all the commandments, remember Him Who said: "When you have done all this, say that we are unprofitable slaves, for we were obliged to do what we have done" (Luke 17:10) – and all the more when we have not even attained as yet to the fulfilling of a single commandment.

Thus one should always think and reproach oneself at every good deed and say to oneself: I do not know whether it is pleasing to God. It is a great work to do according to God's Will, and yet greater to fulfill the Will of God: this is the joining of all the commandments; for to do something according to God's Will is a private matter and is less than fulfilling the Will of God.

Therefore the Apostle said: "Forgetting what is behind, and stretching forth to what is ahead" (Philemon 3:13). And no matter how much he stretched out to what was ahead, he did not stop and always saw himself as insufficient, and he advanced; for he said: "whatever is perfect, think on this"(Philemon 3:15), that is, so as to advance. "   bid

---

Repentance and humility establish the soul. Charity and meekness strengthen it.   Evagrius

---

Self-accusation before God is something that is very necessary for us; and humility of heart is extremely advantageous in our lives, above all at the time of prayer. For prayer requires great attention and needs a proper awareness, otherwise it will turn out to be unacceptable and rejected, and `it will be turned back empty' to our bosom.   Martyrius of Edessa

---

Self-accusation before God is something that is very necessary for us; and humility of heart is extremely advantageous in our lives, above all at the time of prayer. For prayer requires great attention and needs a proper awareness, otherwise it will turn out to be unacceptable and rejected, and `it will be turned back empty' to our bosom.   Martyrius of Edessa

Self-accusation before God is something that is very necessary for us; and humility of heart is extremely advantageous in our lives, above all at the time of prayer. For prayer requires great attention and needs a proper awareness, otherwise it will turn out to be unacceptable and rejected, and `it will be turned back empty' to our bosom.   Symeon the New Theologian

Some visitors came to the Thebaid one day to visit an old man, bringing one possessed with a devil that he might heal him. When they persistently asked him, the old man said to the devil, "Come out of God's creature." And the devil said to the old man, "I am going to come out, but I am going to ask you a question. Tell me, who are the goats and who are the sheep?" The old man said, "I am one of the goats, but as for the sheep, God alone knows who they are." When he heard this, the devil began to cry out with a loud voice, "Because of your humility, I am driven away!" and he departed at the same hour.   The Desert Fathers

Tame your steed with the bridle of knowledge, lest, looking here and there, he become inflamed with lust towards women and men and throw you, the horseman, to the ground. Pray to God, that He may turn "your eyes, lest they see vanity" (Psalms 118:37). Also, when you will acquire a manful heart, warfare will depart from you.

Cleanse yourself, as wine cleanses wounds, and do not allow stench and filthiness to accumulate in you. Acquire weeping, so that it might remove from you freedom (looseness) in your relations, which destroys the souls that adopt it. Do not throw away the implement without which fertile land cannot be worked. This implement, made by the Great God, is humility: it uproots all the tares from the field of the Master and gives grace to those who dwell in it. Humility does not fall, but raises from a fall those who possess it. Love weeping with all your heart, for it also is a participant in this good work.

Labor in everything to cut off your own will, for this is accounted to a man for sacrifice. This is what is meant by: "For You we are mortified all the day, we are accounted as sheep for slaughter" (Psalms 43:22). Do not weaken yourselves by conversations, for they will not allow you to prosper in God. Firmly bridle the organs of your senses: sight, hearing, smelling, taste, and feeling, and you will prosper by the grace of Christ. Without tortures no one is a martyr, as the Lord also has said: "In your patience possess you your souls" (Luke 21:19), and the Apostle says, "in much endurance, in sorrows" (2 Corinthians 6:4). "   Barsanuphius and John

---

The Lord said, 'When you have done all that is commanded you, say: We are useless servants: we have only done what was our duty' (Luke 17:10). Thus the kingdom of heaven is not a reward for works, but a gift of grace prepared by the Master for His faithful servants.   Hesychius the Priest

---

The One Who used humble words with Paul, His persecutor, used the same humble words with the Pharisee. Humility is so powerful that even the all-conquering God did not conquer without it. Humility was even able to bear the burden of a stiff-necked nation in the desert. Moses, the humblest of men, was given charge of the nation that was the most stubborn of all men. God, Who needed nothing to save His people, later found Himself in need of the humility of Moses just to abide the grumbling and complaining of (His) critics. Only humility could tolerate the perversity of a nation that dismissed signs in Egypt as well as wonders in the desert. Whenever pride caused divisions in the nation, the prayer of humility healed their divisions. Now, if the humility of a tongue-tied man endured six hundred thousand, how much more does His humility endure, Who granted speech to the tongue-tied! For the humility of Moses is a (mere) shadow of the humility of our Lord.

Ephrem the Syrian

The Russian ascetic, Father Tychon, who lived sixty years on Mt. Athos after he had visited three hundred monasteries in Russian, said, "God blesses with one hand in the morning the entire world, and uses both hands to bless the humble man. A humble person is above the whole world."

Athonite Gerontikon

The appearance of this holy vine is one thing during the winter of the passions, another in the spring of fruit-blossom, yet another in the actual harvest of the virtues. Yet all these different stages concur in gladness and fruit-bearing, and therefore, they all have their own signs and sure indications of fruit to come. For as soon as the cluster of holy humility begins to blossom within us, we at once begin, though with an effort, to hate all human glory and praise, and to banish from ourselves irritation and anger. When this queen of virtues makes progress in our soul by spiritual growth, we regard all the good deeds accomplished by us as nothing, or rather as an abomination, supposing that everyday we add more and more to our burden by a dissipation that we do not comprehend. We suspect the very abundance of the Divine gifts showered upon us to be beyond our deserts and to aggravate our punishment. So our mind remains unplundered, reposing securely in the casket of modesty, only hearing the knocks and jeers of the thieves, without being subject to any of their threats; because modesty is an inviolable safe.

John Climacus

The brothers surrounded the same Abbot John (Cassian) was at the point of death and ready to depart eagerly and joyously to God. They asked him to leave them a concise and salutary saying as their inheritance, which would enable them to become perfect in Christ. Groaning he said to them, "I have never done my own will, not taught anything which I had not previously carried out."   The Desert Fathers

The first kind of humility is to hold my brother to be wiser than myself, and in all things to rate him higher than myself, and simply, as that holy man said, to put oneself below everyone. The second kind is to attribute to God all virtuous actions. This is the perfect humility of the saints. It is generated naturally in the soul by the performance of the commandments. It is just like a tree bearing much fruit: it is the fruit that bends the branches and lowers them down, but when there is no fruit, the branches point upwards and grow straight.   Dorotheos of Gaza

The heights of humility are great and so are the depths of boasting; I advise you to attend to the first and not to fall into the second.   Isidore of Pelusia

The humbler our opinion of ourselves, the more swiftly our prayer rises to God. So soon as we lose humility, each and every ascetic effort is nullified. If pride is active in us, or fault-finding, or unfriendliness, the Lord stands remote from us.   Archimandrite Sophrony

The more a person thinks in his soul that he is the most sinful of men, the more does hope increase and flourish within his heart by this humility, giving us the confidence that it will be our salvation.   Symeon the New Theologian

The natural property of the lemon tree is such that it lifts its branches upwards when it has no fruit, but the more the branches bend down the more fruit they bear. Those who have the mind to understand will grasp the meaning of this.   John Climacus

The old man (Abbot Moses) was asked, "What is the good of the fasts and watchings which a man imposes on himself?" and he replied, "They make the soul humble. For it is written, "Consider my affliction and my trouble, and forgive all my sins" (Psalm 25:18). So if the soul gives itself all this hardship, God will have mercy on it."   The Desert Fathers

The one who has come to understand the weakness of human nature has had experience of the divine power, and such a person who because of it has succeeded in some things and is eager to succeed in others never looks down on anyone. For he knows that in the same way that God has helped him and freed him from many passions and hardships, so can He help everyone when He wishes, especially those who are striving for His sake. Although for His own reasons He does not deliver all from their passions right away, still as a good and loving physician He heals in His own good time each one of those who are striving.   Maximus the Confessor

The power to bear Mysteries, which the humble man has received, which makes him perfect in every virtue without toil, this is the very power which the blessed apostles received in the form of fire. For its sake the Savior commanded them not to leave Jerusalem until they should receive power from on high, that is to say, the Paraclete, which, being interpreted, is the Spirit of consolation. And this is the Spirit of divine visions. Concerning this it is said in divine Scripture: 'Mysteries are revealed to the humble' [Ecclus 3:19]. The humble are accounted worthy of receiving in themselves this Spirit of revelations Who teaches mysteries.   Isaac the Syrian

The question of Abbot Dorotheus to the Great : I am being strongly attacked by sexual passion; I am afraid that I may fall into despondency, and that from the infirmity of my body I will not be able to restrain myself; pray for me, for the Lord's sake, and tell me, my Father, what I should do?

A: Brother! The devil, out of envy, has raised up warfare against you. Guard your eyes and do not eat until you are full. Take a little wine for the sake of the body's infirmity of which you speak. Acquire humility, which rends all the nets of the enemy.

And I, who am nothing, will do what I can, entreating God that He might deliver you from every temptation and preserve you from every evil. Do not yield to the enemy, Oh brother, and do not give yourself over to despondency, for this is a great joy to the enemy. Pray without ceasing, saying: "Lord Jesus Christ, deliver me from shameful passions," and God will have mercy on you, and you will receive strength by the prayers of the Saints. Amen. "   Barsanuphius and John

The soul that really loves God and Christ, though it may do ten thousand righteousnesses, esteems itself as having wrought nothing, by reason of its insatiable aspiration after God. Though it should exhaust the body with fastings, with watchings, its attitude towards the virtues is as if it had not yet even begun to labor for them.   Macarius the Great

The way of humility is this: self-control, prayer, and thinking yourself inferior to all creatures.   Abbot Pimen

There are certain kinds of trees, which never bear any fruit as long as their branches stay up straight, but if stones are hung on the branches to bend them down they begin to bear fruit. So it is with the soul. When it is humbled it begins to bear fruit, and the more fruit it bears the lowlier it becomes. So also the saints; the nearer they get to God, the more they see themselves as sinners.   Dorotheos of Gaza

There are certain kinds of trees, which never bear any fruit as long as their branches stay up straight, but if stones are hung on the branches to bend them down they begin to bear fruit. So it is with the soul. When it is humbled it begins to bear fruit, and the more fruit it bears the lowlier it becomes. So also the saints; the nearer they get to God, the more they see themselves as sinners.

I remember once we were speaking about humiliation and one of the great lights of Gaza, hearing us say, "The nearer a man is to God the more he sees himself to be a sinner," was astonished, and said, "How is this possible?" He did not know, and wanted to know the answer. I said to him, "Tell me, how do you regard yourself in respect to the other citizens here?"

And he said, "I regard myself as great, and among the first of the citizens." I said then, "If you went away to Caesaraea, how would you regard yourself then?" "I would value myself somewhat less than the great folk there." So I said, "If you went away to Antioch, what then?" And he replied, I would regard myself as one of the common people." I said, "And if you went into the presence of the Emperor, what would you think of yourself then?" He replied, "I should think of myself as just one of the poor." Then I said to him, "There you are! In the same way, the saints, the nearer they approach to God, the more they see themselves as sinners."   Dorotheus of Gaza

---

There is a humility that comes from the fear of God, and there is a humility that comes from the fervent love of God. One man is humbled because of his fear of God, another is humbled because of his joy. The man humbled from fear of God is possessed of modesty in his members, a right ordering of his senses, and a heart contrite at all times. But the man humbled because of joy is possessed of great exuberance and an open and insuppressible heart.

Isaac of Syria

Therefore, brothers, let us strive with all our heart, bearing death before our eyes every hour, and every moment imagining the fearful punishment. But these things the mind comes to perception and the soul is weighed down weeping, but it is also made contemplative and prepared to be turned toward God, undistracted by earthly things. And not only this, but once humility is worked out by these, the soul is persuaded to become compassionate and without vainglory, lowly and made a stranger to all worldly mentality.

Pachomius, Armand Veilleux

They used to say that on one occasion when Abbot Arsenius the Great fell ill in Scete, a priest went and brought him to the church, and he spread a palm-leaf mat for him, and placed a small pillow under his head; and one of the old men came to visit him and saw that he was lying upon a mat that he had a pillow under his head, and he was offended and said, "And this is Arsenius lying upon such things!"

Then the priest took the old man aside privately, and said unto him, "What labor did you do in your village?" And the old man said unto him, "I was a shepherd." And the priest said unto him, "What manner of life did you lead in the world?" And he said unto him, "A life of toil, and great want."

And when the old man had described all the tribulation, which he had endured in the world, the priest said unto him, "And here what manner of life do you lead?" And the old man said unto him, "In my cell I have everything comfortable, and I have more than I want." And the priest said unto him, "Consider the position of Abbot Arsenius when he was in the world! He was the father of kings, and a thousand slaves, girt about with gold-embroidered vests, and with chains and ornaments around their necks, and clothed in silk, stood before him; and he had the most costly couches and cushions to lie upon. But you were a shepherd, and the comforts which you never enjoyed in the world, you have here; but his man Arsenius has not here the comforts which he enjoyed in the world, and now you are at ease while he is troubled."

Then the mind of the old man was opened, and he expressed contrition and said, "Father, forgive me; I have sinned. Verily this is the way of truth. He has come to a state of humility, while I have attained to ease."

And the old men having profited went his way.   Desert Fathers

---

This is the mark of Christianity--however much a man toils, and however many righteousnesses he performs, to feel that he has done nothing, and in fasting to say, "This is not fasting," and in praying, "This is not prayer," and in perseverance at prayer, "I have shown no perseverance; I am only just beginning to practice and to take pains"; and even if he is righteous before God, he should say, "I am not righteous, not I; I do not take pains, but only make a beginning every day.   Macarius the Great

---

This subject sets before us as a touchstone, a treasure preserved in earthen vessels, that is to say in our bodies, and it is of a quality that baffles all description. This treasure has an inscription, which is incomprehensible because it comes from above, and those who try to explain it with words give themselves great and endless trouble. And the inscription runs thus: Holy Humility.   John Climacus

---

Those who seek humility should bear in mind the three following things: that they are the worst of sinners, that they are the most despicable of all creatures since their state is an unnatural one, and that they are even more pitiable than the demons, since they are slaves to the demons. You will also profit if you say this to yourself: how do I know what or how many other people's sins are, or whether they are greater than or equal to my own? In our ignorance you and I , my soul, are worse than all men, we are dust and ashes under their feet. How can I not regard myself as more despicable than all other creatures, for they act in accordance with the nature they have been given, while I, owing to my innumerable sins, am in a state contrary to nature.

Gregory of Sinai

Throughout all his years as pastor Peter of Alexandria sat on a footstool at the times appointed for sitting, though the people and clergy often entreated him to be seated upon his throne. One day, after the Divine Liturgy,   Peter explained to them, 'Do you know why I do not sit on my throne or ascend the steps leading to it? It is because when I draw near, I see a heavenly light shining on it and sense the presence of a divine power. I am filled with terror and do not dare sit there, for I know myself to be unworthy. Instead, I sit on the footstool, and still feel fear...For this reason the people sat   Peter upon his throne after his death, crying, 'Pray for us, God's holy favorite"

Peter of Alexandria

True discrimination comes to us only as a result of true humility, and this in turn is shown by our revealing to our spiritual fathers not only what we do but also what we think, by never trusting our own thoughts, and by following in all things the words of our elders, regarding as good what they have judged to be so.   John Cassian

---

What salt is for any food, humility is for every virtue. To acquire it, a man must always think of himself with contrition, self-belittlement and painful self-judgment. But if we acquire it, it will make us sons of God.

Isaac of Syria

When a man penetrates the depths of humility and recognizes that his is unworthy to be saved, his sorrow releases springs of tears, and as a consequence spiritual joy floods out in his heart. In this way, hope rises out of this spring, grows with it, and strengthens our certainty of being saved.

Symeon the New Theologian

When anyone out of kindness praises you to others, and they pass on these praises to you, do not consider them as a just tribute of esteem really due you, but ascribe them solely to the kindness of heart of the person who spoke of you in this way, and pray for him that God may strengthen him in his kindness of heart and in every virtue; but acknowledge yourself to be the greatest of sinners, not just out of humility, but truthfully, actually, knowing as you do your evil deeds.   John of Kronstadt

When pride retreats from a man, humility begins to dwell in him, and the more pride is diminished, so much more does humility grow. The one gives way to the other as to its opposite. Darkness departs and light appears. Pride is darkness, but humility is light.   Tikhon of Zadonsk

Where humility is combined with the remembrance of God that is established through watchfulness and attention, and also with recurrent prayer inflexible in its resistance to the enemy, there is the place of God, the heaven of the heart in which because of God's presence no demonic army dares to make a stand.   Philotheos of Sinai

Where there is humility, there is also simplicity and innocence, and this Divine branch will not experience God's judgment.   Leo of Optina

Wondrous are the works of humility that lead a person to divine and glorious heights of honor and grace. There was a monk of Anne's (on Mt Athos), a vessel of grace, who was the first chanter at the Patriarchate. This monk went to the spiritual father of Anne's to make his confession and to ask his advice.

"What kind of work did you do?" asked the spiritual father.

"I was the leading chanter at the Patriarchate, holy Father."

"If you want to be saved," the confessor said, "you will not tell anyone that you are a chanter, because here on the Holy Mountain there are many celebrations and you will be asked to go and sing, and so you will have no real chance to be a monk. I will put you under the obedience of a good father. You will only read well; you will never sing well. You will be out of tune and you will pretend that you are unable to read music."

"Let it be blessed, holy Father," said the novice who was then sent to a pious elder.

A considerable time went by before the spiritual confessor asked the elder, "How is everything going with the novice?"

"Good," he replied. "He is obedient. The only thing is that he cannot sing. But he does read very well."

The years went by. The spiritual father, who was clairvoyant, foresaw that the chanter who was in hiding was near his end. One Anne's feast day the central church was celebrating. The spiritual father had been appointed typikaris of the skete. He ordered the chanter-in-hiding to prepare himself to sing the Cherubic Hymn for the Divine Liturgy. The monk was sad, for he did not want to be revealed. It was such a grace for him not to be known, "to exist in secrecy." He pretended that he had forgotten the music with the passing of time. Even so, he obeyed his spiritual father and agreed to it.

When it was time for the Cherubic Hymn, the typikaris pulled the monk to where the chanters were. The others were sad, thanking that the typikaris had made a mistake. After they had heard the singing however, and the evident musical knowledge of this unknown nobleman and chanter, they said to each other, "And he, the blessed one, was listening to us all this time and he said nothing!"

After the Liturgy ended, the father confessor took the monk with him to his hut. Two days later he fell ill and reposed in the Lord. No one would have known the victorious struggle of humility had the spiritual father not revealed it.   Athonite Gerontikon

Believe that dishonors and reproaches are medicines that heal the pride of your soul, and pray for those who reproach you, as for true physicians of your soul, being assured that he who hates dishonor, hates humility, and he who avoids those who grieve him, flees from meekness.   Dorotheos

Remember that by your own power you will gain nothing. Always call upon the Lord Jesus Christ for help in all situations. Then, your praiseworthy attitude will be aided by God's Might, which curtails all sin - All wiles of the demons. If you overcome some sinful influence, do not credit yourself, you will again fall into the same sins.   Abbot Nikon

Since salvation comes to you as a free gift, give thanks to God your Savior. If you wish to present Him with gifts, gratefully offer from your widowed soul two tiny coins, humility and love, and God will accept these in the treasury of His salvation more gladly than the host of virtues deposited there by others. Dead through the passions, pray like Lazarus to be brought to life again, sending to God these two sisters to intercede with Him; and you will surely attain your goal.   Theognostos

The man who endures accusations against himself with humility has arrived at perfection. He is marveled at by the holy angels, for there is no other virtue so great and so hard to achieve.   Isaac of Syria

The mind that realizes it's own weakness has discovered whence it might enter upon salvation and draw near to the light of knowledge and receive true wisdom which does not pass away with this age."   Gregory Palamas

Where poverty of spirit is perceived, there is also the sorrow that is full of joy.   Symeon the New Theologian

---

Paul writes, 'I know of nothing against myself, yet I am not justified by this' (1 Cor. 4:4). You see he does not exalt himself, but humbles and abases himself in every way, and that just when he had reached the summit. And the Three Children were in the fire, in the midst of the furnace, and what did they say? 'For we have sinned and transgressed by departing from You; and we have done evil in every way' (Dan. 3:29). This is what it is to have a contrite heart.   John Chrysostom

---

Since salvation comes to you as a free gift, give thanks to God your Savior. If you wish to present Him with gifts, gratefully offer from your widowed soul two tiny coins, humility and love, and God will accept these in the treasury of His salvation more gladly than the host of virtues deposited there by others. Dead through the passions, pray like Lazarus to be brought to life again, sending to God these two sisters to intercede with Him; and you will surely attain your goal.   Theognostos

---

111. Humility consists, not in condemning our conscience, but in recognizing God's grace and compassion.   Kosmas Aitolos

---

You should not even get the fleeting idea that you are better. Before God whoever thinks that it is possible that all others are better than he wins.

John Chrysostom

Hypocrisy

Hypocrisy is the mother of lying, and often its occasion. For some define hypocrisy as none other than meditation on falsehood, and an inventor of falsehood which has a reprehensible oath intertwined with it.   John Climacus

---

87. Presumption and boastfulness are causes of blasphemy. Avarice and self-esteem are causes of cruelty and hypocrisy.   Kosmas Aitolos

---

Idle Talk

Know that nothing quenches the Spirit more than idle talk.
                                                        Anthony the Great

---

Idolatry

He who refuses to give into passions does the same as he who refuses to bow down and worship idols.   Theophan the Recluse

---

If you speak of pagan abuses, these abuses do not make our veneration of images loathsome. Blame the pagans, who made images into gods! Just because the pagans used them in a foul way, that is no reason to object to our pious practice. Sorcerers and magicians use incantations and the Church prays over catechumens; the former conjure up demons while the Church calls upon God to exorcise the demons. Pagans make images of demons which they address as gods, but we make images of God incarnate, and of His servants and friends, and with them we drive away the demonic hosts....If the Scripture says, The idols of the nations are silver and gold, the work of men's hands (Ps. 135:15), it is not forbidden to bow before inanimate things, or the handiwork of men, but only before those images which are the devil's work.   John of Damascus

He who refuses to give into passions does the same as he who refuses to bow down and worship idols.   Theophan the Recluse

Ignorance

Better poverty with knowledge than riches with ignorance.   Abbot Evagrius

Where sin enters, there too enters ignorance; but the hearts of the righteous are filled with knowledge.   Ibid

The first among all evils is ignorance; next comes lack of faith.

Kosmas Aitolos

As Maximos has said, "To think that one knows prevents one from advancing in knowledge." John Chrysostom points out that there is an ignorance, which is praiseworthy: it consists in knowing consciously that one knows nothing. In addition, there is a form of ignorance that is worse than any other: not to know that one does not know. Similarly, there is a knowledge that is falsely so called, which occurs when, as Paul says, one thinks that one knows but does not know (see I Corinthians 8:2).

Peter of Damaskos

Illness

Amma Syncletica said: "If illness weighs us down, let us not be sorrowful as though, because of the illness and the prostration of our bodies, we could not sing, for all these things are for our good, for the purification of our desires. Truly fasting and sleeping on the ground are set before us because of our sensuality. If illness then weakens this sensuality, the reason for these ascetic practices is superfluous. For this is the great asceticism: to be self-controlled in illness and to sing hymns of thanksgiving to God." The Desert Fathers

Disease, more than this, is a punishment and takes the place of fasting and even more – for one who bears it with patience, thanks God, and through patience receives the fruit of his salvation; for instead of weakening his body by fasting, he is already sick without that. Give thanks to God that you have been delivered from the labor of fasting. Even if you will eat ten times in a day, do not grieve; you will not be judged for this, for you are doing this not at the demon's instigation, and not from the weakening of your thought; but rather, this occurs to us for our testing and for profit to the soul.

Barsanuphius and John

The body is a slave, the soul a sovereign, and therefore it is due to Divine mercy when the body is worn out by illness: for thereby the passions are weakened, and a man comes to himself; indeed, bodily illness itself is sometimes caused by the passions. Abbot Tithoes

The body is a slave, the soul a sovereign, and therefore it is due to Divine mercy when the body is worn out by illness: for thereby the passions are weakened, and a man comes to himself; indeed, bodily illness itself is sometimes caused by the passions.   Seraphim of Sarov

When we become unduly distressed at falling ill, we should recognize that our soul is still the slave of bodily desires and so longs for physical health, not wishing to lose the good things of this life and even finding it a great hardship not to be able to enjoy them because of illness. If, however, the soul accepts thankfully the pains of illness, it is clear that it is not far from the realm of dispassion; as a result it even waits joyfully for death as the entry into a life that is more true.   Diadochos of Photiki

Images

The heart, which is constantly guarded, and is not allowed to receive the forms, images and fantasies of the dark and evil spirits, is conditioned by nature to give birth from within itself to thoughts filled with light. For just as coal engenders a flame, or a flame lights a candle, so will God, who from our baptism dwells in our heart, kindle our mind to contemplation when He finds it free from the winds of evil and protected by the guarding of the intellect.

Hesychios the Presbyter

It is well known how powerfully corrupt images act upon the soul, no matter in what form they may touch it! How unfortunate is the child who, closing his eyes, or being left alone and going within himself, is stifled by a multitude of improper images -- vain, tempting, breathing of the passions. This is the same thing for the soul as smoke is for the head.

Theophan the Recluse

Imagination

Not to accept some temptation through one sense or another is easily managed; but it is very difficult to control the imagination and memory of it, once it is accepted. For example, to see or not to see some face, or to look at it with passion or without passion, is not very difficult and does not need much effort; but after you have seen it and looked at it with passion, to banish from your memory the image of this face is already not easy, but demands much effort and no small inner struggle. And the enemy can play with your soul as with a ball, tossing your attention from one memory to another, stirring up desires and passions beneath them, and so keeping you always in a passionate state. Therefore, I say to you: stay awake and, above all, watch imagination and memory.   Lorenzo Scupoli

The devil has a very close relationship and familiarity with the imagination, and of all the power of the soul he has this one as the most appropriate organ to deceive man and to activate his passions and evils. He indeed is very familiar with the nature of the imagination. For he, being created by God originally as a pure and simple mind without form and image, as the other divine angels, later came to love the forms and the imagination. Imagining that he could set his throne above the heavens and become like God, he fell from being an angel of light and became a devil of darkness. Dionysius spoke about this devil. "What is the evil in the devils? Irrational anger; unreasonable desire; and reckless imagination.

Nicodemos of the Holy Mountain

Incarnation

"The law of grace directly teaches those who are led by it to imitate God Himself. For it is permitted to speak in this way despite the fact that because of sin we were His enemies.

God loved us so much more than Himself that, although He is beyond every being, He entered without changing into our being, supra-essentially took on human nature, became man and, wishing to reveal Himself as a man among men, did not refuse to make His own the penalty we pay.

And as in His providence He became man, so He deified us by grace, in this way teaching us not only to cleave to one another naturally and to love others spiritually as ourselves, but also, like God, to be more concerned for others than for ourselves, and as proof of our love for each other readily to choose, as virtue enjoins, to die for others. For as Scripture tells us, there is no greater love than to lay down one's life for a friend" (cf. John 15: 13).

The incorporeal and incorruptible and immaterial Word of God entered our world. In one sense, indeed, He was not far From it before, for no part of creation had ever been without Him Who, while ever abiding in union with the Father, yet fills all things that are. But now He entered the world in a new way, stooping to our level in His love and Self-revealing to us.

Athanasius the Great

Now if Christ is God, as indeed He is, but took not human nature upon Him, we are strangers to salvation. Let us then worship Him as God, but believe that He also was made Man. For neither is there any profit in calling Him man without Godhead, nor any salvation in refusing to confess the Manhood together with the Godhead.   Cyril of Jerusalem

He Who created us ... took on the form of being which He Himself had created, in order, as man, to manifest to us in our flesh the perfection of the Father to which we, too, are called. 'Be of good cheer; I have overcome the world' (John 16:33)."   Archimandrite Sophrony

Although this union of the immortal Son of God with our human nature, all men were clothed with incorruption in the promise of the resurrection... For the solidarity of mankind is such that, by virtue of the Word's indwelling in a single human body, the corruption which goes with death has lost its power over all. You know how it is when some great king enters a large city, and dwells in one of its houses; because of his dwelling in that single h use, the whole city is honored, and enemies and robbers cease to molest it. Even so is it with the King of ail; He has come into our country and dwelt in one body amidst the many, and in consequence the designs of the enemy against mankind have been foiled, and the corruption of death, which formerly held them in its power, has simply ceased to be. For the human race would have perished utterly had not the Lord and Savior of all, the Son of God, come among us to put an end to death.   Athanasius the Great

The Divine Logos took on Himself human flesh and thereby showed that God is not a fantasy of man's imagination, born of ignorant fear of unknown phenomena, but actual reality.   Archimandrite Sophrony

And being clothed with the Spirit, they [the prophets] saw that none among the creatures was able to heal that great wound, but only the bounty of God, that is to say His Only-begotten, Whom He sent to be the Savior of all the world, for He is the great Physician, Who is able to heal the great wound. And they asked God and of His bounty the father of creatures spared not His Only-begotten for our salvation, but delivered Him up for us all and for our iniquities. And He humbled Himself, and by His stripes we all were healed. And by the word of His power He gathered us out of all lands, from one end of the world to the other end of the world, and raised up our hearts from the earth, and taught us that we are members one of another.   Anthony the Great

For His it was once more both to bring the corruptible to incorruption, and to maintain intact the just claim of the Father upon all. For being Word of the Father, and above all, He alone of natural fitness was both able to recreate everything, and worthy to suffer on behalf of all and to be ambassador for all with the Father. For this purpose, then, the incorporeal and incorruptible and immaterial Word of God comes to our realm, howbeit He was not far from us before. For no part of creation is left void of Him: He has filled all things everywhere, remaining present with His own Father. But He comes in condescension to show loving-kindness upon us, and to visit us.

Athanasius of Alexandria

For by the sacrifice of His own body, He both put an end to the law, which was against us, and made a new beginning of life for us, by the hope of resurrection, which He has given us. For since from man it was that death prevailed over men, for this cause conversely, by the Word of God being made man has come about the destruction of death and the resurrection of life; as the man which bore Christ says: For since by man came death, by man came also the resurrection of the dead. For as in Adam all die, so also in Christ shall all be made alive: and so forth. Fort no longer now do we die as subject to condemnation; but as men who rise from the dead we await the general resurrection of all, `which in its own times He shall show,' even God, Who has also wrought it, and bestowed it upon us. Athanasius of Alexandria

For since from man it was that death prevailed over men, for this cause conversely, by the Word of God being made man has come about the destruction of death and the resurrection of life; as the man which bore Christ says: 'For since by man came death, by man came also the resurrection of the dead. For as in Adam all die, so also in Christ shall all be made alive.'

Athanasius of Alexandria

For what principle did the Blood of His Only-Begotten Son delight the Father, Who would not receive even Isaac, when he was being offered by his father, but changed the sacrifice, putting a ram in the place of the human victim? Is it not evident that the Father accepts Him, but neither asked for Him nor demanded Him; but on account of the Incarnation, and because humanity must be sanctified by the Humanity of God, that He might deliver us Himself, and overcome the tyrant, and draw us to Himself by the mediation of His Son, Who also arranged this to the honor of the Father, Whom it is manifest that He obeys in all things? So much we have said of Christ; the greatest part of what we might say shall be reverenced with silence.   Gregory the Theologian

God's Majesty that had clothed Itself in all sorts of similitudes saw that humanity did not want to find salvation through this assistance, so He sent His Beloved One who, instead of the borrowed similitude with which God's Majesty had previously clothed Itself, clothed Himself with real limbs, as the First-born, and was mingled with humanity: He gave what belonged to Him and took what belonged to us, so that this mingling of His might give life to our dead state.   Ephraim the Syrian

How could anyone doubt that the nature of God the Word is filled with true and regal dominion? Certainly we must understand this nature as being in the very heights befitting to God. Since He appeared as a man, however, a being upon whom all things are bestowed as gifts, He received as a man, even though He is full and gives to all from His own fullness (Jn. 1:16). He made our poverty His own, and we see in Christ the strange and rare paradox of Lordship in servant's form and divine glory in human abasement. That which was under the yoke in terms of the limitations of manhood was crowned with royal dignity, and that which was humble was raised to the most supreme excellence.   Cyril of Alexandria

If it was for us that the Word of God in His incarnation descended into the lower parts of the earth and ascended above all the heavens, while being Himself perfectly unmoved, He underwent in Himself through the incarnation as man our future destiny. Let the one who is moved by a love of knowledge mystically rejoice in learning of the great destiny that He has promised to those who love the Lord.   Maximus the Confessor

---

If the divine Logos of God the Father became son of man and man so that He might make men gods and the sons of God, let us believe that we shall reach the realm where Christ Himself now is; for He is the head of the whole body (cf. Col. 1:18), and endued with our humanity has gone to the Father as forerunner on our behalf. God will stand 'in the midst of the congregation of gods' (Ps. 82:1.LXX) - that is, of those who are saved - distributing the rewards of that realm's blessedness to those found worthy to receive them, not separated from them by any space."   Maximos the Confessor

---

In saying that the Apostles were eyewitnesses of the substantial and living Word, the Evangelist agrees with John, who says, that the Word was made flesh, and tabernacled in us, and His glory was seen, the glory as of the Only begotten of the Father. For the Word became capable of being seen by reason of the flesh, which is visible and tangible and solid; whereas in Himself He is invisible. And John again in his Epistle says, That which was from the beginning, That which we have heard, That which we have seen with our eyes, and our hands have handled around the Word of Life, and the Life became manifest. Do you not hear that he speaks of the Life as capable of being handled? This he does that you may understand that the Son became man, and was visible in respect to the flesh, but invisible as regards His divinity."   Cyril Patriarch of Alexandria

---

It was unworthy of the goodness of God that creatures made by Him should be brought to nothing through the deceit wrought upon man by the devil; and it was supremely unfitting that the work of God in mankind should disappear, either through their own negligence or through the deceit of evil spirits. As, then, the creatures whom He had created reasonable, like the Word, were in fact perishing, and such noble works were on the road to ruin, what then, was God, being God, to do? Was He to let corruption and death have their way with them? In that case, what was the use of having made them in the beginning? Surely it would have been better never to have been created at all than, having been created, to be neglected and perish; and, besides that, such indifference to the ruin of His own work before His very eyes would argue not goodness in God but limitation, and that far more than if He had never created men at all....

Was He to demand repentance from men for their transgression? You might say that that was worthy of God, and argue further that, as through the Transgression they became subject to corruption, so through repentance they might return to incorruption again. But repentance would not guard the Divine consistency, for, if death did not hold dominion over men, God would still remain untrue. Nor does repentance recall men from what is according to their nature; all that it does is to make them cease from sinning. Had it been a case of a trespass only, and not of a subsequent corruption, repentance would have been well enough; but when once transgression had begun, men came under the power of the corruption proper to their nature and were bereft of the grace that belonged to them as creatures in the Image of God. No, repentance could not meet the case.

What-- or rather Who was it that was needed for such grace and such recall as we required? Who, save the Word of God Himself, Who also in the beginning had made all things out of nothing? His part it was, and His alone, both to bring again the corruptible to incorruption and to maintain for the Father His consistency of character with all. For he alone, being Word of the Father and above all, was in consequence both able to recreate all, and worthy to suffer on behalf of all and to be an ambassador for all with the Father.

For this purpose, then, the incorporeal and incorruptible and immaterial Word of God entered our world. In one sense, indeed, He was not far from it before, for no part of creation had ever been without Him Who, while ever abiding in union with the Father, yet fills all things that are, But now He entered the world in a new way, stooping to our level in His love and Self-revealing to us. He saw the reasonable race, the race of men that, like Himself, expressed the Father's Mind, wasting out of existence, and death reigning over all in corruption. He saw that corruption held us all the closer, because it was the penalty for the Transgression; He saw, too, how unthinkable it would be for the law to be repealed before it was fulfilled He saw how unseemly it was that the very things of which He Himself was the Artificer should be disappearing. He saw how the surpassing wickedness of men was mounting up against them; He saw also their universal liability to death. All this He saw and, pitying our race, moved with compassion for our limitation, unable to endure that death should have the mastery, rather than that His creatures should perish and the work of His Father for us men come to nothing, He took to Himself a body, a human body even as our own. Nor did He will merely to become embodied or merely to appear; had that been so, He could have revealed His divine majesty some other and better way. No, He took our body, and not only so, but He took it directly from a spotless, stainless virgin, without the agency of human father--a pure body, untainted by intercourse with man. He, the Mighty One, the Artificer of all, Himself prepared this body in the Virgin as a temple for Himself, and took it for His very own, as the instrument through which He was known and in which He dwelt. Thus, taking a body like our own, because all our bodies were liable to the corruption of death, He surrendered His body to death in place of all, and offered it to the Father. This He did out of sheer love for us, so that in His death all might die, and the law of death thereby be abolished because, when He had fulfilled in His body that for which it was appointed, it was thereafter voided of its power for men. This He did that He might turn again to incorruption men who had turned back to corruption, and make them alive through death by the appropriation of His body and by the grace of His resurrection. Thus He would make death to disappear from them as utterly as straw from fire   Athanasius the Great

---

Jesus Christ, radiant center of glory, image of our God, the invisible Father, revealer of His eternal designs, prince of peace; Father of the world to come. For our sake he took the likeness of a slave, becoming flesh in the womb of the Virgin Mary, for our sake, wrapped in swaddling bands and laid in a manger adored by the shepherds and hymned by the angelic powers, who sang: Glory to God in the heavens and on earth peace and good to men. Make us worthy, Lord, to celebrate and to conclude in peace the feast which magnifies the rising of Your light, by avoiding empty words, working with justice, fleeing from the passions, and raising up the spirit above earthly goods. Bless Your Church, formed long ago to be united with You through Your life-giving blood. Come to the aid of Your faithful shepherds, of the priests and the teachers of the Gospel. Bless Your faithful whose only hope is in Your mercy; Christian souls, the sick, those who are tormented in spirit, and those who have asked us to pray for them. Have pity, in Your infinite clemency, and preserve us in fitness to receive the future, endless, good things. We celebrate Your glorious Nativity with the Father who sent you for our redemption, with the life-giving Spirit, now and for ever and through all ages. Amen

Like a flaming pillar in the deepest darkness, so is the coming of God among men. The news of this coming began with an angel and a maiden, with a conversation between heavenly and earthly purity. When an impure heart converses with a pure one, there is strife. When an impure heart converses with a pure one, there is strife. Only when a pure heart converses with a pure one is there joy, peace and a great wonder   Nicolai Velimirovich

Men forsook God, and made carved images of men. Since therefore an image of man was falsely worshipped as God, God became truly Man, that the falsehood might be done away.   Cyril of Jerusalem

Now the Word of God in His man's nature was not like that; for He was not bound to His body, but rather was Himself wielding it, so that He was not only in it, but was actually in everything, and while external to the universe, abode in His Father only. Now this was the wonderful thing that He was at once walking as man, and as the Word was quickening all things, and as the Son was dwelling with His Father. So that not even when the virgin bore Him did He suffer any change, nor by being in the body was [His glory] dulled; but, on the contrary, He sanctified the body also. For not even by being in the universe does He share in its nature, but all things, on the contrary, are quickened and sustained by Him.   Athanasius the Great

Our Lord was pleased to assume the likeness of every poor man and compared Himself to every poor man in order that no man who believes in Him should exalt himself over his brother, but, seeing his Lord in his brother, should consider himself less and worse than his brother, just as he is less than his Creator; and should take the poor man in and honor him, and be ready to exhaust all his means in helping him, just as our Lord Jesus Christ exhausted His blood for our salvation.   Archimandrite Sophrony

The Devil had used the flesh as an instrument against us; and Paul knowing this says, 'But I see another law in my members warring against the law of my mind, and bringing me into captivity' (Rom. 7:23). By the very same weapons, therefore, wherewith the Devil used to vanquish us, have we been saved. The Lord took on Him from us our likeness, that He might save man's nature: He took our likeness, that He might give greater grace to that which lacked; that sinful humanity might become partaker of God.

Cyril of Jerusalem

The Son of God has become Son of Man in order to make us...sons of God, raising our race by grace to what He is Himself by nature, granting us birth from above through the grace of the Holy Spirit and leading us straightway to the kingdom of heaven, or rather, granting us this kingdom within us (Luke 17:21), in order that we should not merely be fed by the hope of entering it, but entering into full possession thereof should cry: our 'life is hid with Christ in God.' (Col. 3:3)."   Simeon the New Theologian

The Word of God thus acted consistently in assuming a body and using a human instrument to vitalize the body. He was consistent in working through man to reveal Himself everywhere, as well as through the other parts of His creation, so that nothing was left void of His Divinity and knowledge. For I take up now the point I made before, namely that the Savior did this in order that He might fill all things everywhere with the knowledge of Himself, just as they are already filled with His presence, even as the Divine Scripture says, "The whole universe was filled with the knowledge of the Lord.

Athanasius

The Word, having unveiled the truth, showed to men the summit of salvation, so that either repenting they might be saved, or refusing to obey, they might be condemned. This is the proclamation of righteousness: to those who obey, rejoicing; to those who disobey, condemnation."   Clement of Alexandria

The Word, then, visited that earth in which He was yet always present; and saw all the evils.... For this purpose, then, the incorporeal and incorruptible and immaterial Word of God comes to our realm, howbeit he was not far from us before. For no part of Creation is left void of Him: He has filled all things everywhere, remaining present with His own Father. But He comes in condescension to show loving kindness upon us, and to visit us.

Athanasius the Great

The final end of Orthodoxy is pure knowledge of the two dogmas of faith - the Trinity and the Duality; to contemplate and know the Trinity as indivisible and yet not merged together; to know the Duality as the two natures of Christ joined in one person - that is, to know and to profess one's faith in the Son of God both before incarnation, and after incarnation, to praise Him in His two natures and wills unmerged, the one Divine and the other human.   Gregory of Sinai

The mystery of the incarnation of the Logos is the key to all the arcane symbolism and typology in the Scriptures, and in addition gives us knowledge of created things, both visible and intelligible. He who apprehends the mystery of the cross and the burial apprehends the inward essence of created things; while he who is initiated into the inexpressible power of the resurrection apprehends the purpose for which God first established everything.   Maximos the Confessor

The perfect Teacher of babes (Rom. 2:20) became a babe among babes, that He might give wisdom to the foolish. The Bread of Heaven came down on earth (John 6:32,33,50) that He might feed the hungry.   Cyril of Jerusalem

---

The purpose of the advent of the Savior, when He gave us His life-giving commandments as purifying remedies in our passionate state, was to cleanse the soul from the damage done by the first transgression and bring it back to its original state. What medicines are for a sick body, that the commandments are for the passionate soul.   Isaac of Syria

---

The purpose of the incarnate economy of God the Word, which is proclaimed by all the divine scriptures and which we read but do not understand, is surely summed up by saying that He has shared in what was ours to let us share in what was His. The Son of God became the Son of Man in order to make us men the sons of God. By grace He lifts up our race to what He is by nature. He gives birth to us from on high in the Holy Spirit, and then straightway leads us into the kingdom of heaven; or rather, He gives us the grace to have this kingdom within us. We therefore have more than just the hope of entering here; we really possess it as we cry out: 'Our life is hidden with Christ in God.'   Symeon the New Theologian

---

The reason for the coming of the New Adam, Jesus Christ, can be said to be our liberation from seeking and loving only the visible things, and at the same time our exaltation to love and enjoy the spiritual realties, thus indicating our true transference to what is indeed better. Those who wanted to achieve this very goal with ease, that is, the cutting off of worldly pleasures and the enjoyment of the spiritual ones, were the true philosophers and ascetics who abandoned the inhabited places where there are always so many causes for sinful attacks and went to live in deserts and caves. Not finding there the usual causes of worldly pleasures, they were more readily able to subdue the senses and in relatively short periods of time were able to rise up to the sweetest enjoyment of the spiritual and divine realities.

Through Eve yet virgin came death; through a virgin, or rather from a virgin, must the Life appear: that as the serpent beguiled the one, so to the other Gabriel might bring good tidings.   Cyril of Jerusalem

---

Through His Incarnation, God gave us the model for a holy life and recalled us from our ancient fall. In addition to many other things, He taught us, feeble as we are, that we should fight against the demons with humility, fasting, prayer, and watchfulness.   Hesychios the Priest

---

Through the fall our nature was stripped of divine illumination and resplendence. But the Logos of God had pity upon our disfigurement and in His compassion He took our nature upon Himself, and on Tabor He manifested it to His elect disciples clothed once again most brilliantly. He shows what we once were and what we shall become through Him in the age to come, if we choose to live our present life as far as possible in accordance with His ways.   Gregory Palamas

---

We were created for eternal life by our Creator, we are called to it by the word of God, and we are renewed by holy Baptism. And Christ the Son of God came into the world for this, that He should call us and take us there, and He is the one thing needful. For this reason your very first endeavor and care should be to receive it. Without it everything is as nothing, though you have the whole world under you.   Tikhon of Zadonsk

---

"The law of grace directly teaches those who are led by it to imitate God Himself. For -- it is permitted to speak in this way -- despite the fact that because of sin we were His enemies.

God loved us so much more than Himself that, although He is beyond every being, He entered without changing into our being, supra-essentially took on human nature, became man and, wishing to reveal Himself as a man among men, did not refuse to make His own the penalty we pay. And as in His providence He became man, so He deified us by grace, in this way teaching us not only to cleave to one another naturally and to love others spiritually as ourselves, but also, like God, to be more concerned for others than for ourselves, and as proof of our love for each other readily to choose, as virtue enjoins, to die for others. For as Scripture tells us, there is no greater love than to lay down one's life for a friend" cf. John 15: 13.

"...there has been appointed over the spiritual Sion, that is, over the Church, a prince and a teacher who was not promoted at the time when He is said to have acceded to that office. For the Word that was born from the Virgin was and is always king and Lord of all.

But when He became man, He made the limitations of humanity His own. For in this way we could believe truly and without hesitation that He became as we are. Therefore although it might be said that He received dominion over all things, this refers to His accepting the dispensation of the flesh, not to His pre-eminence by which He is regarded as Master of all things."

<u>Cyril of Alexandria</u>

Incensive Power

When through self-control we have purified our body, and when through divine love we have made our incensive power and our desire incentives for virtue, and when we offer to God our intellect cleansed by prayer, then we will possess and see within ourselves the grace promised to the pure in heart (cf. Matt. 5:8). <u>Gregory Palamas</u>

---

ngratitude

...he who has received a gift from God, and is ungrateful for it, is already on the way to losing it..." <u>Peter of Damaskos</u>

---

nsensibility

A little fire softens a large piece of wax. So, too, a small indignity often softens, sweetens and wipes away suddenly all the fierceness, insensibility and hardness of our heart. <u>John Climacus</u>

He who has lost sensibility is a witless philosopher, a self-condemned commentator, a self-contradictory windbag, a blind man who teaches others to see. He talks about healing a wound, and does not stop irritating it. He complains of sickness, and does not stop eating what is harmful. He prays against it, and immediately goes and does it. And when he has done it, he is angry with himself; and the wretched man is not ashamed of his own words. "I am doing wrong," he cries, and eagerly continues to do so. His mouth prays against his passion, and his body struggles for it. He philosophizes about death, but he behaves as if he were immortal. He groans over the separation of soul and body, but drowses along as if he were eternal. He talks of temperance and self-control, but he lives for gluttony. He reads about the judgment and begins to smile. He reads about vainglory, and is vainglorious while actually reading. He repeats what he has learnt about vigil, and drops asleep on the spot. He praises prayer, but runs from it as from the plague. He blesses obedience, but he is the first to disobey. He praises detachment, but he is not ashamed to be spiteful and to fight for a rag. When angered he becomes bitter, and he is angered again at his bitterness; and he does not feel that, after one defeat, he is suffering another. Having overeaten he repents, and a little later again gives way. He blesses silence, and praises it with a spate of words. He teaches meekness, and during the actual teaching frequently gets angry. Having woken from passion he sighs, and shaking his head, he again yields to passion. He condemns laughter, and lectures on mourning with a smile on his face. Before others he blames himself for being vainglorious, and in blaming himself is only angling for glory for himself. He looks people in the face with passion, and talks about chastity. While frequenting the world, he praises those who live in stillness without realizing that he shames himself. He extols almsgivers, and reviles beggars. All the time he is his own accuser, and he does not want to come to his senses -- I will say cannot. <u>John Climacus</u>

Insensibility both in the body and in the spirit is deadened feeling, which, from long sickness and negligence, lapses into loss of feeling.

<u>John Climacus</u>

---

nstructions

...here is a general means for making peace in the heart, when some affliction tries to disturb it: with all your strength make firm your faith in the goodness of God's Providence towards you and revive in your soul a devoted submission to God's will. <u>Lorenzo Scupoli</u>

If you happen to be wounded by succumbing to some sin through weakness, or through the faulty nature of your character...do not lose heart and fall into senseless turmoil. Above all do not dwell on yourself, do not say: 'How could I be such as to allow and suffer it?' This is a cry of proud self-opinion. Humble yourself and, raising your eyes to the Lord, say and feel: 'What else could be expected of me, Oh Lord, weak and faulty as I am.' Thereupon give thanks to Him that the thing has gone no further, saying: 'If it were not for Your boundless mercy, Oh Lord, I would not have stopped at that, but would certainly have fallen into something much worse.'   Lorenzo Scupoli

---

Never accuse anyone of anything, but strive always to please your neighbor. And never think evil of anyone, for through this you become evil yourself, since an evil man thinks evil, and a good man thinks good. When the thought comes to you: "They say about me...", know that it is the enemy who whispers it in your ear. Never have suspicions. Endure everything with joy and gladness, for great is the reward of endurance. As to demons -- do not trust them, for reality is not as they represent it. All they care about is to confuse you in every possible way.   Barsanuphius and John

---

Remember that by your own power you will gain nothing. Always call upon the Lord Jesus Christ for help in all situations. Then, your praiseworthy attitude will be aided by God's Might, which curtails all sin --- all wiles of the demons. If you overcome some sinful influence, do not credit yourself but the Lord; and thank Him for helping you conquer the sin. If you credit yourself, you will again fall into the same sins.   Abbot Nikon

---

Stop pleasing yourself and you will not hate your brother; stop loving yourself and you will love God.   Maximos the Confessor

---

Therefore, casting out of our souls all faithlessness, sloth, and hesitation, let us draw near with all our heart, with unhesitating faith and burning desire, like slaves who have been newly purchased with precious blood. In deed, with reverence for the price paid on our behalf, and with love for our Master Who paid it, and as having accepted His love for us, let us recognize that, if He had not wished to save by means of Himself us who have been purchased,

He would not have come down to earth, nor would He have been slain for our sake. But, as it is written, He has done this because He wills that all should be saved. Listen to Him say it Himself: 'I did not come to judge the world, but to save the world' (Jn. 12:17).   Symeon the New Theologian

---

Insults

A brother came to see Abbot Macarius the Egyptian, and said to him, "Abbot, give me a word, that I may be saved." So the old man said, "Go to the cemetery and abuse the dead." The brother went there, abused them and threw stones at them; then he returned and told the old man about it. The latter said to him, "Didn't they say anything to you?" He replied, "No."

The old man said, "Go back tomorrow and praise them." So the brother went away and praised them, calling them, "Apostles, saints, and righteous men." He returned to the old man and said to him, "Did they not answer you?" The brother said, "No."

The old man said to him, "You know how you insulted them and they did not reply, and how you praised them and they did not speak; so you too, if you wish to be saved, must do the same and become a dead man. Like the dead, take no account of either the scorn of men or their praises, and you can be saved."   "The Desert Fathers"

Avoid praise, but do not be ashamed of reproach.   Nilus of Sinai

---

Intellect

If you distract your intellect from its love for God and concentrate it, not on God, but on some sensible object, you thereby show that you value the body more than the soul and the things made by God more than God Himself.

300

Since the Light of Spiritual Knowledge is the intellect's life, and since this Light is engendered by love for God, it is rightly said that nothing is greater than divine love. (cf. I Cor. 13)   Maximos the Confessor

---

When in the intensity of its love for God the intellect goes out of itself, then it has no sense of itself or of any created thing. For when it is illumined by the Infinite Light of God, it becomes insensible to everything made by Him, just as the eye becomes insensible to the stars when the sun rises.

Maximos the Confessor

---

17. The intellect does many good and bad things without the body, whereas the body can do neither good nor evil without the intellect. This is because the law of freedom applies to what happens before we act.   Kosmas Aitolos

---

The intellect changes from one to another of three different noetic states: that according to nature, above nature, and contrary to nature. When it enters the state according to nature, it finds that it is itself the cause of evil thoughts, and confesses its sins to God, clearly understanding the causes of the passions. When it is in the state contrary to nature, it forgets God's justice and fights with men, believing itself unjustly treated. But when it is raised to the state above nature, it finds the fruits of the Holy Spirit: love, joy, peace and the other fruits of which the Apostle speaks (cf. Ga 5:22); and it knows that if it gives priority to bodily cares it cannot remain in this state. An intellect that departs from this state falls into sin and all the terrible consequences of sin- if not immediately, then in due time, as God's justice shall decide.   Ibid

What a house is to the air, the spiritual intellect is to divine grace. The more you get rid of materiality, the more the air and grace will come in of their own accord; and the more you increase materiality, the more they will go away.   Ibid

ntelligence

People are generally called intelligent through a wrong use of this word. The intelligent are not those who have studied..., but those whose soul is intelligent, who can judge what is good and what evil; they avoid what is evil and harms the soul and intelligently care for and practice what is good and profits the soul, greatly thanking God. It is these alone who should properly be called intelligent.   Antony the Great

People are generally called intelligent through a wrong use of this word. The intelligent are not those who have studied..., but those whose soul is intelligent, who can judge what is good and what evil; they avoid what is evil and harms the soul and intelligently care for and practice what is good and profits the soul, greatly thanking God. It is these alone who should properly be called intelligent.   Ibid

ntemperance

...intemperance and attachment to things cause torrents of passions to flood the soil of the heart and deposit there all the mud and filth of thoughts, thus confusing the mind, darkening the heart and weighing down the body. In the heart and the soul they produce negligence, darkness and death and deprive them of the feeling and disposition natural to them.   Gregory of Sinai

Intention

He who wants to do something and cannot is, in the eyes of God who sees our hearts, as though he has done it. This should be understood as being so in relation to good and evil alike.   Mark the Ascetic

When we fulfill the commandments in our outward actions, we receive from the Lord what is appropriate; but any real benefit we gain depends on our inward intention.   Kosmas Aitolos

If we want to do something but cannot, then before God, who knows our hearts, it is as if we have done it. This is true whether the intended action is good or bad.   Ibid

Jesus Christ

There is, after all, only one Physician: both flesh and spirit, begotten and unbegotten, God Incarnate, in death, true life, both of Mary and of God, first passible, then impassible, Jesus Christ our Lord.   Ignatius of Antioch

The soul and Christ you need…These two guard; do not lose them.

Kosmas Aitolos

Only our Christ is the Son of God and True God, the life of all…Our Teacher is Christ alone. Ibid

---

This is the way we should see Christ. He is our friend, our brother; He is whatever is good and beautiful. He is everything. Yet, He is still a friend and He shouts it out, "You're my friends, don't you understand that? We are brothers. I am not...I do not hold hell in my hands. I am not threatening you. I love you. I want you to enjoy life together with me." Porphyrios

---

Christ is Everything. He is joy, He is life, He is light. He is the true light who makes man joyful, Christ is Everything. He is joy, He is makes him soar with happiness; makes him see everything, everybody; makes him feel for everyone, to want everyone with him, everyone with Christ. Love Christ and put nothing before His Love. Christ is Everything. He is the source of life, the ultimate desire, He is everything. Everything beautiful is in Christ.

Ibid

Somebody who is Christ's must love Christ, and when he loves Christ he is delivered from the Devil, from hell and from death. Ibid

---

"[Our Savior] has the dignity of His Lordship from nature, and is not called Lord improperly, as we are; but is so in verity, since by the Father's bidding He is Lord of His own works. For our lordship is over men of equal rights and like passions, nay often over our elders, and often a young master rules over aged servants. But in the case of our Lord Jesus Christ the Lordship is not so; but He is first Maker, then Lord: first He made all things by the Father's will, then, He is Lord of the things, which were made by Him.

'Blessed be the God and Father of our Lord Jesus Christ'(2 Cor. 1:3). Blessed also be His Only-begotten Son. For with the thought of 'God' let the thought of 'Father' at once be joined, that the ascription of glory to the Father and the Son may be made indivisible. For the Father has not one glory, and the Son another, but one and the same, since He is the Father's Only-begotten Son; and when the Father is glorified, the Son also shares the glory with Him, because the glory of the Son flows from His Father's honor: and again, when the Son is glorified, the Father of so great a blessing is highly honored.   Ibid

In the character of the Form of a Servant, He [the Son] condescends to His fellow servants, nay, to His servants, and takes upon Him a strange form, bearing all me and mine in Himself, that in Himself He may exhaust the bad, as fire does wax, or as the sun does the mists of the earth; and that I may partake of His nature by the blending. Thus He honors obedience by His action, and proves it experimentally by His Passion. For to possess the disposition is not enough, just as it would not be enough for us, unless we also proved it by our acts; for action is the proof of disposition.

 Gregory Nazianzen

The Savior comes in various forms to each man for his profit. For to those who have need of gladness He becomes a Vine; and to those who want to enter in He stands as a Door; and to those who need to offer up their prayers He stands a mediating High Priest. Again, to those who have sins He becomes a Sheep, that He may be sacrificed for them. He is 'made all things to all men' (1 Cor. 9:22), remaining in His own nature what He is. For so remaining, and holding the dignity of His Sonship in reality unchangeable, He adapts Himself to our infirmities, just as some excellent physician or compassionate teacher...   Cyril of Jerusalem

We were enemies of God through sin, and God had appointed the sinner to die. There must needs therefore have happened one of two things; either that God, in His truth, should destroy all men, or that in His loving-kindness He should cancel the sentence. But behold the wisdom of God; He preserved both the truth of His sentence, and the exercise of His loving-kindness. Christ took our sins 'in His body on the tree, that we by His death might die to sin, and live unto righteousness' (1 Pet. 2:24).   Ibid

A certain God-given equilibrium is produced in our intellect through the constant remembrance and invocation of our Lord Jesus Christ, provided that we do not neglect this constant spiritual entreaty or our close watchfulness and diligence. Indeed, our true task is always the same and is always accomplished in the same way: to call upon our Lord Jesus Christ with a burning heart so that His holy name intercedes for us. In virtue as in vice, constancy is the mother of habit; once acquired, it rules us like nature.

Hesychios the Priest

Adam received the sentence, 'Cursed is the ground in your labors; thorns and thistles shall it bring forth to you' (Gen. 3:17,18). For this cause Jesus assumes the thorns, that He may cancel the sentence; for this cause also was He buried in the earth, that the earth that had been cursed might receive the blessing instead of a curse.   Cyril of Jerusalem

All things which the Savior did, He did in the first place in order that what was spoken concerning Him in the prophets might be fulfilled, 'that the blind should receive sight, and the deaf hear' (Isa. 35:5), and so on; but also to induce the belief that in the resurrection the flesh shall rise entire. For if on earth He healed the sicknesses of the flesh, and made the body whole, much more will He do this in the resurrection, so that the flesh shall rise perfect and entire. In this manner, then, shall those dreaded difficulties of theirs be healed.   Justin Martyr

At the moment before His greatest humiliation, the Lord Jesus, of His own free will and for our instruction and salvation, would not claim all the rights and power that later, risen and glorified, the victorious Lord was to possess. Only when He had risen, when He was glorified in the flesh, and when He was victorious over Satan, the world and death, did the Lord declare to His disciples: 'All power is given unto Me in heaven and in earth' (Mt. 28:18). But we must, to this whole interpretation, add something more, something that shows the Lord's most wise and all-seeing care in the dispensation of man's salvation. He wishes to show that there is here no prejudice, no partiality, 'for there is no respect of person with God' (Rom. 2:11).

Nikolai Velimirovic

Christ calls all to Himself, but not all respond to His voice. Whoever opens his heart to Him becomes His temple. The Lord comes to him and dwells in him. The heart then is filled with peace, and the soul with inexpressible blessedness and love; the will is strengthened in goodness, and the mouth glorified God in heaven.   John Maximovitch

Christ is miracle beyond comprehension. He is the all-perfect revelation of God. He is also the all-perfect manifestation of man.

Archimandrite Sophrony

Christ is the head, we are the body.... He is the foundation, we are the building; He is the Vine, we are the branches; He is the Bridegroom, we are the bride; He is the Shepherd we are the sheep; He is the Way and we are the travelers; again we are the temple and He is the occupant; He is the firstborn, we are the brothers, He is the Heir, we are co-heirs; He is the Life, we are the living; He is the Resurrection, we are the resurrected; He is the Light, we are the illumined.   John Chrysostom

Christ made all things, whether you speak of Angels, or Archangels, of Dominions, or Thrones. Not that the Father wanted strength to create the works Himself, but because He willed that the Son should reign over His own workmanship, God Himself giving Him the design of the things to be made.   Cyril of Jerusalem

He then, Whom no man has seen at any time, whom can we reckon Him to resemble, so that thereby we should understand His generation? And we, indeed, without ambiguity apprehend that our soul dwells in us in union with the body; but still, who has ever seen his own soul? who has been able to discern its conjunction with his body? This one thing is all we know certainly, that there is a soul within us conjoined with the body. Thus, then, we reason and believe that the word is begotten by the Father, albeit we neither possess nor know the clear 'rationale' of the fact. The Word Himself is before every creature eternal from the Eternal, like spring from spring, and light from light.   Gregory the Wonderworker

I want you to know this, that Jesus Christ our Lord is Himself the true Mind of the Father. By Him all the fullness of every rational nature is made in the image of His image, and He Himself is the head of all creation, and of His body the Church (Col. 1:15-18). Therefore we are all members one of another, and the body of Christ, and the head cannot say to the feet, 'I have no need of you'; and if one member suffers, the whole body is moved and suffers with it (Eph. 4:25). But if a member is estranged from the body, and has no communication with the head, but is delighted by the passions of its own body, this means that its wound is incurable, and it has forgotten its beginning and its end. Therefore the Father of creatures, moved with compassion towards this our wound, which could not be healed by any of the creatures, but only by the goodness of the Father, sent forth to us His Only-begotten, who because of our bondage took upon Himself the form of a bondservant, and gave Himself up for our sins; for our iniquities humbled Him, and by His wound we are all healed; and He gathered us out of all regions, till He should make resurrection of our hearts from the earth, and teach us that we are all of one substance, and members one of another. Therefore we ought greatly to love one another. For he who loves his neighbor, loves God: and he who loves God, loves his own soul.

Anthony the Great

If the salvation of the world is in no other, but in Christ alone, then the fathers of the Old Testament were saved by the incarnation and passion of the same Redeemer, by which we also believe and hope to be saved. For although the sacramental signs differed by reason of the times, nevertheless there was agreement in one and the same faith, because through the prophets they learned as something to come the same dispensation of Christ, which we learned through the apostles as something that has been done. For there is no redemption of human captivity [to sinfulness] except in the blood of Him Who gave Himself as a redemption for all.   Bede

---

If, therefore, anyone wishes to show piety towards God, let him worship the Son, since otherwise the Father accepts not his service. The Father spoke with a loud voice from heaven, saying, 'This is my beloved Son, in whom I am well pleased' (Matt. 3:17). The Father was well pleased; unless you also be well pleased in Him. you have not life.   Cyril of Jerusalem

---

In Christ we possess everything. Let every soul approach Him, be it sick with sins of the flesh, infixed by the nails of worldly desires, admittedly still imperfect, progressing by intense meditation, or already perfect in its many virtues. Everyone is in the Lord's power, and Christ is all things to us. If you desire to heal your wounds, He is your doctor; if you are on fire with fever, He is your fountain; if you are burdened with iniquity, He is your justification; if you need help, He is your strength; if you fear death, He is your life; if you desire heaven, He is your way; if you are fleeing from darkness, He is your light; if you are seeking food, He is your nourishment: Taste and see that the Lord is good. Happy is the man who takes refuge in Him. <u>Ambrose of Milan</u>

In Christianity truth is not a philosophical concept nor is it a theory, a teaching, or a system, but rather, it is the living the anthropic hypostasis - the historical Jesus Christ (John 14:6). Before Christ men could only conjecture about the Truth since they did not possess it. With Christ as the incarnate divine Logos the eternally complete divine Truth enters into the world. For this reason the Gospel says: "Truth came by Jesus Christ" (John 1:17).

<u>Justin Popovich</u>

In the life and soul of an Orthodox Christian nothing takes place according to man's desire or will but everything occurs according to the God-man. Through the exercise of evangelical virtues, the Orthodox Christian concentrates on God - his spirit, soul and will concentrate through the aid of the Holy Spirit. Whatever belongs to him is gathered and universalized in the God-man. With his entire being, he understands that the Orthodox Church is always holy and catholic and that the attribute of divine humanity is the unaltered characteristic of the Orthodox Church. <u>Ibid</u>

It is Christ who gives us the power to walk, and He is Himself the Way; He is the lodging where we stay for the night, as well as our final destination.

<u>Nicolas Cabasilas</u>

Jesus Christ, radiant center of glory, image of our God, the invisible Father, revealer of His eternal designs, prince of peace; Father of the world to come. For our sake he took the likeness of a slave, becoming flesh in the womb of the Virgin Mary, for our sake, wrapped in swaddling bands and laid in a manger adored by the shepherds and hymned by the angelic powers, who sang: Glory to God in the heavens and on earth peace and good to men. Make us worthy, Lord, to celebrate and to conclude in peace the feast which magnifies the rising of Your light, by avoiding empty words, working with justice, fleeing from the passions, and raising up the spirit above earthly goods. Bless Your Church, formed long ago to be united with You through Your life-giving blood. Come to the aid of Your faithful shepherds, of the priests and the teachers of the Gospel. Bless Your faithful whose only hope is in Your mercy; Christian souls, the sick, those who are tormented in spirit, and those who have asked us to pray for them. Have pity, in Your infinite clemency, and preserve us in fitness to receive the future, endless, good things. We celebrate Your glorious Nativity with the Father who sent you for our redemption, with the life-giving Spirit, now and for ever and through all ages.

Just as children do not realize the sacrifices their parents and teachers make to bring them up and pass on to them the hard-earned experience of a lifetime, so generally men did not understand Christ - and even the rare exception only partly understood. Thus the Word of Christ, which calls for a radical altering of our whole life, came as a cruel wound. When Christ beheld our distress He suffered more than any of us. And He bore this cross all the years of His service in the world. Golgotha was only the last act, the culminating point, as it were, uniting the whole: the mental distress of an infamous death, the wild vindictive laughter of those to whom He had caused offence, the physical pain of being crucified, the grief of His Spirit because men had spurned the tidings of the Father's love."   Archimandrite Sophrony

Just as the portrait painter is attentive to the face of the king as he paints, and, when the face of the king is directly opposite, face to face, then he paints the portrait easily and well. But when he turns his face away, then the painter cannot paint because the face of the subject is not looking at the painter. In a similar way, the good portrait painter, Christ, for those who believe in him and gaze continually toward him, at once paints according to his own icon a heavenly man. Out of his Spirit, out of the substance of the light itself, ineffable light, he paints a heavenly icon and presents to it its noble a and good Spouse. If anyone, therefore, does not continually gaze at him, overlooking all else, the Lord will not paint his image with his own light. It is necessary that we gaze on him, believing and loving him, casting aside all else and attending to him so that he may paint his own heavenly image and send it into our souls. And thus carrying Christ, we may receive eternal life and even here, filled with confidence, we may be at rest.   Macarius

---

Now the ark of the covenant was placed within this curtain of the temple [Ex. 26:33] because after His passion and resurrection from the dead, the Mediator between God and humankind, the man Christ Jesus, Who alone is privy to the secrets of the Father, has ascended above the highest heaven and sits at the right hand of the Father. The sanctuary and the holy of holies are divided by this curtain because the Church, which consists of the holy angels as well as human beings, partly still sojourns below and partly reigns in the eternal homeland above, as its citizens are still separated from another by the dividing curtain of heaven.   Bede

---

Our Lord and Savior, Jesus Christ, dearly beloved, sometimes connects us by His words and sometimes by His actions. His very deeds are commands, because when He does something silently, He is making known to us what we ought to do. He sent His disciples to preach two by two because there are two commandments of love, of God and neighbor, and there can be no love between fewer than two. Strictly speaking no one is said to have love for himself; love becomes possible when one reaches out toward someone else. The Lord sent His disciples to preach two by two, to inform us silently that no one who has no love for another person should undertake the duty of preaching.   Gregory the Great

---

The God-man Christ is so extraordinarily new and unique that in reality the "Truth" came from Him (Jn. 1:17), and through Him remained in our human world. Before Him and without Him - now and forever - Truth does not exist. Verily, it does not exist because only the Hypostasis of the God-man is Truth. "I am the Truth" (Jn. 14:6). And since man does not exist independently of the God-man there can be no truth for him independently of the God-man.   Justin Popovich

The One Who used humble words with Paul, His persecutor, used the same humble words with the Pharisee. Humility is so powerful that even the all-conquering God did not conquer without it. Humility was even able to bear the burden of a stiff-necked nation in the desert. Moses, the humblest of men, was given charge of the nation that was the most stubborn of all men. God, Who needed nothing to save His people, later found Himself in need of the humility of Moses just to abide the grumbling and complaining of (His) critics. Only humility could tolerate the perversity of a nation that dismissed signs in Egypt as well as wonders in the desert. Whenever pride caused divisions in the nation, the prayer of humility healed their divisions. Now, if the humility of a tongue-tied man endured six hundred thousand, how much more does His humility endure, Who granted speech to the tongue-tied! For the humility of Moses is a (mere) shadow of the humility of our Lord.

Ephrem the Syrian

The Only-begotten Son is Lord of all, but the obedient Son of the Father, for He grasped not the Lordship, but received it by nature of the Father's own will. For neither did the Son grasp it, nor the Father grudge to impart it.

Cyril of Jerusalem

The Son, wishing to assure us of the truth of this, His Divine birth, has appointed His works to serve as an illustration, that from the ineffable power displayed in ineffable deeds we may learn the lesson of the ineffable birth. For instance, when water was made wine, and the five loaves satisfied five thousand men, beside women and children, and twelve baskets were filled with the fragments, we see a fact though we cannot understand it; a deed is done, though it baffles our reason; the process cannot be followed, though the result is obvious. It is folly to intrude in the spirit of carping, when the matter into which we enquire is such that we cannot probe it to the bottom. For even as the Father is ineffable because He is Unbegotten, so is the Son ineffable because He is the Only-begotten, since the Begotten is the Image of the Unbegotten.   Hilary of Poitiers

The Word is the expression of the truth; the truth itself being and deed. The Word precedes every being, every thing, as the cause of their being - past, present, or future. 'I am Alpha and Omega, the beginning and the ending, says the Lord, Which is, and Which was, and Which is to come, the Almighty.' Thus spoke the creative Word of the Father. In Him - in the Word - is the cause of all creatures - present, past, and future.   John of Kronstadt

The child Jesus born within us advances by different ways in those who receive Him in wisdom, in age, and in grace. He is not the same in every person, but is present according to the measure of the person receiving Him. He comes either as an infant, or a child advancing in age, or as one fully grown after the example of the cluster. Christ is never seen with the same form upon the vine, but He changes His form with time - now budding, now blossoming, now mature, now ripe and finally as wine. Thus the vine holds out a promise with its fruit. It is not yet ripe for wine, but it awaits maturity. Meanwhile it does not lack any delight, for it gladdens our sense of smell instead of our taste with its expectation of the future; by its fragrance of hope it sweetens the soul's senses. A faith firm in a grace we hope for becomes a delight for us who wait in patience.   Gregory of Nyssa

The humility of our Lord Jesus Christ is a matter for as great wonder as are

His miracles, together with His Resurrection - that Wonder of wonders. Clothing Himself in the cramped human body of a slave, He became the Servant of His servants... Why do men try to appear greater and better than they are? The grass in the field does not attempt this, and neither do fish in the water or birds in the air. Why, then, do men do this? Because they were, in reality, at one time greater and better than they are now, and the shadow of this memory urges them to exaggeration of their greatness and goodness- on a string pulled taut and let go by the demons"   Nicolai Velimirovich

The one act that makes the God-man Christ, in particular, the most valuable of all beings is that He is the first and only to have completely and effectively resolved the age-old dilemma of life and death. He has done this by revealing in His God-man person, the incarnate one, immortality and eternal life. This is especially demonstrated by His Resurrection and Ascension to the eternal life of the divine One. The entire the anthropic life of Christ both before and after His resurrection is evident proof that He is the personification of immortality and eternal life and therefore the master over death. by His resurrection He insured for human nature victory over death, and by His Ascension immortal life in the eternity of the Triune God. For this reason, he alone among the human race is justified in saying: "I am the Resurrection and the life..   Justin Popovich

The prophets, after they had received special insight from Him, prophesied concerning Him. And He submitted so that He might break the power of Death and demonstrate the resurrection from the dead -- thus it was necessary for Him to be manifested in the flesh. Also [He submitted] so that He might fulfill the promise to the fathers and, while He was preparing the new people for Himself and while He was still on earth, to prove that after He has brought about the resurrection He will judge.   he Letter of Barnabas

The transcendently and absolutely perfect Goodness is Intellect; thus what else could the which proceeds from It as from a source be except intelligence-content or Logos? But the divine Logos is not to be understood in the same way as the human thought-form that we express orally, for that proceeds not from the intellect but from a body activated by the intellect...Thus the supreme Logos is the Son, and is so described by us, in order that we may recognize Him to be perfect in a perfect and individual hypostasis, since He comes from the Father and is in no way inferior to the Father's essence, but is indistinguishably identical with Him, although not according to hypostasis; for His distinction as hypostasis is manifest in the fact that the Logos is begotten in a divinely fitting manner from the Father."

Gregory Palamas

There is realized the most radical, rational, and perfect unity of the present life with the life that lies beyond in the divine-human person of Christ. Likewise, there is also found in the person of Christ the unity of the present knowledge and the knowledge of the beyond as well as the unity of human and divine feelings. This means that the life, thought, and feelings of man have bridged the abyss, which separates man from God, the abyss between this world and the other. It is for this reason that a man living a life in Christ vividly experiences the unity of this world with the other, the unity of God with man, the worldly with the transcendent, and the natural with the supernatural.   Justin Popovich

---

There remains, I conceive, no possibility of doubt but that the words, `I and the Father are One,' were spoken with regard to the nature which is His by birth. The Jews had rebuked Him because by these words He, being a man, made Himself God. The course of His answer proves that, in this `I and the Father are One,' He did profess Himself the Son of God, first in name, then in nature, and lastly by birth. For 'I and the Father' are the names of substantive Beings; `One' is a declaration of Their nature, namely, that it is essentially the same in Both; `are' forbids us to confound Them together; `are one,' while forbidding confusion, teaches that the unity of the Two is the result of a birth. Now all this truth is drawn out from that name, the Son of God, which He being sanctified by the Father, bestows upon Himself; a name, His right to which is confirmed by His assertion, `I and the Father are One.' For birth cannot confer any nature upon the offspring other than that of the parent from whom that offspring is born.   Hilary of Poitiers

Throughout his entire history, man appears as a unique type of creature who has laboriously sought the fundamental and essential truth upon which the foundation of the cosmos rests. Man has attempted to answer the quest for truth in various ways -- mythologically, philosophically, atheistically, spiritually, and materialistically. However, he has not been able to solve the problem since he has tried to solve it with the categories of pure, autonomous, and atheistic humanism. Only in the miraculous person on the God-man Christ is the entire eternal Truth revealed, without any defects. Further, the search for eternal truth is completed in the revelation of the absolute divine Truth within the boundaries of human nature. Thus, from the mouth of the God-man Christ came the most courageous declaration that a human being could possibly give: 'I am the Truth' (Jn 14:6). This means that the God-man Christ, as a person, is the truth in all His the anthropic perfection and reality.   Justin Popovich

We in accordance with the true doctrine speak of the Son as neither like, nor unlike the Father. Each of these terms is equally impossible, for like and unlike are predicated in relation to quality, and the divine is free from quality.   Basil

We preach not one advent only of Christ, but a second also, far more glorious than the former. For the former gave a view of His patience; but the latter brings with it the crown of a divine kingdom. For all things, for the most part, are twofold in our Lord Jesus Christ: a twofold generation; one, of God, before the ages; and one, of a Virgin, at the close of the ages: His descents twofold; one, the unobserved, 'like rain on a fleece' (Ps. 72:6); and a second His open coming, which is to be. In His former advent, He was wrapped in swaddling clothes in the manger; in His second, He 'covers Himself with light as with a garment' (Ps. 104:2). In His first coming, 'He endured the Cross, despising shame' (Heb. 12:2); in His second, He comes attended by a host of Angels, receiving glory.   Cyril of Jerusalem

What is the essence of Orthodoxy? It is the God-man Christ. Everything that is Orthodox has a divine-human character: knowledge, the senses, the will, the mind, morality, dogma, philosophy, and life. Divine humanity is the only category in which all the manifestations of Orthodoxy are received and fully operate. In all creation, God occupies the first place, man the second. God leads while man is led; God acts and man cooperates. God does not act transcendentally. He is not the abstract God of deism, but rather the God of the most immediate historic reality, the God of revelation, the God who became man and lived within the categories of our human existence while appearing everywhere as absolute holiness, goodness, wisdom, justice and truth.   Justin Popovich

---

What is truth?" inquired Pilate of the incarnate Truth, wanting to hear with his own ears that which he did not perceive with his eyes, as though it was not the same soul that was hearing through his ears and seeing through his eyes. The God-man Christ is the Truth, not as word, neither as teaching nor as concrete energy, but as a most perfect and eternally living divine-human Hypostasis. It is only as a the anthropic Personality that He is the criterion of truth. It is for this reason that the God-man not only said, "I am the Truth," but also that, "I am the Way" (Jn. 14:6), that is, He is the way to Truth itself, the criterion of Truth itself, the essence of Truth itself. The criterion of Truth is the Truth itself, and the Truth is the God-man Christ. Thus, whatever does not come from Him is not from the Truth. The Truth cannot ontologically exist outside of his divine-human personality.   Ibid

---

You look into a mirror so that you may know what is in your face, whether there are any blemishes in it, and having seen blemishes, you cleanse them. Let the immaculate life of Christ be a mirror to your soul, look into it often and know what is in your soul. Does it desire the same things that Christ desires? And does it do what Christ did when He lived on earth? An in it you will see what is contrary to the life of Christ, and you will cleanse it all like blemishes with repentance and contrition of heart. Christ the Lord despised honor, glory and riches in this world, though He was able to have everything as the Master of all. Do you not seek honor, riches, and glory in this world?

Coal is by nature wood, only it is entirely filled with fire and acquires its power and energy. Our Lord Jesus Christ, Himself, in my view, may very appropriately be conceived of in the same way. 'For the Word became flesh and dwelt among us' (Jn. 1:14). But although He was seen by us as a man, in accordance with the dispensation of the Incarnation, the fullness of the Godhead nevertheless dwelt in Him, by means, I would emphasize, of the union. Thus it may be seen that He has the energies most appropriate to God operating through His own flesh. Accordingly, he touched the bier and raised the widow's dead son (cf. Lk. 7:11-16). And indeed by spitting and anointing their eyes with mud, he enabled the blind to see (cf. Jn. 9:6,7). Emmanuel is therefore very appropriately compared to a burning coal (cf. Isa. 6:6), for when He touches our lips He wipes away our sins completely and cleanses us of our transgression.   Cyril of Alexandria

Every kind of help comes to our souls through Him, and an appropriate title has been devised for each particular kind of care. When He presents a blameless soul to Himself, a soul that like a pure virgin has neither spot nor wrinkle, He is called Bridegroom, but when He receives someone paralyzed by the devil's evil strokes, and heals the heavy burden of his sins, He is called Physician. Because He cares for us, will this make us think less of Him? Or will we not be struck with amazement at our Savior's mighty power and love for mankind, Who patiently endured to suffer our infirmities with us, and condescended to our weakness?   Basil the Great

There is, after all, only one Physician: both flesh and spirit, begotten and unbegotten, God Incarnate, in death, true life, both of Mary and of God, first passible, then impassible, Jesus Christ our Lord.   Ignatius of Antioch

319

Jesus Prayer

At your work, flee conversation; only measured words in case of need. The hands should work for the needs of the body, and the mind should say the sweetest name of Christ, so that the need of the soul, which we must not forget even for moment, also will be provided for.   Ephraim of Philotheou

---

Continually say the Prayer [of Jesus] intensely, with zeal, with longing; only thus does one become strong in soul. Avoid idle words by means of all sacrifice, for they weaken the soul and it does not have the strength to struggle.   Ibid

---

Because the nous can get tired by the reciting of all the words of the Jesus Prayer, it is necessary to make it shorter: "Lord Jesus Christ, have mercy on me." Or, "Lord have mercy on me." Or, "Lord Jesus." As the Christian progresses in the work of the Jesus Prayer, he can decrease the words. He can even sometimes insist on the word "Jesus," which he says repeatedly (Jesus, Jesus, Jesus, my Jesus) a wave of calmness and joy rises in him.

He should remain in this sweetness, which appears, and not stop the prayer, even if his usual rule of prayer is finished. He should seize and keep this warmth of his heart and take advantage of this gift of God! For it is a great gift which God sends from on high. The warmth of the heart helps the nous effectively to be fixed on the words of the Jesus Prayer ... If one wants to spend all day in prayer, he should follow the recommendation of the Holy Fathers. He should pray for an hour, read for an hour and then again spend an hour in prayer. When he is engaged in manual work too, he should try to say the Jesus Prayer.   Hierotheos Vlachos

---

... men should have, as their constant practice and occupation, the invoking of His [Christ's] holy and most sweet name, bearing it always in the mind, in the heart and on the lips. They should force themselves in every possible way to live, breathe, sleep and wake, walk, eat and drink with Him and in Him, and in general so to do all that they have to do.

For as in His absence all harmful things come to us, leaving no room for anything to profit the soul, so in His presence all evil is swept away, no good is ever lacking and everything becomes possible, as the Lord Himself says: 'He that abides in me, and I in him, the same brings forth much fruit: for without me you can do nothing' (John 15:5).   Callistus and Ignatius

---

...with the Name of Jesus flog the foes, for there is no surer weapon against them, either on earth or in heaven.   Gregory of Sinai

---

Unceasing calling upon the name of God cures one not only of passions, but also of actions; and as a medicine affects a sick man without his comprehension, similarly the invocation of the name of God destroys passions in a manner beyond our comprehension.   Barsanuphius the Great

---

All Christians, clergy, laity and monks, when rising from sleep must first think of and remember Christ. They must offer this remembrance to Christ as a sacrifice and first-fruits of every thought (Hebrews 13:15). For we must remember, before every thought, Christ Who saved us and has loved us so greatly, for we are, and are called, "Christians". We put him on by divine Baptism (Gal. 3:27), and we were sealed with His Chrism. We have partaken, and do partake, of His holy Body and Blood. We are His members (1 Cor. 12:27) and His temple (2 Cor. 6:16). Him do we put on, and He dwells in us. For this reason we are obliged to love Him and remember Him always. Wherefore, let everyone devote time, according to his ability, and have a certain amount of this prayer as an obligation. And this suffices concerning this matter, for this is a sufficient amount of instruction for those who seek concerning it.   Simeon of Thessalonica

An Athonite elder said, "It is as necessary for a man to say the Jesus Prayer as it is for a ship in danger to send out steadily the S.O.S. signal: Lord Jesus Christ have mercy on me.   Athonite Gerontikon

An elderly Athonite monk said: We should not miss any chance to us to say the Jesus Prayer. We must not let our mind wander in vain things. In saying the Jesus Prayer one's mind finds rest and joy. It is like small children who for the whole day run around, shouting and playing and hitting each other. But the one thing that gives them rest and great joy is when at night they find themselves in their mother's arms. This way also one's mind instead of being scattered about, out to be devoted to mental prayer.   Athonite Gerontikon

As soon as you wake up in the morning, pray for a while, saying: 'Lord Jesus Christ, Son of God, have mercy upon me.' Then your first work should be to shut yourself in your own heart, as if taking up position in an arena. Having established yourself there, bring yourself to the consciousness and feeling that your enemy and the passionate urge against which you struggle at the moment are already there, on your left, ready for immediate attack; therefore rouse against them a firm resolve to conquer or die, but never to submit. Realize also that on your right there stands, invisibly present, your Commander, our Lord Jesus Christ, with His Holy Mother and a host of holy Angels, with Archangel Michael at their head, ready to come to your aid. So take heart and be of good cheer.   Lorenzo Scupoli

As the Christian progresses in the work of the Jesus Prayer, he can decrease the words. He [or she] can even sometimes insist on the word Jesus, which he says repeatedly ('Jesus', 'Jesus', 'Jesus', 'Jesus') - - a wave of calmness and joy rises in him.

He should remain in this sweetness, which appears, and not stop the prayer, even if his usual rule of prayer has finished. He should seize and keep this warmth of his Heart and take advantage of this gift of God! For it is a great gift which God sends from on high.

The warmth of the Heart helps the nous [Eye of the Soul, Single Eye] effectively to be fixed on the words of the Jesus Prayer, to come down into the Heart and remain there.

If one wants to spend all day in prayer, he should follow the recommendation of the Holy Fathers. He should pray for an hour, read for an hour and then again spend an hour in prayer. When he is engaged in manual work too, he should try to say the Jesus Prayer.   Hierotheos Vlachos

---

At first it may appear very difficult to you, but be assured, as it were from Almighty God, that this very name of our Lord Jesus Christ, constantly invoked by you, will help you to overcome all difficulties, and in the course of time you will become used to this practice and will taste how sweet is the name of the Lord. Then you will learn by experience that this practice is not impossible and not difficult, but both possible and easy. This is why Paul, who knew better than we the great good, which such prayer would bring, commanded us to pray without ceasing. He would not have imposed this obligation upon us if it were extremely difficult and impossible, for he knew beforehand that in such case, having no possibility of fulfilling it, we would inevitably prove to be disobedient and would transgress his commandment, thus incurring blame and condemnation. The Apostle could have had no such intention.   Gregory Palamas

---

At this point the zealous man looks inward, and what do you think he finds there? Ceaseless wandering of thoughts, constant onslaughts from the passions, hardness and coldness of heart, obstinacy and disobedience, desire to do everything according to his own will. In a word, he finds everything within himself in a very bad state. And seeing this, his zeal is inflamed, and he now directs strenuous efforts to the development his inner life, to controlling his thoughts and the dispositions of his heart. >From directions on inner spiritual life he discovers the necessity of paying attention to oneself, of watching over the movements of the heart. In order not to admit to anything bad, it is necessary to preserve the remembrance of God. And so he sets to work to achieve this remembrance. But his thoughts can no more be arrested than the wind; his bad feelings and worthless impulses can no more be evaded than the stench of a corpse; his mind, like a wet and frozen bird, cannot rise to the remembrance of God. What is to be done? Be patient, they say, and go on working. Patience and labor are exercised, but all within remains the same. At last someone of experience is found who explains that all is inwardly in disorder because the forces within are divided: mind and heart each go their own way. Mind and heart must be united; then wandering of thoughts will cease, and you will gain a rudder to steer the ship of your soul, a lever by which to set in movement all your inner world. But how can one unite mind and heart? Acquire the habit of praying these words with the mind in the heart, 'Lord Jesus Christ, Son of God, have mercy upon me'. And this prayer, when you learn to perform it properly, or rather when it becomes grafted to the heart, will lead you to the end that you desire It will unite your mind with your heart, it will cut off your wandering thoughts, and give you the power to govern the movements of your soul.   Theophan the Recluse

---

Blessed are those who acquire the habit of this heavenly practice (unceasing prayer in the name of Jesus, for by it they overcome every temptation of the evil demons, as David overcame the proud Goliath. It extinguishes the unruly lusts of the flesh, as the three men extinguished the flames of the furnace. This practice of inner prayer tames passions as Daniel tamed the wild beasts. By it the dew of the Holy spirit is brought down upon the heart, as Elijah brought down rain on Mount Carmel.   Gregory Palamas

---

Chastise your soul with the thought of death, and through remembrance of Jesus Christ concentrate your scattered intellect.   Joseph of Volokalamsk

---

Continuity of attention produces inner stability; inner stability produces a natural intensification of watchfulness; and this intensification gradually and in due measure gives contemplative insight into spiritual warfare. This in its turn is succeeded by persistence in the Jesus Prayer and by the state that Jesus confers, in which the intellect, free from all images, enjoys complete quietude. Hesychios the Priest

Do not hesitate to go late at night to those places where you usually feel afraid. But if you yield only a little to such weakness, then this childish and ridiculous infirmity will grow old with you. As you go on your way, arm yourself with prayer. When you reach the place, stretch out your hands. Flog your enemies with the name of Jesus, for there is no stronger weapon in heaven or earth. When you get rid of the disease of fear, praise Him who has delivered you. If you continue to be thankful, He will protect you forever.

John Climacus

For the complete fulfillment of its [the intellect's] purpose we should give it nothing but the prayer 'Lord Jesus'...Those who meditate unceasingly upon this glorious and holy name in the depths of their heart can sometimes see the light of their own intellect. For when the mind is closely concentrated upon this name, then we grow fully conscious that the name is burning up all filth, which covers the surface of the soul; for it is written: 'our God is a consuming fire' (Deut. 4:24). Then the Lord awakens in the soul a great love for His glory...This is the pearl of great price which a man can acquire by selling all that he has, and so experience the inexpressible joy of making it his own. Diadochos of Photiki

Grace abides in us from the time of our holy baptism; but, through our inattention, vanity and the wrong life we lead it is stifled, or buried. When a man resolves to lead a righteous life and is zealous for salvation, the fruit of his whole labor is, therefore, the restoration in force of this gift of grace. It comes to pass in a two-fold manner: first, this gift becomes revealed through many labors in following the commandments; insofar as a man succeeds in following the commandments, this gift becomes more radiant and brilliant. Secondly, it manifests and reveals itself through constant invocation of the

Lord Jesus in prayer. The first method is powerful, but the second is more so, so that even the first method gains power through it. Thus, if we sincerely wish to open the seed of grace concealed in us, let us hasten to train ourselves in this latter exercise of the heart, and let us have only this work of prayer in our heart, without forms, without images, till it warms our heart and makes it burn with ineffable love of the Lord.   Gregory of Sinai

Half an hour of the Jesus Prayer is worth as much as three hours of deep sleep. The prolonged Jesus Prayer rests and calms us.   Hierotheos Vlachos

If you, being offended by anything, do sense that grief and wrath have seized you, preserve silence, and say naught until unceasing prayer pacifies your heart.   Ammon of Nitria

In the grim struggle with the invisible enemies of our salvation, the supreme weapon is the prayer of Jesus. `All the nations' - the vociferous and wily demons are called nations - `surround me,' says David, `and in the name of the Lord I repulsed them. They encircled and surrounded me like bees, and they burnt like fire among thorns; and in the name of the Lord I repulsed them' (Ps. 117:10-12). With the name of Jesus flog the foes, because there is no stronger weapon in heaven or earth.   Ignatius Brianchaninov

Join to every breath a sober invocation of the name of Jesus and the thought of death with humility. Both these practices bring great profit to the soul.

Abbot Evagrius

Just as it is impossible to cross the sea without a boat, so it is impossible to repulse the provocation of an evil thought without invoking Jesus Christ.

Hesychios

Let every pious man continually repeat this Name as a payer in his mind and with his tongue. Let him always constrain himself to do this while standing, travelling, sitting, resting, speaking, and doing all things. Then he shall find great peace and joy, as those who have occupied themselves with it know from experience. This activity is both for those in worldly life, and for those monks who are in the midst of turmoil. Each one must strive to occupy himself with this prayer, even if to a limited extent only. All, clergy, monks and laymen, must have this prayer as a guide, practicing it according to their ability.   Simeon of Thessalonica

---

Let no one think, my brother-Christians, that it is the duty only of priests and monks to pray without ceasing, and not of laymen. No, no; it is the duty of all of us Christians to remain always in prayer.

For look what the most holy Patriarch of Constantinople, Philotheus, writes in his life of Gregory of Thessalonica. This saint had a beloved friend by the name of Job, a very simple but most virtuous man. Once, while conversing with him, His Eminence said of prayer that every Christian in general should strive to pray always, and to pray without ceasing, as Apostle Paul commands all Christians, "Pray without ceasing" (1 Thessalonians 5:17), and as the prophet David says of himself, although he was a king and had to concern himself with his whole kingdom: "I foresaw the Lord always before my face" (Psalms 15:8), that is, in my prayer I always mentally see the Lord before me. Gregory the Theologian also teaches all Christians to say God's name in prayer more often than to breathe.

So, my Christian brethren, I too implore you, together also with Chrysostom, for the sake of saving your souls, do not neglect the practice of this prayer. Imitate those I have mentioned and follow in their footsteps as far as you can.

Let those who are in the world work at this as a sealing of themselves a sign of their faith, a protector, sanctification, and expeller of every temptation.

Simeon of Thessalonica

Let us work with the body and pray with the soul. Let our outer man perform his bodily tasks, and let the inner man be entirely dedicated to the service of God, never abandoning this spiritual practice of mental prayer, as Jesus, God and Man, commanded us, saying: "But you, when you pray, enter into your closet, and when you have shut your door, pray to your Father which is in secret" (Matthew 6:6).

The closet of the soul is the body; our doors are the five bodily senses. The soul enters its closet when the mind does not wander hither and thither, roaming among things and affairs of the world, but stays within, in our heart.

Our senses become closed and remain closed when we do not let them be attached to external sensory things, and in this way our mind remains free from every worldly attachment, and by secret mental prayer unites with God its Father. "And your Father which sees in secret shall reward you openly," adds the Lord. God who knows all secret things sees mental prayer and rewards it openly with great gifts.

< For that prayer is true and perfect which fills the soul with Divine grace and spiritual gifts. As chrism perfumes the jar the more strongly the tighter it is closed, so prayer, the more fast it is imprisoned in the heart, abounds the more in Divine grace.   Gregory Palamas

---

Man's chief aim should be to find God. In finding God, he finds true happiness. The interior prayer we have been discussing [the Prayer of Jesus] leads man to Him. We can never thank God sufficiently for revealing Himself to us. We can never even thank Him enough for the other goods He bestows upon us. God need not have created man: He had hosts of angels. Yet He created man and countless marvelous things for him.

Joseph of New Skete

Moreover, bear in mind the method of prayer – how it is possible to pray without ceasing, namely by praying in the mind. And this we can always do if we so wish. For when we sit down to work with our hands, when we walk, when we eat, when we drink we can always pray mentally and practice this mental prayer – the true prayer pleasing to God.   Gregory Palamas

---

One time Nicodemos, on a feast day, was walking toward the Great Lavra (on Mt Athos). On his way he came across a kellion where he spent the night. At midnight he saw an elder and his accompanying monks entering the church. He secretly went in also, and there he saw the elder and his subordinate monks uttering the Jesus Prayer ("Lord Jesus Christ, Son of God, have mercy on me"), sometimes in a kneeling position, sometimes standing up. And at the time of the Holy Communion, he saw all their faces shining only a little less dimly than the sun.   Athonite Gerontikon

---

Prayer is the mind's dialogue with God, in which words of petition are uttered with the intellect riveted wholly on God. For when the mind unceasingly repeats the name of the Lord and the intellect gives its full attention to the invocation of the divine name, the light of the knowledge of God overshadows the entire soul like a luminous cloud.   Theoliptos

---

Remembrance of wrongs is an interpreter of Scripture, which explains the words of the Spirit allegorically in order to suit its own disposition. Let it be put to shame by the Prayer of Jesus that cannot be said with it.

John Climacus

The clergy must be diligent in this prayer as though it were apostolic work and divine preaching, as the one activity, which brings about divine effects - one that demonstrates the love of Christ.　　　　Simeon of Thessalonica

---

The incessant invocation of God's name is a medicine, which mortifies not just the passions, but even their influence. Just as the physician puts medications or dressings on a wound that it might be healed, without the patient even knowing the manner of their operation, so also the name of God, when we invoke it, mortifies all passions, though we do not know how that happens.　　　　Barsanuphius the Great

---

The late Athonite Father Tikhon used to say: The prayer, "Lord Jesus have mercy on us" is worth one hundred drachmas, but "Glory to God" is word one thousand. Glorifying God is more valuable than anything else, because in the first instance, people often say the Jesus Prayer when needing something; but when one glorifies God in the midst of suffering, it is an ascesis.

Athonite Gerontikon

The monks are dedicated, and have an indispensable obligation to do this even thought they are in labors which are in the midst of turmoil. They must constrain themselves to say the prayer constantly, praying to the Lord unceasingly (1 Thess. 5:17), even though they are wandering in thoughts and in midst of that confusion which is called "captivity of the mind". They must not be neglectful because their thoughts are stolen by the enemy, but must return to the prayer, rejoicing. Simeon of Thessalonica

---

The more the rain falls on the earth, the softer it makes it; similarly, Christ's holy name gladdens the earth of our heart the more we call upon it.

Hesychius the Priest

The power given by the Lord to His seventy disciples is given to all Christians (Mk. 16:17). Use it, Christian! With the name of Jesus cut off their heads, that is the first appearances of sin in our thoughts, fancies and feelings. Destroy within you the devil's rule over you; destroy all his influence over you; acquire spiritual freedom. The foundation for your struggle is the grace of holy baptism; your weapon is prayer in the name of Jesus. Ignatius Brianchaninov

---

The practice of the prayer of Jesus holy David, or more accurately the Holy Spirit by the mouth of David, offers to all Christians without exception: 'The kings of the earth and all people, princes and all judges of the earth, young men and maidens - let elders with the young praise the name of the Lord, for His name alone is exalted (PS. 148:11-13).' A literal understanding of the states enumerated here would be perfectly permissible, but their essential meaning is spiritual. Ibid

---

This mental prayer reaches to the very throne of God and is preserved in golden vials, sending forth their odors before the Lord, as John the Divine saw in the Revelation, "Four and twenty elders fell down before the Lamb, having every one of them harps, and golden vials full of odors, which are the prayers of the saints" (Revelation 5:8).

This mental prayer is the light that illumines man's soul and inflames his heart with the fire of love of God. It is the chain linking God with man and man with God. Oh the incomparable blessing of mental prayer! It allows a man constantly to converse with God. Oh truly wonderful and more than wonderful – to be with one's body among men while in one's mind conversing with God. Angels have no physical voice, but mentally never cease to sing glory to God. This is their sole occupation and all their life is dedicated to this.   Gregory Palamas

Those who have truly decided to serve the Lord God should practice the remembrance of God and uninterrupted prayer to Jesus Christ, mentally saying: Lord Jesus Christ, Son of God, have mercy on me, a sinner.

Dimitry of Rostov

Those who have truly decided to serve the Lord God should practice the remembrance of God and uninterrupted prayer to Jesus Christ, mentally saying: Lord Jesus Christ, Son of God, have mercy upon me a sinner.

Seraphim of Sarov

To fast in the soul means keeping silent more and praying more frequently by oneself saying, "Lord, Jesus Christ, Son of God, have mercy on me, a sinner." At first this prayer will be only in our minds, then, because of the mind's prayerful effort, suddenly, we know not how, this prayer passes into our hearts. It is possible that at this moment we may even weep and in this way we are baptized anew in the unseen font of our tears. There are all kinds of tears: tears of exaltation, tears of joy, tears of sadness, but the most precious are tears of compunction and repentance.   Paschal Encyclical

What should one do so that the mind might be constantly occupied with God? If we do not acquire the three following virtues: love for God and men, continence, and the Prayer of Jesus, then our mind cannot be completely occupied with God. For love makes anger meek, continence weakens fleshly desire, and prayer draws the mind away from thoughts and banishes every hatred and high-mindedness.   Paisius Velichkovsky

Whenever we are filled with evil thoughts, we should throw the invocation of our Lord Jesus Christ in their midst. Then, as experience has taught us, we shall see them instantly dispersed like smoke in air. Once the intellect is left to itself again, we can renew our constant attentiveness and our invocation. Whenever we are distracted, we should act in this way.   Hesychios the Priest

The sun rising over the earth creates the daylight; and the venerable and holy name of the Lord Jesus, shining continually in the mind, gives birth to countless intellections radiant as the sun.   Ibid

.Because the nous can get tired by the reciting of all the words of the Jesus Prayer, it is necessary to make it shorter: "Lord Jesus Christ, have mercy on me." Or, "Lord have mercy on me." Or, "Lord Jesus." As the Christian progresses in the work of the Jesus Prayer, he can decrease the words. He can even sometimes insist on the word "Jesus," which he says repeatedly (Jesus, Jesus, Jesus, my Jesus) -- a wave of calmness and joy rises in him. He should remain in this sweetness, which appears, and not stop the prayer, even if his usual rule of prayer is finished. He should seize and keep this warmth of his heart and take advantage of this gift of God! For it is a great gift which God sends from on high. The warmth of the heart helps the nous* effectively to be fixed on the words of the Jesus Prayer......If one wants to spend all day in prayer, he should follow the recommendation of the Holy Fathers. He should pray for an hour, read for an hour and then again spend an hour in prayer. When he is engaged in manual work too, he should try to say the Jesus Prayer.   Hierotheos

By rubbing wood against wood fire is kindled, and by the prayerful words of rumination within the heart the fire of love is ignited. Through ardent yearning for God it bursts into flame.   Isaac the Syrian

Watchfulness and the Jesus Prayer, as I have said, mutually reinforce each other, for close attentiveness goes with constant prayer, while prayer goes with close watchfulness and attentiveness of intellect.   Hesychios the Priest

Please put this commandment into practice. Cultivate love towards the Person of Christ to such an extent that, when you pronounce His name, tears fall from your eyes. Your heart must really burn. Then He will become your teacher. He will be your Guide, your Brother, your Father, and your.

Amphilochios Makris

Cultivate the Jesus Prayer and a time will come when your heart will leap with joy, just as it does when you are about to see a person who you love very much.   Ibid

Brethren, let us also occupy yourselves with noetic prayer…, and seeking God's mercy, cry out with a humble heart from morning till night and if possible all night long, saying constantly: "Lord Jesus Christ, Son of God, have mercy on us."   John Chrysostom

Joy

"Rejoice in the Lord," said Paul (Philemon 3:1). And he was right to say, "in the Lord." For if our joy is not in the Lord, not only do we not rejoice, but in all probability we never shall. Job, as he described the life of men, found it full of every kind of affliction (Job 7:1-21), and so also did Basil the Great.

Gregory of Nyssa said that birds and other animals rejoice because of their lack of awareness, while man, being endowed with intelligence, is never happy because of his grief. For, he says, we have not been found worthy even to have knowledge of the blessings we have lost. For this reason nature teaches us rather to grieve, since life is full of pain and effort, like a state of exile dominated by sin.

Now if a person is constantly mindful of God, he will rejoice: as the psalmist says, "I remembered God, and I rejoiced" (Psalms 77:3). For when the intellect is gladdened by the remembrance of God, then it forgets the afflictions of this world, places its hope in Him, and is no longer troubled or anxious.   Peter of Damaskos

Freedom from anxiety makes it (the heart) rejoice and give thanks; and the grateful offering of thanks augments the gifts of grace it has received. And as the blessings increase, so does the thankfulness, and so does the pure prayer offered with tears of joy. Slowly the man emerges from the tears of distress and from the passions, and enters fully into the state of spiritual joy.   Ibid

Through the things that bring him pleasure, he (man) is made humble and grateful; through trials and temptations his hope in the world to come is consolidated; in both he rejoices, and naturally and spontaneously he loves God and all men as his benefactors. He finds nothing in the whole of creation that can harm him.   Ibid

oyful Sorrow

Where poverty of spirit is perceived, there is also the sorrow that is full of joy
                                                    <u>Symeon the New Theologian</u>

---

udging Others

Keep your mind from malicious thoughts of your neighbors, knowing that such thoughts are hurled by diabolical power, to keep your mind from your own sins and from seeking God.   <u>Elias of Egypt</u>

When we judge our brother, we censure ourselves in a great sin. When therefore, we shield our brother, God will also shield us from great sins. When we uncover our brother, we drive off the grace of God from over us and we are given over to fall into the same things, so that we learn that we are all weak and the grace of God carries us. Whoever guards his tongue, that one guards his soul from great sins and falls.   <u>Ephraim of Philotheou</u>

If something pushes you to criticism about some business or other of a brother or of a monastery, you, rather, try to pray about the matter, without passing it under judgment of your reason.   <u>Ibid</u>

Be attentive, my child, that you not judge any soul. For God steps aside from

---

the one who judges his neighbor, and he falls, in order to learn to have sympathy for his sick brother. <u>Ibid</u>

Do not judge one another, for you transgress the evangelical law, and "every transgression and disobedience received a just retribution" (Heb. 2:2). "Who are you to pass judgment on the servant of another?" (Rom. 14:4). Do you not know that the one who passes judgment goes astray through pride, and that everyone who exalts himself will be humbled (Luke 14:11) by the Lord, when temptation seizes him? <u>Ibid</u>

My children, avoid criticism -- a very great sin. God is grieved whenever we criticize and loathe people. Let us concern ourselves only with our own faults -- for these let us feel pain; let us criticize ourselves and then we will find mercy and grace from God. <u>Ibid</u>

Did you see that brother who was negligent and lazy, who did not go down to the all-night vigils and did not do his duties, whom the brothers knew and held to be a negligent brother? When, therefore, he became sick and the hour of his death drew near, the brothers gathered to hear something beneficial, or to comfort him, or in case he wanted to say something to them, but they saw him rejoicing, cheerful.

One brother was scandalized and said, But what do we see in you, brother? We see you rejoicing, while you approach death? But our thought says to us that you were not a violent man and how do you have this courage and this rejoicing face? On what do you base this thing?

Yes, brothers, he said, really I was a negligent person and I did not fulfill my duties. But I achieved one good thing, by the grace of God -- not to criticize any brother and not to scandalize anyone; and never did I allow my heart to have something against my brother of the monastery when the sun set. And inasmuch as I did not judge my brother, I believe that God will not judge me, even me, for He said, Judge not, that you not be judged (Mt. 7:1); and as long as I did not judge, I will not be judged.

The brothers marveled and said, Brother, very easily you found the way of salvation. And the brother died with much joy   .   Ibid

---

A brother who shared a lodging with other brothers asked Abbot Bessarion, "What should I do?" The old man replied, "Keep silence and do not compare yourself with others."   Bessarion the Egyptian

---

Abbot Ammonas came one day to eat in a place where there was a monk of evil repute. Now it happened that a woman came and entered the cell of the brother of evil reputation. The dwellers in that place, having learnt this, were troubled and gathered together to chase the brother from his cell. Knowing that Bishop Ammonas was in the place, they asked him to join them. When the brother in question learnt this, he hid the woman in a large cask.

The crowd of monks came the place. Now Abbot Ammonas saw the position clearly but for the sake of God he kept the secret; he entered, seated himself on the cask and commanded the cell to be searched. Then when the monks had searched everywhere without finding the woman, Abbot Ammonas said, "What is this? May God forgive you!" After praying, he made everyone go out, then taking the brother by the hand he said, "Brother, be on your guard." With these words, he withdrew.   Desert Fathers

---

An old man said to a brother: Do not measure your heart against your brother, saying that you are more serious or more continent or more understanding than he. But be obedient to the grace of God, in the spirit of poverty, and in charity unfeigned. The efforts of a man swollen with vanity are futile. It is written, "Let him that thinks he stands take heed lest he falls." In your spirit be seasoned with salt -- and so be dependent upon Christ.

Batiushka [affectionate term for "Father"] said regarding condemnation and criticism of other's faults and sins: "You need to pay such close attention to your own internal life, that you not focus on what is happening around you. Then you will not condemn."   Amvrossy of Optina

Be kind, for everyone you meet is fighting a great battle. Philo of Alexandria

CAT"1corinthians10-12 Abbot Or used to say this, "Do not speak in your heart against your brother like this: 'I am a man of more sober and austere life than he is,' but put yourself in subjection to the grace of Christ, in the spirit of poverty and genuine charity, or you will be overcome by the spirit of vainglory and lose all you have gained. For it is written in the Scriptures: 'Let him who stands take heed lest he fall.' (1 Corinthians 10:12) Let your salvation be founded in the Lord."   Desert Fathers

Christians should judge no one, neither an open harlot, nor sinners, nor dissolute people, but should look upon all with simplicity of soul and a pure eye. Purity of heart, indeed, consists in seeing sinful and weak men and having compassion for them and being merciful.   Abbot Macarius the Great

Do not condemn today as base and wicked the man whom yesterday you praised as good and virtuous, changing love to hatred, because he has criticized you, but even though you are still full of resentment, commend him as before, and you will soon recover your same saving love.   Maximos

Do not condemn, even if you see with your eyes, for they are often deceived.

John Climacus

Do not listen gleefully to gossip at your neighbors' expense or chatter to a person who likes finding fault.   Maximos the Confessor

Do not pass judgment when you give advice, for you know not God's mysteries.   Ephraim the Syrian

Even if a person's sin is not only obvious, but very grievous and comes from a hardened and unrepentant heart, do not condemn him, but raise your eyes to the wondrous and incomprehensible judgments of God; then you will see that many people, formerly full of iniquity, later repented and reached a high degree of sanctity, and that, on the other hand, others, who were on a high level of perfection, fell into a deep abyss. Take care, lest you also suffer this calamity through judging others.   Theophan the Recluse

He who busies himself with the sins of others, or judges his brother on suspicion, has not yet even begun to repent or to examine himself so as to discover his own sins.   Maximos the Confessor

He who speaks dispassionately of his brother's sin does so either to correct him or to benefit another. If he speaks for any other reason, either to the brother himself or to another person, he speaks to abuse him or ridicule him.

Maximos the Confessor

He who sufficiently knows and judges himself has no time to judge others.

Philaret of Moscow

I suppose that it is sometimes better to fall oneself and rise, than to judge one's neighbor; because one who has sinned is incited to self-abasement and repentance, while he who judges one who has sinned becomes hardened in an illusion about himself and in pride. Therefore everyone must guard himself, as much as possible, so as not to judge.   Abbot Nazarius

In truth, whatever we may suffer, we suffer it because of our sins. If the saints suffered, they suffered for God's name or to demonstrate their virtue for the benefit of many or to gain greater reward from God. As for us wretches, how can we say this? We sin like this daily and in seeking to satisfy our passion, we abandoned the right path, which the Fathers spoke about, that of self-accusation. Each one of us follows the wrong path, tries on every occasion to put the case against his brother and throw the burden of responsibility upon him. Each one of us is negligent and keeps nothing, but demands that our neighbor keeps the commandments.   Abbot Dorotheus

It was said of Abbot Arsenius that once when he was ill at Scetis, the priest came to take him to church and put him on a bed with a small pillow under his head. Now behold, and old man who was coming to see him, saw him lying on a bed with a little pillow under his head and he was shocked and said, "Is this really Abbot Arsenius, this man lying down like this?"

The priest took him aside and said to him, "In the village where you lived, what was your trade?" "I was a shepherd," he replied. "And how did you live?" "I had a very hard life." Then the priest said to him, "And how do you live in your cell now?" The other replied, "I am more comfortable." Then the priest said to him, "Do you see this Abbot Arsenius? When he was in the world he was the guardian of the emperor, surrounded by thousands of slaves with golden girdles, all wearing collars of gold and garments of silk. Beneath him were spread rich coverings. While you were in the world as a shepherd you did not enjoy even the comforts you now have, but he no longer enjoys the delicate life he led in the world. So you are comforted while he is afflicted."

At these words, the old man was filled with compunction and prostrated himself saying, "Father, forgive me, for I have sinned. Truly the way this man follows is the way of truth, for it leads to humility, while mine leads to comfort." So the old man withdrew, edified.   Desert Fathers

---

Love sinners, but hate their works, and do not despise them for their faults, lest you be tempted by the same. Remember that you share the earthly nature of Adam and that you are clothed with his infirmity.   Isaac the Syrian

---

Love sinners, but hate their works, and do not despise them for their faults, lest you be tempted by the same. Remember that you share the earthly nature of Adam and that you are clothed with his infirmity.   Ibid

---

Never allow yourself boldly to judge your neighbor; judge and condemn no one, ... rather have compassion and pity for him, but let his example be a lesson in humility to you; realizing that you too are extremely weak and as easily moved to sin as dust on the road, say to yourself: 'He fell today, but tomorrow I shall fall.'   Lorenzo Scupoli

---

Practice self-observation. And if you want to benefit yourself and your fellow men, look at your own faults and not those of others. The Lord tells us: "Judge not, that you be not judged," condemn not that you be not condemned. And the Apostle Paul says: "Who are you that judge another man's servant?"   Arsenios of Paros

---

Since the enemy watches you constantly, waiting for an opportunity to sow evil in you, be doubly watchful over yourself, lest you fall in the nets spread for you. As soon as he shows you some fault in your neighbor, hasten to repel this thought, lest it take root in you and grow. Cast it out, so that no trace is left in you, and replace it by the thought of the good qualities you know your neighbor to possess, or of those people generally should have. If you still feel the impulse to pass judgment, add to this the truth that you are given no authority for this and that the moment you assume this authority you thereby make yourself worthy of judgment and condemnation, not before powerless men, but before God, the all-powerful Judge of all.

Theophan the Recluse

Paul ... says, ... 'By judging another you condemn yourself' (Rom. 2:1). But men have given up weeping for their own sins and have taken judgment away from the Son. They themselves judge and condemn one another as if they were sinless.   Maximos the Confessor

---

The Lord's most important commandments are "Judge not, and you shall not be judged; condemn not, and you shall not be condemned; forgive, and you

---

shall be forgiven.". Moreover, those desirous of salvation should always keep in mind the words of Peter Damascene, that creation takes place between fear and hope.   Amvrossy of Optina

---

This reversal of thoughts is the strongest means, not only for repelling accidental critical thoughts, but also for completely freeing yourself of this vice.   Theophan the Recluse

---

Those who want to be saved scrutinize not the shortcomings of their neighbor but always their own and they set about eliminating them. Such was the man who saw his brother doing wrong and groaned, `Woe is me; him today-me tomorrow!' You see his caution? You see the preparedness of his mind? How he swiftly foresaw how to avoid judging his brother? When he said `me tomorrow' he aroused his fear of sinning, and by this he increased his caution about avoiding those sins which he was likely to commit, and so he escaped judging his neighbor; and he did not stop at this, but put himself below his brother, saying, `He has repented for his sin but I do not always repent. I am never first to ask for forgiveness and I am never completely converted.'   Dorotheos of Gaza

---

To bear a grudge and pray, means to sow seed on the sea and expect a harvest.   Isaac of Syria

---

We should look upon each believer alike, and suppose that Christ abides in each; we must have such loving disposition towards him as to be ready to lay down our life for him. We should never think or say that someone is evil, but, as is said, should see everyone as good. If you see someone attacked by passions, hate not the brother but the passions attacking him. And when you see someone succumbing to the tyranny of lusts and bad habits, have a still greater compassion for him, lest you suffer a similar temptation - since you are changeable and under the influence of changeable matter.

Simeon the New Theologian

When we see sinners we must always weep for ourselves first over their failure. Perhaps we have fallen in the same way; or we can fall, if we have not yet. And if the judgment of the teaching office must always eradicate vices by the power of discipline, we must nevertheless make careful distinctions: we should be uncompromising about vice, but compassionate to human nature. If a sinner has to be punished, a neighbor has to be supported. When he has nullified what he has done by his repentance, our neighbor is no longer a sinner. With the righteousness of God he turns against himself, and what the divine righteousness reproves he punishes in himself.

Gregory the Great

When you go to your spiritual father for confession, do not bring yourself as an accuser of other people, saying, "he said this," and "so-and-so said that". . . but speak about your own doings, so that you may obtain forgiveness.

Daniel of Kantounakia

Wherefore a man can know nothing about the judgments of God. He alone is the One Who takes account of all and is able to judge the hearts of each one of us, as He alone is our Master. Truly it happens that a man may do a certain thing (which seems to be wrong) out of simplicity, and there may be something about it which makes more amends to God than your whole life; how are you going to sit in judgment and constrict your own soul? And should it happen that he has fallen away, how do you know how much and how well he fought, how much blood he sweated before he did it? Perhaps so little fault can be found in him that God can look on his action as if it were just, for God looks on his labor and all the struggle he had before he did it, and has pity on him. And you know this, and what God has spared him for, are you going to condemn him for, and ruin your own soul? And how do you know what tears he has shed about it before God? You may well know about the sin, but you do not know about the repentance.   Dorotheos of Gaza

Your past and present torments and sufferings are poured down upon you to test your faith and 'steel' it; they also work to curb your lusts and passions. Humble yourself. God gives help to the humble. Judgment of others, insistence on their shortcomings, can only increase the bitterness of your sorrow. Choose the better part.   Macarius of Optina

Do not disdain those who are handicapped from birth, because all of us will go to the grave equally privileged.   Isaac of Syria

Love sinners, but hate their works; and do not despise them for their faults, lest you be tempted by the same trespasses.   Ibid

"Do not judge and do not belittle anyone, because from this the heart grows faint and the mind is blinded, and from this, negligence appears and unfeelingness of heart is born. Keep ceaseless vigil, learning in the law of God, for through this the heart is warmed by heavenly fire, as is said: 'In my meditation a fire was kindled'."   Barsanuphius

Do not rail against anyone, but rather say 'God knows each one.' Do not agree with him who slanders, do not rejoice at his slander and do not hate him who slanders his neighbor. This is what it means not to judge."

Moses the Ethiopian

Through the things that bring him pleasure, he (man) is made humble and grateful; through trials and temptations his hope in the world to come is consolidated; in both he rejoices, and naturally and spontaneously he loves God and all men as his benefactors. He finds nothing in the whole of creation that can harm him.

Then we say: "Forgive us our trespasses as we forgive those who trespass against us." Brothers, praying thus, we should very much fear lest the Lord reply to these words of our prayer: "The judgments you give are the judgments you will get, and the amount you measure out is the amount you will be given." And you who ask this, see whether you did to no one what you did not want done to you. Therefore before we hear these words of the Lord, brethren, let us first examine our hearts as to whether we are with justice asking of the Lord what we have not denied to those asking us. We ask that our trespasses be forgiven us. God hears and He wants to forgive us, but only if we first pardon those who ask us to do likewise.   Benedict

Judgment

On that dreadful and amazing day, You shall say to us sinners, Oh Lord: "You men know well what I have undergone for you...what have you suffered for Me?" What shall I say to that; I who, though penitent, am evil, sinful and polluted? The martyrs will point to their wounds, their sufferings, the severed parts of their bodies, and to their endurance to the end. The ascetics will point to their asceticism, to their long fasts and vigils, to their liberality, their tears and their endurance to the end. But I, idle, sinful, transgressing as I am, what shall I be able to point to? Spare me, Oh merciful One! Spare me, Oh You Lover of mankind!"   Ephraim the Syrian

---

[Jesus], in administering the righteous judgment of the Father to all, assigns to each what is righteous according to his works. ... Justification will be seen in the awarding to each that which is just; to those who have done well, there will be justly assigned eternal happiness. The lovers of wickedness will be assigned eternal punishment. ... But the righteous will remember only the righteous deeds by which they reached the heavenly kingdom."   Hippolytus

---

A brother asked Abbot Sisoes, 'What shall I do, Abbot, for I have fallen?' The old man said to him, 'Get up again.' The brother said, 'I have got up again, but I have fallen again.; The old man said, 'Get up again and again.; So then the brother said, 'How many times?' The old man said, 'Until you are taken up either in virtue or in sin. For a man presents himself to judgment in the state in which he is found.'   Desert Fathers

---

Kingdom of God

The kingdom of God is knowledge of the Holy Trinity, extending as far as the state of one's mind permits, and filling it with an endlessly blessed life.

Abbot Evagrius

Kingdom of Heaven

Let us cut sin out of our heart, and we will find within us the Kingdom of Heaven.   Philotheos of Sinai

---

The kingdom of God is always present for him who desires and wills it. When a man's disposition and way of life are like that of an angel, most assuredly this is the kingdom of God. For God indeed is said to rule as King when nothing worldly meddles in the governing of our souls and when in every respect we live not of this world. This manner of life we have within us, that is to say, we have it within us when we desire and will it. We do not need to wait a long time, or until our departure from this life; instead, faith and a God-pleasing life, which accompanies faith, are very near us.

Theophylact

The present age is temporal. In comparison with the future one it is like a drop in the oceans. So no longer attach your mind to temporal and earthly things, but to the incorruptible and heavenly things. Let us long with our whole soul for heavenly things, and with God's help we shall obtain them. Let your recollections, says Yperechios, be in the Kingdom of Heaven, and you shall quickly inherit it. So please, my brethren, let us not be negligent and drowsy.   Philotheos

Knowledge

...we should search the Scriptures in accordance with the Lord's commandment, so that we may find eternal life in them (cf. John 5:39); and we should pay attention to the meaning of the psalms and troparia, becoming in this way totally aware of our ignorance. For if one does not taste of knowledge, says Basil the Great, one does not know how much one lacks.

Peter of Damaskos

A life of spiritual endeavor is the mother of sanctity; from it is born the first experience of perception of the mysteries of Christ -- which is called the first stage of spiritual knowledge.   Isaac of Syria

---

BROTHER: To what extent is a man held capable of revelation?

OLD MAN: To the same extent as a man is capable of stripping off sin, both internally and externally. For when a man dies by spiritual sacrifice, he dies to all the words and deeds of this habitation of time, and when he has committed his life to the life, which is after the revivification, divine grace bestows itself upon him, and he becomes capable of divine revelations. For the impurity of the world is a dark covering before the face of the soul, and it prevents it from discerning spiritual wisdom   Desert Fathers

---

Better poverty with knowledge than riches with ignorance. "Instructions to Cenobites and Others"   Abbot Evagrius

---

We also know that the fulfillment of the commandments of God gives true knowledge, since it is through this that the soul gains health. How could a rational soul be healthy, if it is sick in its cognitive faculty? So we know that the commandments of God also grant knowledge, and not that alone, but deification also.   Gregory Palamas

---

He is not yet a faithful servant who bases himself on bare knowledge alone; a faithful servant is he who professes his faith by obedience to Christ, Who gave the commandments.   Mark the Ascetic

---

If you love knowledge, love also work, for bare knowledge puffs a man up.

Mark the Ascetic

If you will keep in mind that, according to the Scriptures, the Lord's "judgments are in all the earth" (Psalms 104:7), then every event will teach you knowledge of God.   Ibid

---

If you wish to be saved and to come to the knowledge of truth, always urge yourself to rise above sensory things and to cling with hope to God alone. Thus compelling yourself to turn inwards, you will meet principalities and powers, which wage war against you by suggestions in thoughts. If you overcome them by prayer and remain in good hope, you will receive Divine grace, which will free you from the wrath to come.   Ibid

---

Knowledge is an excellent thing; it helps prayer, inciting the power of the mind to the contemplation of Divine knowledge.   Nilus of Mt Sinai

---

Knowledge that is occupied with visible things and receives instruction concerning them through the senses, is called natural. But knowledge that is occupied with the noetic power that is within things and with incorporeal natures is called spiritual, since perception in this case is received by the spirit and not by the senses. In both of these kinds of knowledge matter comes to the soul from without to give her comprehension. But that knowledge which is occupied with Divinity is called supranatural, or rather, un-knowing and knowledge-transcending.   Isaac the Syrian

---

Knowledge without corresponding practice is still insecure, even if it is true. All is made firm by practice.   Mark the Ascetic

---

Love is preceded by passionlessness; knowledge is preceded by love.

Abbot Evagrius

Some hold that the practice of the virtues constitutes the truest form of spiritual knowledge. In that case, we should make every effort to manifest our faith and knowledge throughout our actions. Whoever trusts blindly to knowledge alone should call to mind the words: "They claim to know God, but in their actions they deny Him" (Titus 1:16).   John of Karpathos

---

The bosom of the Lord is knowledge of God; he who rests therein will be a theologian.   Abbot Evagrius

---

The highest adornment of the head is the crown; the highest adornment of the heart is knowledge of God.   Ibid

---

The knowledge of God is a mountain steep indeed and difficult to climb - the majority of people scarcely reach its base. If one were a Moses, he would ascend higher and hear the sound of trumpets that, as the text of the history says, becomes louder as one advances. For the preaching of the divine nature is truly a trumpet blast, which strikes the hearing, being already loud at the beginning but becoming yet louder at the end.   Gregory of Nyssa

There is a knowledge that precedes faith, and there is a knowledge born of faith. Knowledge that precedes faith is natural knowledge; and that which is born of faith is spiritual knowledge. What is natural knowledge? Knowledge is natural that discerns good from evil, and this is also called natural discernment, by which we know to discern good from evil naturally, without being taught. God has implanted this in rational nature, and with teaching it receives growth and assistance; there is no one who does not have it.

Isaac the Syrian

Therefore, there is no other way of attaining to spiritual knowledge except by following this order, which one of the prophets has neatly expressed: 'Sow for yourselves unto righteousness; reap the hope of life; enlighten yourselves with the light of knowledge' (Hosea 10:12). First, then, we sow for ourselves unto righteousness - that is, we must increase practical perfection by works of righteousness. Then we must reap the hope of life - that is, we must gather the fruit of spiritual virtues by expelling our carnal vices. Thus we shall be able to enlighten ourselves with the light of knowledge.   John Cassian

When he who is filled with knowledge and he who practices good meet one another, the Lord is between them.   Abbot Evagrius

Where sin enters, there too enters ignorance; but the hearts of the righteous are filled with knowledge.   Ibid

But also know that the fulfillment of the commandments of God gives true knowledge, since it is through this that the soul gains health. How could a rational soul be healthy, if it is sick in it's cognitive faculty? So we know that the commandments of God also grant knowledge, and not that alone, but deification also.   Gregory Palamas

---

If you love true knowledge, devote yourself to the ascetic life; for mere theoretical knowledge puffs a man up (cf. 1Co 8:1).   Kosmas Aitolos

---

Even though knowledge is true, it is still not firmly established if unaccompanied by works. For everything is established by being put into practice.

Often our knowledge becomes darkened because we fail to put things into practice. For when we have totally neglected to practice something, our memory of it will gradually disappear.

For this reason Scripture urges us to acquire the knowledge of God, so that through our works we may serve Him rightly.   Ibid

---

Each man's knowledge is genuine to the extent that it is confirmed by gentleness, humility and love.   Ibid

---

Knowledge of created beings is one thing, and knowledge of the divine truth is another. The second surpasses the first just as the sun outshines the moon.

Ibid

As Maximos has said, "To think that one knows prevents one from advancing in knowledge." John Chrysostom points out that there is an ignorance, which is praiseworthy: it consists in knowing consciously that one knows nothing. In addition, there is a form of ignorance that is worse than any other: not to know that one does not know. Similarly, there is a knowledge that is falsely so called, which occurs when, as Paul says, one thinks that one knows but does not know (see I Corinthians 8:2).

Peter of Damaskos

The End of this Text

This Volume completes Book 2 of this Set of Four

Visit us at your local bookstore on the web at our web site

http://Revelationinsight.tripod.com

All works available in *Kindle* via Amazon

I-Pad E-Books via Apple Book Store

Nook via Barnes &Noble

All works always at least 10% off retail, through our store

The Spurgeon Library

Collected Works   Vol. 1-6

1st segment

The Andrew Murray Library

Collected Works   Volumes 1-5

Women of Faith Series

Volumes 1-4

1st segment

Teresa of Avila	Interior Castle
Collected Works	Julian of Norwich
Dialogues	Catherine of Sienna
Passion of Christ	Anne Catherine Emmerich

2nd segment

Vol. 5-7

Select Jewels	Jessie Penn-Lewis
Women (According to Bonaventure)	E. Therese
Immaculate Conception	Aquinas, Bonaventure & D. Scotus

Works of the Catholic Classics Series

Volumes 1-5

1st segment

Explanation of the Rule of St Augustine	Hugh of St. Victor

Treatise of the Spiritual Life Books 1-3	Bishop Morozzo O.Cist
Imitation of Christ	Thomas a' Kempis

Note: vol. 2-4 are fraternal twins writings

2nd segment

Vol. 5-6

Little Book of Wisdom	Henry Suso
Spiritual Exercises with Commentary	Ignatius

Works of the Desert Fathers Series

Volumes 1-4

1st segment

Wisdom of the Desert	James O' Hanney
Desert Fathers Books 1 & 2	Countess Hahn-Hahn
Evigarius Essentials	Evigarius

2nd segment

Vol. 5-6

Selected Works	Ephraim the Syrian
Steps to Paradise with Commentary by L Granada	John Climacus

Works for the Master

"Philosopher's Palate" Series

Vol. 1-4

1st segment

Divine Names	Pseudo Dionysius
First Principle	Duns Scotus
Consolation of Philosophy	Boethius
Pensees	Paschal

2nd segment

Vol. 5-8

The Greek Thinkers   Theodor Gomperz

"Philip Schaff Library "

Vol 1-6

Church History   Philip Schaff

The Thomas Aquinas Library

Volumes 1-4

1st segment

The Companion to the Summa   Walter Farrell O.P.

2nd segment

Vol. 5-8

Contra Gentiles   Thomas Aquinas

3rd segment

Vol. 9-12

Catena Aurea Thomas Aquinas

(a.k.a Commentary on the four Gospels)

Works for the Journeyman

Great Christian Mystical Writings

Volumes 1-4

1st segment

Ascent of Mount Carmel   St. John of the Cross

Dark Night of the Soul   St. John of the Cross

A Cell of Knowledge   Anonymous

Divine Consolation   Angelina Foligno

2nd segment

Vol. 5-6

A Cloud of Unknowing   Walter Hilton

Mysticism of Francis of Assisi   D. Nicholson

The Poetry Series

1st segment

Volumes 1-3

The Complete Poetry Works   Adam of St. Victor

72nd segment

Vol. 4

Mystical Poetry   Ramon Lull

The Contemplative Series

Volumes 1-4

1st segment

Ladder of Perfection   Walter Hilton

Selection of Hugh of St Victor   Hugh of St Victor

Golden Treatise of Mental Prayer   Peter of Alcantra

Third Spiritual Alphabet   Francisco de Osuna

French Enlightenment Series

Volumes 1-4

1st segment

Selections	Francis de Fenelon
Selections	Francis de Sales Book. 1&2
Great Works	Gene Gerson

2nd segment

Vol. 5-8

Selections	St Bernard

3rd segment

Selections	Reginald Garriough

Research Essentials Series

Volumes 1-5

1st segment

Medieval to Modern English Dictionary	R /I Publishing Staff
Contemplative Life	St. Bruno
Ecclesiastical History	Bede
Church Creeds	Various

2nd segment

Vols. 5-6

Bible Customs and Manners	OT/NT (2 Bks)	James Freeman

Works for the Apprentice

The Initial Series

Pilgrim's Pantry

Volumes 1-4

1st segment

The Kneeling Christian	Anonymous
Passion of Christ	Bro Smith SGS
Way of Perfection	Teresa of Avila
Augustine Essentials	Augustine

2nd segment

Vols. 5-7

Ascent of the Pilgrim	Various Authors
Best Works	E. Bounds
Grammar of Assent	John H. Newman

The Monastic Series

Volumes 1-2

1st segment

| A Short Overview of Monasticism | Alfred Wishart |
| Monasticism from Egypt to the 4th Cent | W. Mackean |

2nd segment

Vols. 3-6

A Monk's Topical Bible in 4 Books.

Cologne Cadre

1st Segment

| Best of Luther | Martin Luther |
| Three Friends of God | Frances Bevin |

Church Fathers Series

(All works to be completed in their respective segments)

ANF, NF, PNF

Anti-Nicene Fathers

Volume 1-9

Vol 1: The Apostolic Fathers with Justin Martyr and Irenaeus

(Presented via 2 Bks)

Bk 1: Clement of Rome, Mathetes, Polycarp, Ignatius, Barnabas, Papias,

Bk 2: Justin Martyr, Irenaeus.

Rare Books

(All works have been out of print at least 60 plus years)

Treatise of the Spiritual Life Books 1-3   Bishop Morozzo O.Cist

Ascent to Mount Sion   Bernardo de Laredo

Mystical Poetry   Ramon Lull

Selected Works   Ephraim the Syrian

Great Works   Jean Gerson

Women (According to Bonaventure)   E. Therese

Immaculate Conception   Aquinas, Bonaventure & D. Scotus

Steps to Paradise with Commentary by L Granada   John Climacus

www.ingramcontent.com/pod-product-compliance
Lightning Source LLC
Chambersburg PA
CBHW020654270326
41928CB00005B/119